Lessons in Creativity from Musical Theatre Characters

James C. Kaufman and
Dana P. Rowe

LONDON AND NEW YORK

Designed cover image: © Original image by master1305, Envato Elements; Adapted by Dana P. Rowe.

First published 2024
by Routledge
4 Park Square, Milton Park, Abingdon, Oxon OX14 4RN

and by Routledge
605 Third Avenue, New York, NY 10158

Routledge is an imprint of the Taylor & Francis Group, an informa business

© 2024 James C. Kaufman and Dana P. Rowe

The right of James C. Kaufman and Dana P. Rowe to be identified as authors of this work has been asserted in accordance with sections 77 and 78 of the Copyright, Designs and Patents Act 1988.

All rights reserved. No part of this book may be reprinted or reproduced or utilised in any form or by any electronic, mechanical, or other means, now known or hereafter invented, including photocopying and recording, or in any information storage or retrieval system, without permission in writing from the publishers.

Trademark notice: Product or corporate names may be trademarks or registered trademarks, and are used only for identification and explanation without intent to infringe.

British Library Cataloguing-in-Publication Data
A catalogue record for this book is available from the British Library

Library of Congress Cataloging-in-Publication Data
Names: Kaufman, James C., author. | Rowe, Dana P., author.
Title: Lessons in creativity from musical theatre characters / James C. Kaufman and Dana P. Rowe.
Description: [1.] | New York: Routledge, 2023. | Includes bibliographical references and index.
Identifiers: LCCN 2023027353 (print) | LCCN 2023027354 (ebook) | ISBN 9781032485638 (hardback) | ISBN 9781032485621 (paperback) | ISBN 9781003389668 (ebook)
Subjects: LCSH: Musical theater—Vocational guidance. | Music trade—Vocational guidance. | Performing arts—Vocational guidance. | Creative ability. | Creation (Literary, artistic, etc.)
Classification: LCC ML3795.K28 2023 (print) | LCC ML3795 (ebook) | DDC 780.23—dc23/eng/20230628
LC record available at https://lccn.loc.gov/2023027353
LC ebook record available at https://lccn.loc.gov/2023027354

ISBN: 9781032485638 (hbk)
ISBN: 9781032485621 (pbk)
ISBN: 9781003389668 (ebk)

DOI: 10.4324/9781003389668

Typeset in Times New Roman
by codeMantra

Lessons in Creativity from Musical Theatre Characters

Lessons in Creativity from Musical Theatre Characters marries art and science with a new and exciting collaboration between one of the world's leading creativity scholars and an internationally renowned musical theatre composer. This book will help readers tap into their creativity and unleash their own creative potential as they start their careers.

Blending cutting-edge research, juicy anecdotes, lived experience, hands-on activities, and gentle advice, authors James C. Kaufman and Dana P. Rowe take readers on a journey to explore and enhance their own creativity. Each chapter addresses a key aspect of creativity, from how to overcome blocks to understanding one's personal strengths all through the lens of Musical Theatre characters along with insights from those within the industry. Kaufman and Rowe shatter creativity myths (such as the tormented artist or having one big break) that may be harming the reader's potential growth. Probing questions, fun quizzes, and engaging exercises will help the reader reflect on the material and develop strategies for their next step. All throughout, the readers can learn from the tales of Sweeney Todd, Maria Von Trapp, Alexander Hamilton, Christine Daaé, and countless others to inspire their own creativity.

This book is ideal for aspiring theatre professionals, students of performing arts, and theatre and creativity scholars.

James C. Kaufman is a Professor of Educational Psychology at the University of Connecticut, USA. He has written/edited more than 50 books, including *The Creativity Advantage*. A former president of the American Psychological Association's Division 10, he has won numerous awards.

Dana P. Rowe is the composer of 11 musicals, including the off-Broadway hit *Zombie Prom*, and the Olivier-nominated West End shows *The Witches of Eastwick* and *The Fix*. As a certified personal development coach, he specializes in working with creative professionals.

We would like to dedicate this book to:

Alan and Nadeen Kaufman
Cleve and Beulah Rowe
For introducing us to the magic of musical theatre

and

Allison Kaufman
Andrew Scharf
For being our favorite theatre-going companions

Contents

List of Activities   ix
Acknowledgments   xi

Overture: Waiting in the Wings   1

PART I
Your Creative Spark   5

1 Making Your Entrance: Finding Your Original Voice   7
2 Hitting Your Mark: The Importance of Appropriateness   28
3 Thinking on Your Feet: The Creative Process   43
4 Finding Your Light: Your Creative Aspirations   58

PART II
Your Creative Tools   73

5 Keeping It Fresh: Staying Open to New Things   75
6 What's Your Motivation?: Passion and Balance   90
7 Showing Them What You've Got: The Creative Self   115
8 Crying on Cue: Monitoring Your Mood   130

PART III
Your Creative Life   149

9 Leaving the Drama on the Stage: The Myth of the Mad Genius   151
10 Taking Your Show on the Road: Know When to Make a Change   167

11 Dreaming Your Dream: Your Journey of Success	182
Exit Music: The Show Must Go On	197
Index	*199*

Activities

Chapter 1

Your Creative Map	9
Uniquely You	19

Chapter 2

The Abacus of Balance	38

Chapter 3

Musical Theatre Idea Generation	45
Remote Theatrical Associations	53

Chapter 4

The Twelve F-Words	64

Chapter 5

Increasing Openness with Random Random Random	77
Too Perfect: Does Your Attitude Need Adjusting?	83

Chapter 6

The Driving Range: Enjoyment, Success, and Growth	99

Chapter 7

Using 1950s Musicals to Distinguish Self-Beliefs, Self-Efficacy, and Metacognition	118
Test Your Creative Metacognition	126

Chapter 8

A Showtune for Every Mood	135
What Would Norma Desmond Do?	140

Chapter 9

Let's Put On a Show! 152
The Auditorium and the Affirmation 161

Chapter 10

The Change Flowchart 173

Chapter 11

Rodgers and Hammerstein Values Wheel 190

Acknowledgments

This book has been a long and rewarding journey. We would like to start by thanking our amazing team at Routledge, especially our editor Claire Margerison and Steph Hines. Stephen Acerra from Cambridge University Press made the excellent suggestion to approach Routledge. Heartfelt thanks to our many wonderful readers who gave terrific advice on earlier drafts: Barbara Bengels, Annelies Gentile, Allison B. Kaufman, Nadeen L. Kaufman, John Pigate, Ron Renaud, Jennie K. Singer, and Jennifer Zarin-Nickman. Amanda Osmanlli helped us tremendously with the preparation of the manuscript. We would like to give an extra special thanks to Alan S. Kaufman and Andrew Scharf, whose detailed and thoughtful comments greatly shaped the book.

We reached out to many top theatre people who graciously answered our questions and shared their thoughts. Much love to Rosemary Ashe, the late Bob Avian, Sierra Boggess, Leanne Borghesi, Kevin Cahoon, John Dempsey, James Gardiner, Kaitlin Hopkins, Rachel Bay Jones, Marc Kudisch, Jerry Mitchell, Marta Sanders, Emily Skinner, Avery Sommers, Ginger Tidwell-Walker, André Ward, and Jim Walton. We also drew from interviews with luminaries John Barrowman, Jeff Blumenkrantz, Randy Graff, Denis O'Hare, and Cameron Mackintosh from Dana's podcast, *Take It From The Top: Life Lessons from Creative Maestros to Awaken Your Artistic Soul*.

Finally, we send all of our love to our support team – our spouses Allison Kaufman and Andrew Scharf and our children Amber Berntsen, Asher Kaufman, Jacob Kaufman, and Landon Rowe.

Overture
Waiting in the Wings

There is no single best way to be creative, just as there is no one path to being successful in theatre, the arts, or life. It's about discovering the path that is most aligned with what you value, desire, and can offer the world. To paraphrase the showtune master Jerry Herman, you are who you are. Your ideal self might be a Broadway star or the CEO of the company. Perhaps, instead, you want to be part of a bigger whole. In the theatre world, that might be anything from acting in the ensemble, operating the front of house, working backstage, or simply being part of the audience. In real world, you can be creative in almost any arena you can imagine.

You might find your spotlight anywhere – on stage in your hometown or on Broadway. Conversely, the magic might come to you in the kitchen, a corporate boardroom, on your laptop, or carefully tending to a blooming rosebush. We are both people with a passion for theatre whose creativity has flourished on- and off-stage. James has spent most of career doing psychological research and being in the classroom, yet he has also worked to help creators (including theatre folk) reach their potential. Dana has seen his shows flourish around the world, yet one of his most memorable experiences was singing at a retirement community and seeing the older generations moved to tears.

Throughout this book, we present different creative hurdles that everyone encounters at some point in their lives. In each chapter, we present two classic characters from musical theatre to serve as metaphors for positive and negative approaches for each hurdle. One character represents Success, who presses on, overcomes the obstacle, and moves forward. The other character represents Suppress, who stays in place, reaches moments of clarity too late, and hits every bump and snag on the creative journey. In addition, each chapter will have at least one hands-on activity designed to offer insight or practical tools to help your own creativity.

Meet Your Authors

Your two authors seem to have little in common. Dana is a composer and James is a psychologist. Yet we share a deep passion for creativity on multiple levels. We are each creators and also devote a great deal of time trying to help others reach their creative potential; we have just taken different paths. We draw our combined expertise from several different sources – lived experience, mentoring others, scientific studies and theories, and the world of the performing arts.

Both theatre and the creative process have been a mutual calling. For both of us, it started in childhood. Music spoke to Dana – but not the rock music his brother Mike played in his garage band. It was the music of musical theatre. After randomly seeing *Gypsy* and *West Side Story* on television, Dana took to scanning the newspaper for the listings for movie musicals while his mom bought him remaindered studio cast recordings. He played along on the piano with those rudimentary vinyl records, picking out the music by ear because he couldn't yet read music (besides, musical scores were expensive and rare). Dana would pore over the liner notes and credits to see who did what and learn more about this wonderful world so different from the one he was experiencing in 1960s Columbus, Ohio. He memorized every note and nuance of the soundtracks of *The Sound of Music* and *Mary Poppins* and, of course, promptly fell in love with Julie Andrews. Dana sang "Spoonful of Sugar," complete with the vocal cadenza, for his second grade show-and-tell. He went from entertaining his family with rousing renditions of "I'm a Little Teapot" to performing in his first professional musical at age eight (*Oliver!*). He remembers, like yesterday, the excitement of sitting with the cast during vocal rehearsals and feeling their vibrant voices and harmonies surround him. He looked down at the music he was singing from and had this epiphany: "One day, I want a score of my very own."

After *Oliver!* closed, Dana checked out the scores and corresponding vinyl records that filled the shelves of his local library. He started a ritual of listening to and memorizing each musical, playing it on the piano, and analyzing how the music advanced the story and conveyed emotions. After high school, Dana attended Indiana University School of Music as a double major in piano and voice. Subsequent years saw him performing, coaching vocalists, re-orchestrating musicals, musical direction, musical supervision, arranging, creating children's shows, and writing special material, all of which helped him move toward writing his first full-length musical. As *Zombie Prom* (with lyrics by John Dempsey) began rehearsals for its Off-Broadway opening, Dana realized that he finally had "a score of his very own."

After *Zombie Prom* came *The Fix*, which led to *The Witches of Eastwick*, *The Ballad of Bonnie & Clyde*, *See Jane Run*, *Brother Russia*, *Frida*, and *Blackbeard*. One of the delightful side effects of writing his own musicals was being able to work closely with many of the same people whose cast albums inspired Dana in childhood. As he continued to compose, mentor, and coach artists, his curiosity about psychology and neuroscience led him to think about the broader construct of creativity. Dana started a podcast, *Take It From The Top: Life Lessons from Creative Maestros to Awaken Your Artistic Soul*. He began with theatre icon Cameron Mackintosh and continued with deep conversations about craft, process, and purpose with such eminent professionals as John Barrowman, the late and much missed Bob Avian, Sierra Boggess, and Jerry Mitchell. We will occasionally get words of wisdom throughout from the luminaries on the podcast.

Dana and James met through the podcast and realized they were kindred spirits. James had grown up singing along to the original brown covered version of *Jesus Christ Superstar*, being hooked by a college production of *Sweeney Todd*, and then getting to see a pre-Broadway *Into the Woods* in seventh grade in the front row (due to a wonderful teacher, the late Shari Mount Essex, who gave up her prime location to sit in the back with the other students). He found a moment of bliss when the grandmother, Meryl Louise (the original Beggar Woman from *Sweeney Todd*), winked at him in the Act One Finale.

As vinyl gave way to compact discs in the 1980s (before the trend reversed back), James spent his college days digging through Los Angeles' CD stores (Aron's, Tower Records on Sunset Boulevard, Amoeba) for new show albums. He discovered old shows, obscure shows, and flops and loved nearly all of them. A double major in Psychology and Creative Writing, James came to a crossroads. He knew his passion was for creating theatre but doubted whether he was talented enough to succeed (and didn't think he would cut it as a waiter – too clumsy). So he went to his back-up plan, which turned out to be getting a Ph.D. in cognitive psychology. After two years of struggling to find his niche, he finally combined his passions by studying creativity. Between classes, he continued to write plays and see them sporadically produced. With his first full-time job, however, his playwriting time dwindled.

James became a university professor and creativity researcher. His only connection to the world of theatre was as audience member until several things conspired to bring him back to the theatre world. His musical *Discovering Magenta* was accepted into the NYC Thespis Festival, so James and his composer (Michael Bitterman) got to work revising the show. The creative muse began to emerge. An actor friend, Gordon Goodman, convinced him that people in theatre would be interested in the creativity research James did. Finally, he connected with Dana, who composed one of his favorite all-time musicals (*The Fix*).

How about you?

How are you, dear reader? What is your goal with your creativity? Do you want to be creative to advance at your job or start your own business? Do you want to be creative in your hobbies or daily life because it's fun or it makes you feel better? Maybe you want to become more creative or figure out the best use of your abilities or consider new ways to channel your imagination. Perhaps you are interested in pursuing or continuing a journey in the performing arts as either a hobby or career. You may find your creative spotlight in front of a large crowd, with a small circle of friends, or all by yourself. Your creative peaks don't need to come in a starring role; they happen as you play with your kids, train your pets, cook an impromptu meal, or toss out a perfect bon mot. Such moments of inspiration can sustain us through the trials and mundanities of both the creative process and life itself.

So many people want to be creative but do not know how. Or they are creative but are trying to reignite their spark. Others know they like being creative but need a push getting started. We hope that this book can help all of these people – and you. Musical theatre is our language of examples, stories, and metaphors, but it is not the intended default domain (or area). We want to use your love of *Hamilton* or *Six* or *West Side Story* or *Mamma Mia* to talk to you about being creative in any area – not just on stage or anywhere else in the theatre world.

All creativity, whether at home, work, school, or daily life hits stumbling blocks and unexpected turns. How many people at the beginning of 2020 foresaw a year largely spent at home in a world that may not have provided the same opportunities and challenges it did the year before? Circumstances can change suddenly with little time to choose the best pathway. We hope that this book can help you think about your choices, your aspirations, and even your values – while also giving you practical tips that can boost your creative output.

Our goal is to strike a balance between wisdom from the scientific and artistic worlds. We will use a mix of anecdotes, studies, conversations, and questionnaires designed for this book to weave a narrative of how to take center stage. We will share stories from theatre people as part of this journey. Between Dana's podcasts and our discussions with talented friends and colleagues as we write this book, we believe their insights will inspire you as they have inspired us. Throughout, we will root our tale of creativity in the world of musical theatre, from classic shows to current hits. We will use examples of heroes, ingénues, villains, and sidekicks as we illustrate different concepts with your favorite (or least favorite) musical theatre characters. We will suggest creative hurdles that you can leap over. Our goal is not to tell you what to do (although we may be guilty of that at times) but rather to challenge you to question yourself and get your own answers.

Our enthusiasm can only go so far, though; we want to get YOU excited. Will you accept our challenge and travel with us on this road of discovery? We want you to think about the different characters we discuss, try the tools we offer, answer our questions, and talk back to us. Whether you've established yourself and want to dig deeper or if you're just starting out, we want YOU to add your own story to the ones you will read in the pages to come. As we invite you into our lives, minds, and hearts, we hope you will welcome us into yours! At any point, feel free to check in with us at our website, *Creating Your Spotlight!*, at https://creatingyourspotlight.com/, where we will have our latest projects and thoughts.

Onward!

Part I

Your Creative Spark

Chapter 1

Making Your Entrance

Finding Your Original Voice

> Christine Daaé (*Phantom of the Opera*), Success
> Lt. Cable (*South Pacific*), Suppress
> Myth: Wait for the Muse to Call
> Activity: Your Creativity Map; Uniquely You

There has been a time you fell in love. Maybe were entranced by another person, a pet, a food, a place, or an idea; regardless of who or what it was, you felt as though you were home. That feeling of love can fill many intense needs. Certainly, the need to belong and to connect with other people is one, but the leading theory of motivation argues that there are several key needs that drive us.[1] We want to feel valued and competent and as though we have something to offer. We want to feel agency and in control of our story. We want to have meaning.

Some people find that love in theatre; maybe you are one of them. Some fall in love with performing and being in front of people. Some find it in collaboration with fellow tech crew, ushers, public relations crew, or set designers. Others have a "moment in a darkened theatre" in the audience, aglow with percolating emotions and insights. However, it came about – a spontaneous trip to accompany a friend to an audition, signing up for backstage work to impress someone, randomly buying a half-price ticket to see an unknown show – many of us find our missing piece in the theatre.

In essence, we are talking about joy. Being creative brings joy to people, regardless of their ability or how they create.[2] Many people also find joy in the theatre, whether as active participant or ardent fan. Some need to be in the spotlight, whereas others get equal enjoyment being part of the world in any role. What everyone we hope to reach with this book (including you) has in common, whether they dream of being on or off stage, is the need to create. There is that desire to feel the thrill of using your imagination, the magic of connecting with other people with your ideas, and the gratification of seeing what was once only in your head suddenly become real. We all yearn, as Sondheim famously put it, to finish the hat.[3]

The first step to starting your creative journey is to find your own voice. What is your special ability or secret power? What new insight do you bring to the table?

DOI: 10.4324/9781003389668-3

As we will do throughout this book, we are using theatre for our examples and narrative. If you are an aspiring theatre artist, then consider these literally; if you are a theatre fan who wants to be more creative in your life or job, consider these musical metaphors.

If you see a show and think (like Mike in *A Chorus Line*), "I can do that!", that is great. However, matching the performance you see is only the first step. It is not only thinking "I could do that," but also following that thought with, "I could do it in my own way." There has to be that thing – that magnetism, drive, perspective, or energy – that makes people perk up their ears and keep their eyes focused on *you*. In the world of creativity research, we call this magical thing "originality."[4]

You may imagine scientists wrestling each other, yelling about the best way to define exactly what creativity is or is not. However, researchers actually have come to a strong agreement about the definition of creativity.[5] There tend to be two components. We will get into the second one (being useful and staying task appropriate) in Chapter 2, but the first aspect of creativity is that something must be original. It must be new or, at least, different enough from what has come before. What is unoriginal[6]? Following a routine or sticking to a habit. Imitating other people or listening perfectly to directions. Remembering something or making a lucky guess. Doing something the same way over and over again.

What is originality? Imagine asking many people the same question or having them do the same type of thing. The responses that are given the least often would be the most original.[7] To take a very basic example, think about what would happen if you asked many different people to name a Broadway musical. Some shows would come up more than others.

Some common responses might be *Hamilton, Six, Waitress, Heathers, Dear Evan Hansen, Fun Home, Hadestown,* or *Kimberly Akimbo*. Depending on their age, taste, culture, and location, others might say *Oklahoma!, The Lion King, Les Misérables, Wicked, West Side Story, Phantom of the Opera, Showboat, My Fair Lady, Rocky Horror Picture Show* or *Into the Woods*. There would also be answers that might only be given by a very small handful of people – shows that are largely unknown to most audiences. Think of *Flahooey, American Psycho, La Strada, Merlin, Hands on a Hard Body,* or *Dude* – or, perhaps, do not.

Someone may come up with a particularly obscure musical for many reasons; maybe they saw a rare local production. Similarly, an original idea may come from many possible places – an unusual association, an unexpected memory, a daydream, or a random thought. How do we go from original to creative? What makes one response be original, but another one be considered just strange? One answer involves the role of the second prong of creativity, the relevance of the response (which, as mentioned, we dive into in Chapter 2). Certainly, there is a line that separates brilliant from bizarre, wonderful from weird, and clever from crazy. But much of the way that your originality can blossom and thrive involves your location on the Creativity Map.

The Creativity Map

If someone asks you where you live, there are many possible answers. James, for example, could (accurately) respond with "Earth," "North America," "the United States," "Connecticut," "somewhere near Hartford," "Glastonbury," or an exact street location. All of these are technically accurate but some are more helpful than others. If James is visiting a friend in Geneva, then the answer "Glastonbury" is not very useful. If James is at a local farmer's market, telling someone he lives on Earth will only get odd sideways glances.

Similarly, if we ask you about how you want to be creative, there are many different ways you can respond. Let us assume that Earth represents the entire possible scope of creativity. There are seven continents on Earth (not counting Zealandia or other aspirants): Africa, Antarctica, Asia, Australia, Europe, North America, and South America. In creativity, there are larger thematic areas consisting of different related domains that represent different ways to be creative.[8] There is no set number of these "creative continents." In addition, everything in creativity overlaps a little bit. In the physical world, you wouldn't have a piece of land that was part of both North and South America (at least not without a military conflict). So interpret our suggested creativity continents with your own opinions and views!

There are many, many possible approaches we could take. If your guidance counselor gave you a test in high school to give you career advice, it probably used a framework of Realistic, Investigative, Artistic, Social, Enterprising, and Conventional interests to tell you if you should be a tap dancer, dentist, or shepherd.[9] The popular theory of Multiple Intelligence proposes linguistic, logical-mathematical, visual-spatial, bodily-kinesthetic, interpersonal, intrapersonal, musical, and naturalist types of intelligence[10] (intelligence and creativity, although related, are not the same thing.[11] We could spend the next several pages detailing comparable attempts in the creativity literature,[12] but we like you too much to do that).

Before we present our proposed creativity map of different possible domains, we will ask a few questions so you can see your pattern on the map.

Activity: Your Creative Map

For each of the activities described below, please indicate your level of interest (or excitement) about each one. Please use the following scale[13]:

0 = No interest   1 = Some interest   2 = Significant interest   3 = Strong interest

1. Telling someone a story
2. Putting down a thought in words
3. Teaching someone how to do something that you can do
4. Expressing your thoughts about a topic to a friend
5. Using poetic or lyrical language or music to communicate
6. Inventing a new type of product or finding a new use for an existing one
7. Figuring out a way to save or make money

8 Fixing, tinkering, or repairing something around the house
9 Coordinating people's schedules and interests to go and have a great time
10 Finding a way to market or promote a product
11 Singing with a group of people
12 Performing a dance or song
13 Acting in a play or musical
14 Making people laugh with a joke or funny face
15 Using your voice or movement to engage other people
16 Analyzing data to find trends or results
17 Designing an experiment or testing a hypothesis
18 Programming a computer or designing a website/app
19 Synthesizing information to explain a larger concept
20 Understanding or studying the natural world around us
21 Drawing or painting a picture
22 Making a sculpture
23 Arranging visual elements in an esthetically pleasing way
24 Bringing out the natural beauty in a person or place
25 Designing or arranging new clothing or fashion

Sum up your scores as follows:

#s 1–5: _____
#s 6–10: _____
#s 11–15: _____
#s 16–20: _____
#s 21–25: _____

What do these scores mean? In order, these scores represent the different continents (or domains) on our creativity map: Communication, Enterprise & Application, Performance, Science & Technology, and Visual Arts. Here is how we define each one:

Communication: An appreciation for the written or spoken word. A desire to connect with people, tell stories, teach, and share information.
Enterprise & Application: A hands-on, real-world feel for organization, promotion, and money management. The ability to actualize and make ideas a reality.
Performance: The use of your talents to help others be enlightened, entertained, and engaged. The aspiration to be seen and make an emotional impact with sounds, movement, voice, and expressions.
Science & Technology: The utilization of a vast array of numbers, nature, and networks to make sense of the world. The need to synthesize, explain, and discover ourselves and our environment.
Visual Arts: An eye for design, beauty, structure, and aesthetics. Using tools of color, shape, and touch to evoke a deeper shade of reality or a new perspective.

Making Your Entrance: Finding Your Original Voice   11

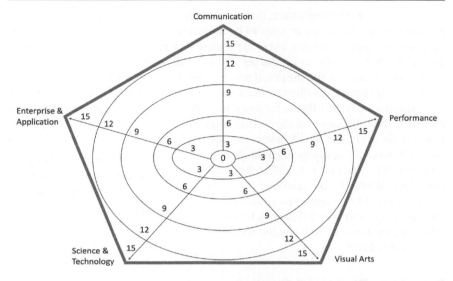

Figure 1.1 A creativity map to fill in. © Kaufman and Rowe (Creating Your Spotlight workbook, in progress)

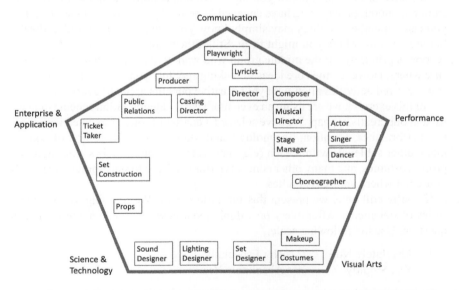

Figure 1.2 A creativity map with theatre examples. © Kaufman and Rowe (Creating Your Spotlight workbook, in progress)

Here is a creativity map for you to fill in; mark each of your five scores to get a visual representation of your perceived creative areas of high and low interest:

We have also created a creativity map giving many theatrical examples for each of the five continents:

As you can see in the map above, there is room for all types of creativity. For those readers who are in theatre or want to be in theatre, this map may offer some new suggestions. Some will want to pursue theatre in a professional way, from scenic design to choreography to producing. Others will want to have a non-theatrical career but continue in the theatrical arts as a hobby, such as those who will act in a community theatre or volunteer at an arts-related non-profit. Others may already have found a perfect fit that is far away from the arts, yet are passionate fans who marvel at the brilliance of a show. This book is meant for everyone; the life and career lessons will generally apply to any field (and we will note when advice may differ for other domains). Whether you consider the Tony Awards to be a holy night, belt showtunes in the shower, or were gifted this book by someone who just doesn't know you too well, you are welcome here!

> Creativity Hurdle to Leap: To find your own voice, find your best creative fit – there are all kinds!

Pursuing a Theatrical Career

As we have discussed, some of you may have had a similar and specific passion from childhood; perhaps you have engaged in pretend play and daydreaming since you can remember.[14] Others may simply know you want to be involved in theatre but are not sure where you might fit in. Still, others are happiest being fans. This section is primarily for the middle group who want to be in the theatre but are not sure where. However, the core ideas of making sure that your personality, interests, and preferred activities align with your creative pursuits apply to everyone.

For this exercise, we are using an even more basic categorization scheme than we used in our creativity map. We have selected a quartet of roles associated with theatre: Performance, Creation, Technology, and Management. There are, of course, many other sublevels within each (e.g., underneath technology is sound, lighting, props, costumes, and many other concepts). But you have to start somewhere. Let's figure out where your passion lies.

If you're still here, we present this fun little survey. We're going to give you a series of statements. After every one, think about how much you agree with each question. Use the following scale:

1 = Absolutely Not   2 = Not Especially
3 = Yes, Slightly   4 = Absolutely Yes

Write the number representing your response inside the shape (or shapes) at the end of the row. If there are two shapes, write your same number in both shapes (we promise it will make sense when you are done).

Making Your Entrance: Finding Your Original Voice   13

Okay! Now let's score it. For each page, add up all of your scores across a vertical line so that you are adding together all of your responses in the circles, then squares, then diamonds, and finally hexagons. Then add the two page scores together.

For the following questions, respond with the following scale:

1 = Absolutely Not   2 = Not Especially   3 = Yes, Slightly   4 = Absolutely Yes

Let's start with some basic questions:

1. Do you want to be on stage?   ○
2. Do you like telling stories?   ☐
3. Do you like figuring out how things work?   ◇
4. Do you like planning?   ⬡
5. Do you have a good attention to detail?   ◇ ⬡
6. Do you prefer to focus on the larger picture?   ☐
7. Do you want to work behind the scenes?   ◇ ⬡
8. Do you want to focus on a character's journey?   ○ ☐
9. Do you enjoy tinkering with your hands and building things?   ◇
10. Are you drawn to applause and public recognition?   ○
11. Does the idea of introducing people to new work appeal to you?   ⬡
12. Do you enjoy expressing yourself with your body?   ○
13. Are you able to manage your checkbook well?   ⬡
14. Do you like being in front of crowds?   ○
15. Do you think about why one show catches on and another one closes early?   ⬡
16. Do you like figuring out how to fix something with limited resources?   ◇
17. Do you consider your voice an instrument?   ○
18. Are you good at coming up with a good spin to sell a show?   ⬡
19. Do you find yourself memorizing monologues or songs and imagining how you would perform them?   ○
20. Do you like the idea of providing jobs for other creators?   ⬡

Page Total:

(Continued)

14 Your Creative Spark

FOR THE FOLLOWING QUESTIONS, RESPOND WITH THE FOLLOWING SCALE:

1 = Absolutely Not   2 = Not Especially   3 = Yes, Slightly   4 = Absolutely Yes

THINK ABOUT WHEN YOU SEE A SHOW:

21. Do you think about how it was created? □
22. Do you have ideas about how the costumes might have been different? ◇
23. Do you imagine what role you'd want to play? ○
24. Do you critique the choices made by the writers? □
25. Do you think about how the actors could make different choices? ○ □
26. Do you consider how you could get other people to see the show? ⬡
27. Do you wonder how else the story could have been told? □
28. Do you notice the quality of the lighting? ◇
29. Do you compare different orchestrations of different productions of a show? □
30. Do you notice how the set, costumes, props, and lighting advance the storytelling and set the mood? □ ◇
31. If you are seeing a revival, do you care about changes made from the original? □
32. Do you like to monitor the audience's reactions? ⬡
33. Do you notice the quality of the sound design? ◇
34. Do you think about how the actors inhabited the roles of the characters? ○
35. Do you ponder how the effects have been created? ◇

PAGE TOTAL: ● ■ ◆ ⬢

Figure 1.3 Theatrical Career Survey, (a) Page One and (b) Page Two. © Kaufman and Rowe (Creating Your Spotlight workbook, in progress)

You should now have four scores. Write them down below:

Circle: _____   Square: _____

Diamond: _____   Hexagon: _____

What do they translate into?

Circle is Performance: You want to take center stage. You want to act, sing, or dance!

Square is Creation: You want to tell a story and invent a world. You want to write, compose, choreograph, or direct!

Diamond is Technology: You want to roll up your sleeves and make theatre magic happen.

You want to build the props and set, work with the lighting and sound, and make the costumes!

Hexagon is Management: You want to promote and proselytize theatre for everyone. You want to produce, stage manage, and market and sell the show!

What do these scores mean? It is important to note that this part is not an exact science. If we wanted to have you truly make life choices based on this survey, we would need to have many theatre professionals complete it and then see if their scores align with their actual jobs. If you want to see how you compare with other people, ask some friends to also take the test and see how the patterns of your scores differ from theirs.

> Creativity Hurdle to Leap: There are many opportunities for your voice to be heard; let your role match what you like to do!

That said, there are some ways of analyzing your scores without having to bug all of your friends. First, see what number is highest and which number is lowest. Is your highest number for a domain that you want to pursue? Is your lowest number a domain that is less exciting to you? Are there any surprises?

Finding Your Niche

> Creativity Hurdle to Leap: Find the niche that matches who you are in the here and now!

Part of finding your voice is figuring out your exact niche. You can't find your dream role if you don't know what to target. This process involves some reflection on your true passions and interests – as well as your strengths and weaknesses. You also need to expose yourself to as much as you possibly can, from different potential careers to diving deep into the paths that compel you. You cannot be original unless you know what has already been done. You will not be able to maximize your own originality unless it fits with your interests, passions, and abilities. For example, consider if your highest creativity map score was on Science & Technology *and* it is consistent with your gut feelings, interests, and feedback from trusted friends. If you are persistently pursuing jobs or classes in Communication or Visual Arts because that is what you think you are "supposed" to do, then you are limiting yourself. Using the "find your voice" metaphor literally, it's hard to sing beautifully if you are entirely out of your vocal register. As hard as it might be to give up childhood dreams or subvert other people's expectations, the process of finding your best voice is unique to you and it can change over time.

Know When to Be Original

Let's turn to Tony-nominated acting legend Emily Skinner (*Side Show, The Full Monty, Billy Eliot*), who shared her wisdom with Dana on his podcast. Skinner described the importance of sensing how much creativity a director would actually want. She suggested that sometimes she has been hired because she is able to direct herself. That is, she can figure out her motivation and develop a living breathing character without requiring a lot of attention or time from the director. This ability may be particularly welcomed for a production with a short rehearsal period, such as a summer stock production of *Mame* or *Mamma Mia!* The director may be busy, first with assigning a traffic pattern or blocking to the actors and then getting immersed in myriad technical details. In this setting, an actor who can sort out her or his own inner journey without needing hand-holding is an asset.

In addition to directing herself when necessary, Skinner is also able to take direction well. She can process what the director asks of her, understand the concept or vision of the show presented to her, and then mirror it back beautifully while making interesting and appropriate choices. This approach is especially great for new pieces when the authors want to see how their writing plays out in the hands of a talented and collaborative actor. These are vastly different creative situations and require different mindsets on the actor's part. "You have to be flexible," Skinner told Dana, "and go with the flow. Go into every new adventure with an open view."

Part of anticipating whether a supervisor wants you to use your own voice or not is to consider when an original idea is not necessarily optimal.[15] Sometimes the most straightforward solution is the best. Let's say that you are trying to fix a hole in your wall.

The natural choice would be to spackle it up. If you do not have spackle, then brainstorming ways to fill the hole (with duct tape or several rolls of wallpaper or hanging a framed picture) is fun and helpful. But if you do have spackle, then doing something original just for the sake of being different isn't particularly useful. As we will discuss in the next chapter, creativity has its own limits. Different is not always good. Deciding to have Macbeth breakdance in the middle of his famous soliloquy may be something your audience has never seen before, but it does not mean that it is a good idea. Indeed, most shows whose rights are controlled by a licensing company (such as MTI, Samuel French, or Rodgers & Hammerstein) are insistent that you follow the script. They will not hesitate to close down a show that deviates from the parameters of the license.

Let us go through some examples. Consider a production of *Jesus Christ Superstar* in which Jesus and Judas are having a lover's spat to give an underlying reason behind Judas's anger during the opening number. Or, perhaps, imagine a *West Side Story* with Maria shooting herself dead at the conclusion, to better follow Juliet's original actions. One production of Dana's *Zombie Prom* asked the audience to provide urine samples before they entered to illustrate the toxicity of the subject matter (and serve as a publicity stunt). It is important to note that we are not making up any of these stories. Are these examples of "good originality" or "bad originality?" We will leave the final decision up to you.

> Creativity Hurdle to Leap: Using your originality also means knowing when (and when not) to be original!

Letting Your Originality Work for You

All of that said, originality is usually a very good thing. Assuming you have some degree of judgment and sense, being original is the key to finding your voice. So if we ask you to sing "Don't Rain on my Parade" or "Everything's Coming up Roses," and you blast out a perfect impression of Babs or the Merm, you might be technically proficient or showing off your pipes (or awesome imitation skills, if you're auditioning for a revival of *Forbidden Broadway*) – but you're not being particularly original. It's a replication.[16] You're copying what's been done before.

The same problem can be found in some community theatre productions of classic shows. Either consciously or subconsciously, they're trying to do the show just like the original cast (or the cast of a televised or filmed adaptation). We've seen countless versions of Mrs. Lovett (from *Sweeney Todd*) over the years, but James's favorite (aside from Angela Lansbury) remains one he saw in a college student production. The actress deliberately didn't watch the existing video and performed Lovett as being incredibly sensuous and sexy, making "Wait" feel more like a seductive temptress number as opposed to a song about delaying revenge.

Dana recalls clearly to this day an audition from over 20 years ago by someone who repurposed the 1960s pop song "Goin' out of My Head." The actor sang it like a desperate, befuddled stalker who followed the object of his desire each morning and barely restrained himself from using the "dangerous" plastic butter knife tucked away in his oversized flasher-inspired trench coat. The entire creative team of the show were on the floor laughing to tears. Indeed, the actor got the gig.

Being original is how you find your voice; it doesn't need to mean doing the most unusual thing you can do. To illustrate, here's a story about a performer being wise enough to hold on to her original approach yet still open enough to try new styles. It's about an actress you just might know, Kristin Chenoweth. When Dana was casting the workshop for *Zombie Prom* in 1994, Chenoweth came in to audition for the role of Toffee. She sang *Candide*'s "Glitter and Be Gay" and managed to both be brilliantly funny and hit the high F# with the ease and confidence of a sharpshooter. But it didn't fit the demands of the role; Toffee had to have comedy chops but also had to be able to deliver a power ballad. Chenoweth was stunningly *bel canto*, but the role needed *can-belt-oh*.

What to do? Dana and the team desperately wanted her in the cast and asked if she could learn how to belt. Already a consummate professional at such a young age, she went away and took a few lessons. A week later, she belted out *Zombie Prom*'s "Easy to Say" in a way that would have made Jennifer Hudson jealous and she earned the role for the workshop. Chenoweth was overqualified; belting only showed some of what she was capable of doing. In between the workshop and the show's Off-Broadway mounting, she caught the attention of Kander and Ebb, who promptly cast her in *Steel Pier*. They wrote a new song for her that showed off the versatility of her vocal range, and she earned a Theatre World Award. Kristin Chenoweth became, well, *Kristin Chenoweth*.

Dana, of course, would have loved her to be part of the original cast of *Zombie Prom* – but Chenoweth made the right call. The part of Toffee wouldn't have shown off everything she had to offer; the confines of the role stifled her originality. Playing Precious in *Steel Pier* displayed all of her gifts. *Zombie Prom* opened Off-Broadway in 1996 with Jessica Snow-Wilson (who has continued to be a Broadway mainstay in her own right) playing Toffee. Dana is convinced that this ultimate outcome was the best thing that could have happened for everyone (though James, the psychologist, suspects that might be a rationalization).

There is a lesson here about staying true to your originality and your own voice. A lesser performer would have been too scared to learn to belt, but Chenoweth had that faith in her abilities. Yet Chenoweth also had the confidence in her unique assets to choose the role that would be the best for her.

> Creativity Hurdle to Leap: Have the confidence to follow where your individual skillset takes you!

Different Pathways to Success

In *Phantom of the Opera*, Christine Daaé (our Success model for this chapter) is a budding opera singer when the Phantom grows enamored of her. He decides to become her vocal coach so she can become the new prima donna of the Opéra Populaire. With his help, she found her voice; indeed, in the original source material, the Phantom met Christine at a time when she had lost her passion for singing. The Phantom taught her and nurtured her and made her a better singer.

There are always times when a good mentor knows to back off and let pupils find their own legs. Yet just when Christine most needed time and space to find her place in the world of opera and theatre, the Phantom pressed on. His infatuation and growing obsession with her made his mentorship become more and more selfish. He pushed Christine to star in his opera *Don Juan Triumphant* (among many unpleasant and forceful actions). Our heroine was at a crossroads: Her mentor had truly helped her learn and grow and yet was now an albatross, his advice now borne of unrequited, selfish love. Christine found the strength to show compassion to the Phantom and yet indicate clearly that she was not his possession. The strong implication of both the musical's end and its flash-forward prologue is that Christine found her own voice and became a famous opera diva.

Another (eventual) Success model can be found with Guido in *Nine*. He is creatively blocked for much of the show as he flits from his wife Luisa to his mistress to his muse. Guido turns inward for inspiration, and in a misguided breakthrough he merges his past, his current life, and his creative ideas to make a deeply personal movie about Casanova. Yet as he finds his voice he is so self-enraptured that he callously hurts people he loves (and captures it on camera). The film is a disaster; his wife, mistress, and muse all leave him, and he contemplates suicide. He finally reaches back into his soul and realizes his passion is and always has been his wife. Everything else has been a distraction. Guido is finally ready to give his attention and time to his wife; he realizes that his true voice is not to be found in his affairs or the trappings of fame, but rather in coming back to and honoring his first love. Luckily for Guido, Luisa sees his sincerity and gives him one more chance. Regardless of his development as an artist, Guido has developed as a human being and may once again be able to offer the world a voice that is true to himself.

Finding your voice can entail a lot of work. It is not only about reflection and exploration but also about deciding which advice to listen to (including ours!), which mentors have your best interests at heart, which life changes are for the best, and which ones are moving you backward. If you were a character in a musical, would the audience be rooting for you? Would they be on the edge of their seat, waiting to see what happens next?

> Creativity Hurdle to Leap: There are many pathways to find your voice!

Activity: Uniquely You

So here we're going to take a break and let you (to paraphrase Lois Lane from *Kiss Me Kate*) be true to you in your fashion.

First, think about what makes you uniquely you. What are the life experiences, talents, passions, interests, values, aspirations, and resources that allow you to bring your own voice to each new show (and the world)? List as many things that separate you from the pack as you can! We are debating how many you can do; Dana thinks you can hit twenty, but James would be happy if you can get five. Feel free to grab a piece of scratch paper or just jot ideas below.

Make Dana Happy	Make James Happy
1	1
2	2
3	3
4	4
5	5
6	
7	
8	
9	
10	
11	

(Continued)

(Continued)	
Make James Happy	*Make Dana Happy*
12	
13	
14	
15	
16	
17	
18	
19	
20	

Second, let's try to help you find new strengths you might have overlooked. To start off, tell us compliments you've heard that you too easily dismiss. This time, James believes in your ability to overlook your own success and thinks you can hit at least 15. Dana would be fine if you can nail five.

Make James Happy	*Make Dana Happy*
1	1
2	2
3	3
4	4
5	5
6	
7	
8	
9	
10	
11	
12	
13	
14	
15	

Next, think about past successful, yet challenging, creative experiences. Why did you ultimately succeed? What was most difficult? What do you think you learned from the experience? We'll leave the goal-setting to you for the rest of this activity.

Think about other people who do what you do. What bothers you most about them?
What qualities or behaviors make you dislike them?
If your life were a showtune, which one would it be? Why?
Finally, what qualities, abilities, talents, or skills do you most wish you possessed?

For the list above, make mental asterisks by the ones that you are able to learn. For example, you can't learn how to be tall.

Now take a look at your answers to the last batch of questions. Think about those positive qualities others may see in you that you do not see in yourself. Think about how you have grown from past challenges. Think about which personal growth goals are attainable.

> Creativity Hurdle to Leap: Don't forget to reflect on everything you can and might someday bring to the table!

Now return to the list you made for the first question. What things might you add?

If you're wondering why we asked you what showtune best captured your life... Well, it was fun, wasn't it? But how about this thought: Is there a different showtune that you wish would capture your life five years from now? How can you move from showtune #1 to showtune #2?

Mentors: The Good

We have been lucky enough to have mentors who have helped us find our own voice (and, luckily, not a Phantom in the bunch). Curiously, we both have also had people who quite literally helped us discover our voice. Dana loved to read in elementary school, but his stutter made oral book reports an agonizing experience. He had been playing the piano since he was eight years old. When his fourth-grade teacher, Mrs. Martin, heard him improvising on the piano during an indoor recess to accompany his classmates' playtime, she got an idea. She suggested that Dana create music to describe key scenes in the books for his oral book reports. The class loved it, and in the excitement of sharing the stories through the music, Dana found his voice through the language of music. He also got his stutter under control.

James (much less dramatically) had a number of speech issues; one of them was speaking so fast as to be unintelligible. Ideas would come so fast that they would tumble from his mouth in one hyper rush of motion. His speech therapist worked on exercises to make him sound out each word, and he eventually adapted this slow, evenly paced tone for anything formal. It continues to be the way that he delivers most talks and lectures (and his wife Allison calls it his "professor voice," and hates when he talks to her with it). Mentors can come at any time and in any role.

As for the more traditional mentors, let's start with James, who was born to psychologist parents who developed IQ tests (such as the KABC-II and the KTEA-3, used worldwide). His mother, Nadeen, read his attempts at fiction as he grew up, red pen in hand, and his father, Alan, taught him statistical analyses with baseball stats, which led to a co-authored book, *The Worst Baseball Pitchers of All Time*, when James was a teen. At the University of Southern California, he found dual mentors. T. Coraghessan Boyle (best-selling author of *The Road to Wellville* and many other well-known novels) evaluated James' later attempts at fiction (and, eventually, theatre) with a gentle yet honest touch. The late John Horn, a legend in the field of intelligence, spent hours with James discussing psychology, research methods, intelligence, and the spirit of scientific inquiry. He also spun stories of his life that James remembers decades later – tales of John serving in the Korean War, being an early civil rights activist, and growing up in poverty.

Both mentors were able to walk that fine balance between being honest (James was not and is not the most gifted novelist or statistician) and encouraging. Both were able to let go – to see James not pursue an MFA in Creative Writing and continue on with a Psychology Ph.D. at somewhere other than USC. As James began his studies in Cognitive Psychology under Robert Sternberg at Yale, he still tried to find his voice. He wrote plays that sounded embarrassingly like the works of David Mamet. He tried to do studies and papers but needed Sternberg to dictate what to do. As discussed earlier, James finally was able to create his spotlight by blending his two loves – but that would have been impossible without a long series of mentors, culminating with Sternberg. Indeed, the legendary scholar (one of the most influential living psychologists) made lists of suggested reading, tolerated countless poor suggestions for studies and edited books, and eventually helped James get his first job by repeatedly calling his future employer until they agreed to hire him. It is certainly possible to find your voice on your own, but finding people willing and able to guide you on your journey is invaluable.

James had a wide array of mentors. Dana primarily had one, but what a mentor it has been! Right after *Zombie Prom* closed Off-Broadway, a stroke of good fortune occurred. *Zombie Prom*'s legendary general manager, Albert Poland, had dinner at the delectable steakhouse Frankie and Johnny's with Sir Cameron Mackintosh. Albert was still thinking of *Zombie Prom* and talked to Cameron about the show's merits. Cameron asked for a tape; Albert (or "Peaches," as he is known) has an eye for talent and had helped discover *Little Shop of Horrors*. Dana suggested that Cameron instead be given a tape of his new show, *Cal, A Tale of Relative Insanity*. Two weeks later, Albert received an early morning phone call from Cameron, who said, "Once again, the Peach is right!" The tape was soon shared with Oscar-winning director Sam Mendes, who would end up helming the show (which was eventually renamed *The Fix*).

Although *The Fix* did not become the hit that they hoped, it did cement Dana and John's relationship with Mackintosh… who then insisted that the writing team ignore the reviews and immediately write another show. This next show was *The Witches of Eastwick*, which Mackintosh produced on London's West End three years after *The Fix* and which continues to have large-scale productions around the world.

Working with Mackintosh was one of the greatest learning experiences of Dana's life. The renowned showman perpetually challenged him to be better and would not settle for any music that was not uniquely Dana. Mackintosh demanded songs that could only have been written by Dana, saying, "Darling, anyone could have written that. It's rather ordinary. I want people to hear it and know instantly that you wrote the music." Such a response could be tough to hear, yet was critical to Dana's growth as a composer. What better way could there be to find your own voice than to be guided by someone who had a vision of, and insisted on, a special sound that only could come from you? When Mackintosh did offer his approval for a song, it was like winning the lottery and offered true validation that Dana had truly found his voice.

Theatre and life is about collaboration. Growth comes not just from mentors but from your contemporaries, your colleagues, your friends, and even your audience. Dana remembers one song that came from actress Maria Friedman's suggestion that her character in *The Witches of Eastwick*, Sukie, would benefit by having a song with lots and lots of words. It was a perfect idea that expanded Sukie's journalistic love of words and her real-life challenge of articulating her aspirations and feelings. Many songs in that show also changed and evolved from dialogue with John Dempsey, his long-time collaborator. Some became more energetic and closer to rock music. Others went from Gershwinesque to sexier, darker, and more seductive. A good collaborator will challenge you when your choices are becoming predictable or when the energy needs to change at a given moment.

> Creativity Hurdle to Leap: Mentors can be invaluable and are worth seeking out!

Mentors: The Bad

However, not all mentors or influences have such a positive effect. The Phantom represents a cautionary tale, but Christine was at least able to overcome him at the end. So instead of rehashing his story again, let's turn to our Suppress model for this chapter: Marine Lieutenant Joe Cable from *South Pacific* – or, at least, the unseen mentors he had back home in Philadelphia. Lt. Cable arrives at an island in the South Pacific in the height of World War II. He soon meets Bloody Mary, a Tonkinese street vendor who sells a wide array of goods to the Navy Seabees. Mary convinces Lt. Cable to come to the magical island Bali Ha'i; and once there, she introduces him to her beautiful daughter, Liat. Lt. Cable and Liat instantly fall in love (or at least in lust) and Bloody Mary rejoices as she imagines the better life that would await Liat in America.

It is here that we meet the ugly side of our influences and mentors. Lt. Cable was raised in a racist family (during quite racist times). All of his friends, teachers, and colleagues back home, both in Philadelphia and at Princeton, were likely of a similar mindset. As the show progresses, he realizes he has internalized the fear of the different and unknown. Unlike Christine Daaé, who is able to recognize in time the dark side of the Phantom, Lt. Cable does not believe that he has the strength to follow his own heart. He breaks up with Liat, leaving both of them brokenhearted. Lt. Cable focuses on a spy mission he needs to undertake; as part of the preparations, he gets to know Emile de Becque, a local French plantation owner.

Emile has experienced his own romantic loss at the hands of Nellie Forbush, who is unable to accept Emile's two Polynesian children. Even after Lt. Cable hears Emile's story and sees the devastation caused by Nellie's racism, he leaves for his mission (with Emile) without reaching out to Liat. Emile survives the mission, giving Nellie a second chance (and the audience a somewhat happy ending), but Lt. Cable is killed.

Lt. Cable himself was not a bad mentor, but he was susceptible to other people's beliefs. His ultimate inability to overcome the prejudices that had been drummed into him caused him to lose his chance at love. Ultimately, they may have led to him losing his life.

> Creativity Hurdle to Leap: Learn how to sift advice so you can distinguish the sage from the saboteur!

Myth: Waiting for the Muse to Call

It is time to tackle our first "myth" (we will dismantle one myth per chapter). Let's begin by discussing the dark side of waiting for inspiration. It is very tempting to believe in "the muse," even if you're being tongue-in-cheek. It takes the responsibility out of your hands, in a way. If you're not "feeling it," that's okay – you can just wait for inspiration to strike. There are many reasons not to indulge in this practice. There is a psychological term called "locus of control.[17]" It is how we assign responsibility for something; it is related to our personality. Locus of control can either be internal or external. The way that you see your creative endeavors – where you place the locus of control – can determine how you chalk up your successes and failures. If you hold off for the muse, you are in essence assigning your control to an external source. You're taking the responsibility for your success out of your hands. Having an internal locus of control – seeing yourself as being responsible for your actions (whether success or failure) tends to be healthier.[18] Having an external locus of control can lead to poor self-esteem or depression.[19] Of course, there are times when events truly are outside your control, and it's important to not blame yourself for failures that are not your fault. If you lost a job or had a gig canceled because of the COVID-19 outbreak and subsequent lockdown, you cannot blame yourself for that. But overall, it is healthy to see yourself in the driver's seat, actively determining your own outcomes. Any external factor – the muse, inspiration, or anything else – risks distracting you. What you ultimately want is to be in the best space to create.

So what is the alternative? Schedule time to work, whether it's writing, composing, building, planning, or just thinking. You need to make space in your life for your art (or science or business) and protect that space. Sometimes it can be hard to protect your time for a project if you are working alone. One way in which good collaborations can truly help is by having other vocal advocates for the project. Working with people can keep you honest and hold you accountable. Sometimes it can be as little as an extra hour or two a week that can give you the insight you need to finish the song, give the monologue an extra spin, perfect the dance move or put the final piece together for your vision of a show – or, for that matter, make the soufflé glaze shine, the blueprints more clear, or the data analysis more sophisticated.

As we will say again and again, creativity takes time. You have to practice your craft on a steady, regular basis – even when you are at your least motivated. You wouldn't go hungry because you're not feeling like you are in a place to prepare your finest meal. Indeed, when Mendes was directing *The Fix*, he encouraged Dana and John to compose new songs with abandon; he called it the "bad movie" version. They could also rewrite and refine the songs later; better to get something out that can be edited later than to wait for inspiration. You are your own muse.

> Creativity Hurdle to Leap: Do not hold out for inspiration – just start to create!

Moving Forward

There is no one path to finding your voice. It can come in childhood. It can be developed with a mentor. It can appear to you suddenly or slowly develop. It may require a dramatic denouement or (more likely) a quiet moment of reflection. Your voice can be drawn from your environment, your family, or your particular set of experiences. There is no one path. Some people live fascinating lives and learn nothing. Other people can have perfectly boring childhoods and yet bring a nuanced lens that gives them insight into the world.

The very word "voice" means communication. What is the best way for you to communicate? What is it you have to say – or, better yet, what is it that you *need* to say? What are the cards you bring to the table? It could be your content, style, perspective, analysis, technique, or any combination that makes you who you are. Finding your voice has many components. It involves discovering your original ideas. It involves casting a wide net to discover everything you might be. It entails deciding which advice or mentor to abide by and which to disregard. One step is to consider where you fit in the creativity map across the broad regions of Communication, Enterprise & Application, Performance, Science & Technology, and Visual Arts.

The next step is to find your balance. There are many components. It means keeping things that are part of your essential core which will help you move forward. It also entails growing and improving in areas in which you may be weak. It further can involve shedding that which is unnecessary, distracting, or destructive. Finding your balance requires juggling, reflecting, deciding, and reaching an agreement about your path. In the next chapter, we will dive into this territory.

Notes

1 Deci & Ryan (2010).
2 Csikszentmihalyi (1996) and Kaufman (2023).
3 Sondheim & Lapine (1991).
4 Barron (1955).
5 Kaufman (2016) and Plucker, Beghetto, & Dow (2004).
6 Simonton (2018).
7 Guilford (1950, 1967) and Torrance (1974, 2008).
8 Baer & Kaufman (2005) and Kaufman & Baer (2004).
9 Holland (1959, 1997).
10 Gardner (2011).
11 Barron & Harrington (1981) and Plucker & Esping (2013).
12 Ivcevic & Mayer (2009), Kaufman (2012) and Kerr & McKay (2013).
13 Kaufman & Rowe (Creating Your Spotlight workbook, in progress).
14 Russ & Wallace (2013) and Singer & Singer (1990).
15 Simonton (2012).
16 Sternberg & Kaufman (2012) and Sternberg, Kaufman, & Pretz (2001, 2002, 2003).
17 Rotter (1990).
18 Peterson (2000).
19 Chubb, Fertman, & Ross (1997) and Kaufman & Baer (2002).

References

Baer, J., & Kaufman, J. C. (2005). Bridging generality and specificity: The Amusement Park Theoretical (APT) Model of creativity. *Roeper Review, 27*, 158–163.
Barron, F. (1955). The disposition toward originality. *Journal of Abnormal and Social Psychology, 51*, 478–485.
Barron, F., & Harrington, D. M. (1981). Creativity, intelligence, and personality. *Annual Review of Psychology, 32*, 439–476.
Chubb, N. H., Fertman, C. I., & Ross, J. L. (1997). Adolescent self-esteem and locus of control: Contributions applied to the arts and letters. *Journal of Creative Behavior, 35*, 75–101.
Csikszentmihalyi, M. (1996). *Creativity: Flow and the psychology of discovery and invention.* New York: HarperCollins.
Deci, E. L., & Ryan, R. M. (2010). *Self-determination.* New York: Wiley.
Gardner, H. (2011). *Frames of mind: The theory of multiple intelligences* (rev. ed.). New York: Basic Books.
Guilford, J. P. (1950). Creativity. *American Psychologist, 5*, 444–454.
Guilford, J. P. (1967). *The nature of human intelligence.* New York, NY: McGraw-Hill.
Holland, J. L. (1959). A theory of vocational choice. *Journal of Counseling Psychology, 6*, 35–45.
Holland, J. L. (1997). *Making vocational choices: A theory of vocational personalities and work environments* (3rd ed.). Odessa, FL: Psychological Assessment Resources.
Ivcevic, Z., & Mayer, J. D. (2009). Mapping dimensions of creativity in the life-space. *Creativity Research Journal, 21*, 152–165.

Kaufman, J. C. (2012). Counting the muses: Development of the Kaufman-Domains of Creativity Scale (K-DOCS). *Psychology of Aesthetics, Creativity, and the Arts, 6*, 298–308.
Kaufman, J. C. (2016). *Creativity 101*. New York: Springer.
Kaufman, J. C. (2023). *The creativity advantage.* New York: Cambridge University Press.
Kaufman, J. C., & Baer, J. (2002). I bask in dreams of suicide: Mental illness and poetry. *Review of General Psychology, 6*, 271–286.
Kaufman, J. C., & Baer, J. (2004). The Amusement Park Theoretical (APT) Model of creativity. *Korean Journal of Thinking and Problem Solving, 14*, 15–25.
Kaufman, J. C., & Rowe, D. P. (in progress). *The creating your spotlight workbook.* Retrived from https://creatingyourspotlight.com/
Kerr, B., & McKay, R. (2013). Searching for tomorrow's innovators: Profiling creative adolescents. *Creativity Research Journal, 25*, 21–32.
Peterson, C. (2000). The future of optimism. *American Psychologist, 55*, 44–55.
Plucker, J. A., Beghetto, R. A., & Dow, G. (2004). Why isn't creativity more important to educational psychologists? Potential, pitfalls, and future directions in creativity research. *Educational Psychologist, 39*, 83–96.
Plucker, J. A., & Esping, A. (2013). *Intelligence 101*. New York, NY: Springer.
Rotter, J. B. (1990). Internal versus external control of reinforcement: A case history of a variable. *American Psychologist, 45*, 489–493.
Russ, S. W., & Wallace, C. E. (2013). Pretend play and creative processes. *American Journal of Play, 6*, 136–148.
Simonton, D. K. (2012). Taking the US Patent Office creativity criteria seriously: A quantitative three-criterion definition and its implications. *Creativity Research Journal, 24*, 97–106
Simonton, D. K. (2018). Defining creativity: Don't we also need to define what is not creative? *Journal of Creative Behavior, 52*, 80–90.
Singer, D. G., & Singer, J. L. (1990). *The house of make-believe: Children's play and the developing imagination.* Cambridge, MA: Harvard University Press.
Sondheim, S., & Lapine, J. (1991). *Sunday in the park with George.* New York: Applause.
Sternberg, R. J., & Kaufman, J. C. (2012). When your race is almost run, but you feel you're not yet done: Application of the Propulsion Theory of Creative Contributions to late-career challenges. *Journal of Creative Behavior, 46*, 66–76.
Sternberg, R. J., Kaufman, J. C., & Pretz, J. E. (2001). The propulsion model of creative contributions applied to the arts and letters. *Journal of Creative Behavior, 35*, 75–101.
Sternberg, R. J., Kaufman, J. C., & Pretz, J. E. (2002). *The creativity conundrum.* Philadelphia, PA: Psychology Press.
Sternberg, R. J., Kaufman, J. C., & Pretz, J. E. (2003). A propulsion model of creative leadership. *Leadership Quarterly, 14*, 455–473.
Torrance, E. P. (1974). *Torrance tests of creative thinking. Directions manual and scoring guide, verbal test booklet B.* Bensenville, IL: Scholastic Testing Service.
Torrance, E. P. (2008). *The Torrance tests of creative thinking norms-technical manual figural (streamlined) forms A & B.* Bensenville, IL: Scholastic Testing Service.

Chapter 2

Hitting Your Mark
The Importance of Appropriateness

George (*Sunday in the Park with George*), Success
Hope Cladwell (*Urinetown*), Suppress
Myth: Creativity has no Constraints
Activity: The Abacus of Balance

In *Sunday in the Park with George*, there are actually two characters named George. One is the famous painter Georges Seurat, best known for his pointillist masterpiece "A Sunday Afternoon on the Island of La Grande Jatte." Seurat is not the one who is our Success model. The painter is portrayed (in a fictional manner) as an obsessed creator who ignores his lover and lets her leave him for another man. His single-minded devotion to his craft isolates him and prevents him from human connection. We are instead talking about the other George, who appears in the second act set in the present day. This George is Seurat's (fictional) descendant who is a modern artist who uses light machines to create elaborate displays.

We meet modern-day George at a reception for his work where he is obliged to woo potential donors and make polite conversation with a wide assortment of critics, patrons, colleagues, and museum and gallery workers whom he does not particularly respect or like. He sings "Putting it Together," a frantic explosion of inner monologue that discusses the other side of being an artist: the pandering, the politicking, the polite conversations, and the endless courting of money and support. George hates having to do this part, but he is also aware that it takes a lot of capital to finance his artistic creations. If he wants to create elaborate art installations, he needs the resources. If he does not make the various intelligentsia and jet setters feel valued, he will lose the commissions he needs.

Compromise isn't sexy. There's a reason why there are no songs that extol the power of dreaming the *possible* dream. Yet without that balance between passion and practicality, you can have the best ideas in the world but they will never be realized.

Creativity Hurdle to Leap: Know when compromise and practicality can serve your voice!

DOI: 10.4324/9781003389668-4

The Role of Task Appropriateness

Remember in Chapter 1, we talked about how originality is one part of the most common definition of creativity? The other part is task appropriateness.[1] We do not mean being socially appropriate – you can be as outrageous as you want – but rather, does the action fit the situation? Are you fulfilling the demands of the task? For example, using fireflies instead of stage lights is quite original, but the odds are quite good the audience wouldn't be able to see terribly well.

In creativity research, originality and task appropriateness are each considered necessary but not sufficient.[2] So something that is highly original but not at all task appropriate isn't creative; it's like multiplying something by zero.[3] It doesn't matter if you're multiplying ten times zero or ten thousand times zero; the end result is still zero.

Being creative feels like it should be daring, maybe even scary. Maybe creativity seems like it would thrive best in chaos. Yet most research shows that the opposite is true. Yes, sudden inspiration and glorious a-ha moments of insight and crazed all-night sessions of bouncing ideas back and forth with no boundaries can be part of being creative. The equally important part, however, is less sexy. It's hard work, consistent practice, learning, preparation, revision, and doing your homework. Finding your voice is essential. But if you don't find your balance, you will be singing by yourself.

Part of finding your balance is figuring out what is task appropriate. As with the right level of originality, the rules about what might be considered appropriate or inappropriate may vary. There are some obvious examples of something being task inappropriate (making a delicious guacamole out of avocados, salt, lime juice, and crushed glass), but many things are up for debate. Let's say you ask a group of children what they want to be when they grow up. Some shout out they want to be a fireman or a doctor; sure, those are perfectly good aspirations. Someone else says he wants to be an astronaut and then another voice says she wants to be a major league baseball player. These are less likely goals (statistically speaking), but certainly possible. A little girl says she wants to be a princess. Well, that's still possible if particularly unlikely. Then a little boy says he wants to be a tractor. Yeah, that's not going to happen. And what about the child who yells out, "Broadway star"?

> Creativity Hurdle to Leap: Chaos is not creative; being relevant is underappreciated!

The Risks of Inappropriateness

Any creator trying to make a living today needs to be aware of the task appropriateness component. As Disney's influence on Broadway continues to grow, many shows – like many organizations – are looking for people to fill roles like cogs in a wheel. One of our friends made callbacks for *Les Misérables*'s Madame

Thénardier, only to lose the role to someone who fit into the dress worn by the last actress. Another friend is an award-winning actor who auditioned for a lead role in a long-running Disney show. He was excited, feeling like he had the role, because his read brought a different dimension to what he felt was a stale character. To his surprise, his follow-up call resulted in a heart-to-heart talk with the casting agent. What he believed was his strength, namely his energy and new perspective, actually cost him the role.

It is easy to want to criticize Disney for looking for cookie-cutter actors who could come off an assembly line. Yet it is important, too, to realize that Disney – and every major producer – has a lot at stake. Their brand represents billions of dollars. They know that many people who come to the show are buying tickets because they fell in love with the original movie or have all of the merchandise. The current fan base has to leave the theatre (or streaming service) satisfied. Giving their audience a memorable experience means providing the same characters, situations, and storylines that they already know and love. Even a character's wardrobe is carefully planned through dozens of meetings, and once established, the costume is not changed (unfortunately for our actress friend). There are similar scenarios for many shows that make it all the way to Broadway, particularly the recent string of jukebox musicals.

This phenomenon is not limited to Broadway. At one point, seeing a show in Ohio or Florida meant seeing either a summer stock show with a former movie or television star or else seeing a community theatre production with its own interpretation. Now, if someone sees that their city is getting the National Tour of *Phantom of the Opera*, they're expecting to see a cloned production of what's on Broadway. There might be some minor adjustments to account for the road, but the experience is supposed to be the same. If a ticket-buyer in Nevada sees *Les Misérables*, they will feel cheated if they see a poor knock-off. They may not know the name of the actor playing Jean Valjean, but they have an image of the show in their minds and this show is the one they want to see. Ticket prices are rising such that a night out at the theatre is no longer a regular occurrence for many people; it may be a treat to experience once in a year (or longer). The cloning of the tours serves as a quality control.

If you're seeking cutting-edge, gritty theatre, then you know you're not going to get it in a cloned show. Similarly, if you're an actor who brings a vibrant independence to the table, then auditioning for the fourth National Touring Company of *Wicked* is not the best decision. Our actor friend was quite depressed about not getting the job, but it was predictable. He thought he was helping them out by showing them better interpretations of the role, but that's not what they were seeking. Ultimately, his originality was not appropriate. Similarly, if you are a props master for a low-budget local theatre, they may not appreciate your new idea for a gold-plated, robotic barber chair for their production of *Sweeney Todd*.

This phenomenon is true in nearly all domains. Most workplaces have a virtual or physical suggestion box. Some offer this option simply for show; they don't want to hear from their employees but feel compelled to pretend they do. Others genuinely strive for improvement. It is essential to discern where your company falls. Even if they are truly requesting feedback, some worker suggestions are easy to implement and will help everyone ("We need better WiFi"). Other recommendations would be dauntingly expensive or risky to try ("We need an open bar"). Someone who proposes the second type of idea would not be seen as a problem-solver or innovator. Instead, they would just seem out of touch.

> Creativity Hurdle to Leap: Make sure your ideas are appropriate for the context!

Learning to Find Balance

Consider Tevye from *Fiddler on the Roof*, who is asked to shift gears to keep up with the changing standards of appropriateness of his times. The show begins with the amazing opening number "Tradition," literally setting the stage for the world in which Tevye lives. Anatevka is in early 1900s Russia, where anti-Jewish pogroms are a fact of life. Gender roles are strict, a father's will is dominant, and Jews only marry Jews. Little by little, Tevye has to shift his beliefs about what constitutes task-appropriate behavior in his role as a father. Yente the matchmaker pairs up his oldest daughter Tzeitel with a well-off butcher, to which Tevye enthusiastically agrees. When Tzeitel begs permission to marry her true love, the poor tailor Motel, Tevye relents (knowing he will be publicly humiliated) and allows them to marry for love. Next, Hodel falls in love with the radical Perchik and asks for Tevye's blessing – but not his permission. Again, after some deliberation, he shifts his beliefs. Finally, his daughter Chava begins a relationship with a Russian Christian, Fyedka, and asks for her father's permission. At last Tevye has been pushed too far; he is unable to see a mixed-religion marriage as ever being acceptable. He refuses permission, yet Chava and Fyedka disobey and elope. By the end, however, Tevye has grown enough that, as he and his family are forced to leave their home, he can wish (albeit indirectly) for Chava to have God be with her.

Ironically, Tevye learned to find his balance over the course of *Fiddler of the Roof* – but the performer who first embodied him, Zero Mostel, seemed to lose his ability to stay on task as he progressed in his career. Always known as an improviser, he would constantly try new interpretations or lines in his shows but usually stay true to characters. As he aged, he got worse. As Ethan Mordden noted in *On Sondheim*, adlibbing was at one point a fixture of theatre but had mostly ended by the 1930s. Mostel was one of the last performers to continue to use the technique. In *A Funny Thing Happened on the Way to the Forum*, for example, he altered a line about a body snatcher owing him a favor to be about the body snatcher owing him a snatch – changing a funny line to be, as Mordden described it, "cheap and stupid."[4] It is not surprising that despite Mostel's accomplishments, he is not looked back on fondly by many of the creators with whom he collaborated.

Finding your balance can mean many things. It can be making sure that your ideas are feasible and not off the wall. It can be modifying your own expectations so that you are not so steeped in the past that you overlook new possibilities. It can be knowing when to compromise and let someone else's voice determine the course of events and when to stay true to your vision no matter what happens.

> Creativity Hurdle to Leap: Find that sweet spot of pleasing yourself vs pleasing others!

Your Creative Investment

There are costs to everything, as we will continue to discuss throughout the book. Being creative in anything requires so many resources: time, money, space, effort, passion, and energy. If you pursued every idea with the same force, you would grow exhausted. One popular theory of creativity[5] uses the metaphor of investment banking (which may not strike you as the sexiest choice imaginable). A successful creator will choose ideas that are currently unpopular or out of fashion ("buying low") and convince others of their appeal and worth. Just as people start agreeing and jumping on the bandwagon, the creator finds a new unpopular idea to pursue ("selling high"). Think about Lin-Manuel Miranda. Before *In the Heights*, Hip Hop had not been used in a successful Broadway show. In addition, the Hispanic American/Latino/a experience had not been shared on Broadway (although a small number of off-Broadway and regional shows, such as *Four Guys Named José and Una Mujer Named Maria*, had been met with some level of success). When *In the Heights* became a Tony-winning hit and made Miranda a star, one would be forgiven for assuming he would stick to the same format. Instead, he used his musical talents to revisit American history.

Historical musicals can certainly be quite memorable; *1776* spurred James's lifelong interest in the Declaration of Independence. But at that point, most Broadway musicals tended to be either movie adaptations or jukebox shows, with the occasional original story (such as *Next to Normal, The Drowsy Chaperone*, or *Memphis*). There had only been a few outstanding shows since 1776 that were based on historical events (such as *The Scottsboro Boys, Allegiance*, or *Grey Gardens*), but these focused on 20th-century events. In the hands of many others, celebrating a founding father who is mostly remembered for dying in a duel would have resulted in a theatrical footnote.

Instead, Miranda's talent and instincts led him to make history himself with one of the most game-changing musicals of all time. As you might have guessed, we are referring to ~~Burr!~~ Hamilton.

> Creativity Hurdle to Leap: Learn when to shake things up and learn when to stay the course!

The basic lessons hold true for everyone. If your ideas are so radical that others cannot understand or appreciate them, you may end up singing to yourself. But if you try to repeat past successes, people may not want to hear a reprise of the same song. Remember, too, that your resources are not infinite. If you jump at every opportunity, you risk spreading yourself too thin. Of course, if you wait for the perfect opening, you may wait your whole life. Everything comes down to balance.

Being Creative Does Not Mean Being a Jerk

Something to think about is that there is a subtle anti-creativity bias in our society. Studies in the workplace have found that creative people are seen as being poor potential leaders.[6] When executives talk about creativity to investors, their market shares take a short-term dive.[7] In an academic setting, other studies have found that teachers may dislike creative students without ever even realizing it.[8] One reason may be that, like our friend who auditioned for the Disney show found out, people like things that are familiar and well known.[9] But another possible reason that has been proposed[10] is that what is disliked isn't creativity. What turns people off is chaotic, unpleasant, disorganized, and just plain bad behavior that some creators indulge in, thinking that it is how to better reach their muse.

Such shenanigans can cost people work. For example, Dana was once involved in the casting process of a show as the creators discussed how to best fill a role that needed a heavy hitter. They needed an actress who would bring fire, bite, and vocal prowess. Several well-known actresses auditioned but no one had the mix of excitement and singing acumen that the producers sought. Finally, the lead producer went around the room asking the team one-by-one, "If we could have anyone in the role, who would you choose?" When Dana suggested one name (whom you've heard of), everyone in the room nodded in agreement – until the producer frowned and said something like, "I can't afford therapy for the entire cast."

One more glorious anonymous story: During the run of one musical known for a portrayal of (literally) naked physical intimacy, an actor hurt his thigh muscle when working out. He rubbed a caustic topical ointment on the sore spot yet forgot to warn his female costar (or cover up the afflicted area). After they finished that scene, the lead actress had to sing a solo. One of the castmates would later remember her singing with tears streaming from her eyes from the quite intense pain of the lotion finding its way into a place where the lotion was not meant to be. It may not be a coincidence that whereas the actress went on to a successful career, the actor did not.

> Creativity Hurdle to Leap: Make sure your voice doesn't include unpleasant tones!

Finding your voice, as we discussed in the first chapter, is essential. Yet if expressing your voice comes at the expense of balance – the balance of the show, the balance of an ensemble, the balance of a collaborative team, or even the balance of your own life – then you need to reassess your priorities.

The Long-Term Danger of Being a Diva

The word "diva" (male or female) has many connotations. Some are positive; many are not. On one hand, a diva is someone who commands attention and often has a powerful voice, strong confidence, and sharp charisma. On the other hand, a stereotypical diva might have outrageous demands, betray secrets, and abuse colleagues. In other words, they're crazy-makers. Such behavior loses work even for established, talented stars, let alone those just starting out. Do not pick up bad habits that you assume should come with the territory.

To give an example from the creativity research world, one study that is often misinterpreted is James's own "Sylvia Plath Effect,[11]" which found that eminent female poets are more likely to show signs of mental illness than other eminent writers and other accomplished women (including actors, artists, businesswomen, and politicians). Why is it often misinterpreted? Sometimes people think it means that all creative people are mentally ill (not true). Other times young poets, particularly young female poets, will think that they are more likely to be mentally ill – which is also, unequivocally, not true. It's not what the study ever said, yet it's what many people want to believe.[12] People love to assume that if two things are related, then that means that one causes the other one. It's not true. Sylvia Plath wasn't a poetic genius because she was mentally ill, and trying to act like Plath will not give you her brilliance. It's the same thing with divas – acting like a diva will certainly not give you an amazing voice and presence, and may, in fact, prevent you from ever being able to take the stage in the first place.

Why do people behave in this way? The answer can often be found in some variation of a flawed logic. Maybe some honestly do not know any better. They have seen other people behave like divas and be accepted (and even celebrated). Or else perhaps they themselves have acted poorly before and had their cast and crew (or colleagues) endure it silently, leading them to assume that such behavior is fine. This type of situation can evolve over time. People begin to believe their own press. What can eventually happen is that they have a distorted understanding of what is needed from them at a given moment. Going back one last time to our friend who lost the Disney job, the casting agent can be seen as an angel of mercy, saving our friend from himself. If our friend had gotten the job, his vision of the role would have clashed with expectations and may have led to stories about him being a "difficult" actor.

When we were trying to think of the best diva behavior stories to tell here, we reached out to our Facebook friends for examples. There was a delicious ongoing thread that resulted, as well as many private messages. What ended up standing out more than any one particular juicy story was that each anecdote was equally about the pushback to the behavior. The stories weren't just of the nature of "Can you believe this incredible behavior?" Nearly all of them ended with some type of comeuppance from the cast, crew, or creative team. Just to give a very vague example, a diva was in a musical where a different (very accomplished) actress played the maid. When the maid did not instantly pick up a jacket dropped by the diva during a dress rehearsal, the diva began screaming about the lack of attentiveness. The actress snapped back, "I'm your maid in the show, not in real life," and stormed off to (possible apocryphal) widespread cheering.

We thought that rather than continuing on with stories of outlandish diva shenanigans, we would instead reiterate the need for every storyteller to include the diva's retribution was even more powerful than the telling of the outburst. It doesn't matter if Patti LuPone, Bernadette Peters, Mandy Patinkin, Ethel Merman, Nathan Lane, or Idina Menzel might be able to theoretically get away with it – anyone can have a bad day. The important thing is that you're probably not Patti LuPone. (If you are, hi Patti! We love you! Please get us comps to your next show.) But otherwise, you can't get away with it. Don't do it. In addition, the world is changing. Toxic behavior is becoming less and less excused or tolerated, regardless of the magnitude of the star.

In some ways, being creative in a professional space is like driving: Unless you hear otherwise, stay in your own lane. To continue to use theatre as our metaphor, people are hired for many different reasons, from being able to hit a high "C" to doing a triple pirouette to delivering a monologue that makes the audience weep. Indeed, having experience and talent in many different areas is a positive attribute. But typically, you're hired for a single job.

Consider an actor who is also a skilled musician to the point where they could also be the music director. This talent may have helped them get the role because the creative team knows they can learn the songs easily. However, that actor is *not* the music director and shouldn't be giving notes to their fellow actors. Many ensemble members in a Broadway show are such good dancers they could easily be the choreographer – but if they're not, they know to stay in their lane and keep their mouths shut. There are always exceptions, and as you progress you will get more astute at determining when to make suggestions. As you start out in whatever your creative endeavor, however, err on the side of caution.

Yes, you can be a working performer and act like a diva if you continue being a star. Yet think about the flip side of diva behavior. When James began regularly seeing shows on Broadway, he noted many of the same names kept popping up in the ensembles and smaller roles – people like Michael X. Martin, Ann Sanders, Michael McCormick, Cameron Adams, and T. Oliver Reid. James doesn't know them (he just loves their work), and perhaps his hunch is wrong. He nonetheless has a strong gut feeling that there is some quality about them – a balance that manifests itself as professionalism, generosity, or collegiality – that, combined with their talent, keeps them constantly working on Broadway while others can go years between roles.

> Creativity Hurdle to Leap:
> Aim for a diva's talent, not a diva's behavior!

Myth: Creativity Has No Constraints

It is easy to feel that creativity means no boundaries, no rules, and nothing holding you back. True creativity should be personal expression run wild. Yet research continually indicates that none of these thoughts are actually true. We've already talked about how task appropriateness is half of the actual definition of creativity. Creativity is not chaos.

Constraints are a natural part of creativity. We often have limited time[13] and money,[14] for example. But such restrictions are not necessarily a bad thing. Constraints can lead to different types of creativity.[15] Even more, several studies have found that when you are given a task or prompt, being given some type of limit actually makes you more creative.[16] It may be that the blank page is intimidating and that having any type of guidance, even if it is telling you what not to do, can help. But it can also be that the actual act of overcoming constraints and figuring out how to do something without the usual array of resources actually inspires creativity by itself.[17]

One of the best examples of the use of constraints in theatre is *The Fantasticks*. The show is traditionally told in a simple space with virtually no set (a titled backdrop held up by a pole). The original orchestration used only a Harp, Bass, and Percussion.[18] The show had a tiny budget; the initial sets, props, lighting, and costumes were all done by the same person. This small show became the longest-running musical ever and is now back in New York after a brief hiatus. The sharp financial limitations that the creators faced in mounting the musical allowed the sweetness of the story and music to resonate with generations of audiences.

It is also interesting to note that there is a cultural angle to this myth. The idea of creativity being a purely individual (almost selfish) activity is a very Western idea.[19] Moreover, some argue that Eastern cultures value task appropriateness more than originality when considering creative work.[20] Certainly, Eastern conceptions of creativity tend to emphasize different components than the West. There tends to be more of a focus on collaboration, adaptation, harmony, and working within traditions and social norms.[21]

The Japanese theatre form of *Kabuki* is steeped in tradition. The combination of dramatic theatre and dance is drawn from many conventions that appear in different Japanese arts. It evolved such that the creativity came with how the story could be told within a rigid and formal structure. Later, when Japan was occupied by American forces, *Kabuki* made a comeback as a way to continue artistic expression even in a hostile environment with extensive censorship.[22] It embodies many traits of Eastern conceptions of creativity; it draws on tradition, and creativity emerges from how these limitations are handled. Small, incremental changes on existing work are a viable and important means of artistic expression.

Constraints can also play a role in how you shape your career. Consider Leanne Borghesi, a cabaret singer/actress who won the 2022 New York Manhattan Association of Cabarets (MAC) Award. Whereas many of her colleagues landed in New York City, she and her wife ended up in San Francisco.

She said "The lack of professional theatre thrust me into local theatre, performance art, and cabaret," Because of these new forms, I was able to create my own theatre and learn how to grow and audience and sustain solo show. By living, boozing, loving, and creating in the moment, I learned a whole bevy of skills that my Broadway-bound colleagues did not. As I watched them leave the business, I kept growing.

The kind of person who can be creative under constraints will be primed to handle sudden changes or adversity. As COVID-19 shut down the theatres and cabarets, Borghesi began teaching music online to young students. She also worked to become a certified coach. Think of how many people across all fields had to scramble, change, adapt, and grow under very strict constraints to thrive, support themselves, and remain creatively fulfilled.

> Creativity Hurdle to Leap: Use constraints and limitations to your advantage!

The Danger of No Constraints

Urinetown is a delightfully absurd musical, so forgive us if this example is a wee wee bit over the top (wink, wink). The danger of having no constraints at all can be seen in Hope Cladwell's character arc, our Suppress model for this chapter. *Urinetown* presents a futuristic dystopia where extreme droughts make toilets a luxury. As a huge corporation charges for toilet use, the police crack down on public urinators. When Hope, the corporation president's daughter, is kidnapped by a revolutionary group, she grows sympathetic to their cause. She ends up capturing and executing her father and the other corporation leaders and allows everyone the freedom to pee wherever and whenever they want. Alas, although her father's policies were unfair, they worked. When Hope changes the rules, she inadvertently causes the water supply to run out and she is torn to shreds by the crowd.

There are many dull parts of creativity. One of the least sexy is that rules and boundaries can serve specific and positive purposes. Yes, creativity can entail breaking rules. More often, however, true creativity involves doing something original within the rules.

> Creativity Hurdle to Leap: Figure out which rules to challenge and which ones might save your butt!

Hope's initial triumph plays into our expectation that revolutionaries fighting for freedom *should* be the heroes, just as creativity *should* be about pushing the limits and fighting the establishment. But sometimes a rule has a very good reason for existing. Maybe you'll be fine if you swim 30 minutes after eating, but you should definitely avoid swimming in shark-infested waters.

Activity: The Abacus of Balance

Once again, we'll take a bit of a break and give you the floor. We're going to show you an abacus – the abacus of balance (cue the music)! We have highlighted five key dimensions required for balance that need to be juggled: Past, Expression, Attainability, Constraints, and Ego (PEACE). We are showing the extremes of each dimension on each side of the abacus. We would like you to circle or color in the ball that represents where you think you are across each dimension.

Your own insight into yourself is very important. However, we may not always be the most objective judge of ourselves. So let us get a second opinion. Go to our website at https://creatingyourspotlight.com/do/ and download the exercises packet,

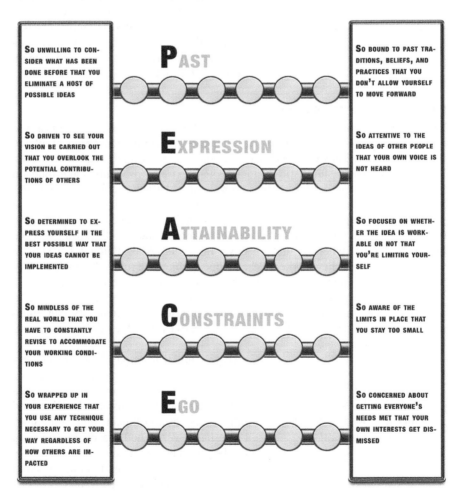

Figure 2.1 Abacus of Balance, Self. © Kaufman and Rowe (Creating Your Spotlight workbook, in progress)

Hitting Your Mark: The Importance of Appropriateness   39

which will include the Abacus of Balance. Give it to someone who knows you and your work very well. It could be a partner (in the personal or professional sense), a colleague, a friend, or a mentor. Have them fill out the abacus *about you* but do not show that person your own version.

Compare your friend's ratings against your own. On which side of the abacus do you tend to lean? How does your judgment of yourself differ from how your friends see you? The way that your own self-perceptions align with how others view you is related to your metacognition, which is how well you understand and can monitor your own strengths and weaknesses.[23] This concept can be applied to creativity, and we will go into more detail in Chapter 7.

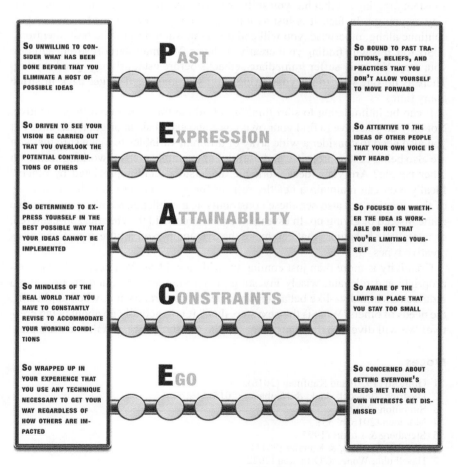

Figure 2.2 Abacus of Balance, Other. © Kaufman and Rowe (Creating Your Spotlight workbook, in progress)

Looking at the different abacuses, where do you have room to grow? Do you tend to err on being too high on each dimension and stifling your own voice in the interests of the greater good? Or do you lean toward the opposite extreme and risk alienating others and sabotaging yourself in your desire to follow your own ideas?

> Creativity Hurdle to Leap: Find the best balance between aiming too big (and failing) and aiming too small!

Moving Forward

Finding your balance on the high-wire act of life is not a one-time activity. It is a constant juggling act that has you shift first one way and then another, feeling your way as you go. In fact, it is just as important that you keep your balance as you continue along; otherwise, you will end up in the water despite the best intentions.

So, too, it is with finding your creative balance. You may start off strong and lose your way. You may suffer immediate setbacks before establishing a good rhythm. There is no one way to hit your stride. And you may need to get back in stride many times.

It can be intimidating to start thinking of all the things required to be creative. Not only do you have to find your own voice and establish an original presence but you also need to consider a wide array of different variables to make sure that you are also being task appropriate and useful. For example, are you working well with other people? Are your ideas workable, understood, and appreciated by others? Ideally, you can maintain a healthy respect for past traditions and the limitations of the situation yet also see these constraints as a challenge to raise your creative game instead of giving up. In essence, you have to avoid the chaotic, self-centered, or unrealistic behaviors that can make the average person a little suspicious of us creative types.

Creativity is more than just coming up with new ideas. You need to be task appropriate and relevant, wisely investing your resources, time, and energy. Avoid indulgences and diva-like behavior while noting constraints and, when applicable, the needs of others. What is the next step, then? It is to actually go about being creative! We will dive into the many stages of the creative process in the next chapter.

Notes

1. Guilford (1950) and Kaufman (2016).
2. Diedrich, Benedek, Jauk, & Neubauer (2015).
3. Simonton (2012).
4. Mordden (2016, p. 53).
5. Sternberg & Lubart (1995).
6. Mueller, Goncalo, & Kamdar (2011).
7. Haselhuhn, Wong, & Ormiston (2022).
8. Aljughaiman & Mowrer-Reynolds (2005) and Westby & Dawson (1995).
9. Eidelman & Crandall (2012).

10 Kaufman, Beghetto, & Watson (2016).
11 Kaufman (2001).
12 Kaufman, Bromley, & Cole (2006).
13 Baer & Oldham (2006).
14 Scopelliti, Cillo, Busacca, & Mazursky (2014).
15 Keinänen, Sheridan, & Gardner (2016).
16 Haught (2015).
17 Stokes (2007).
18 Viagas & Farber (2005).
19 Erez & Nouri (2010) and Sternberg (1985).
20 Leung & Morris (2011).
21 Lan & Kaufman (2012) and Niu & Kaufman (2013).
22 Okamoto (2001).
23 Flavell (1979).

References

Aljughaiman, A., & Mowrer-Reynolds, E. (2005). Teachers' conceptions of creativity and creative students. *Journal of Creative Behavior, 39*, 17–34.
Baer, M., & Oldham, G. R. (2006). The curvilinear relation between experienced creative time pressure and creativity: Moderating effects of openness to experience and support for creativity. *Journal of Applied Psychology, 91*, 963–970.
Diedrich, J., Benedek, M., Jauk, E., & Neubauer, A. C. (2015). Are creative ideas novel and useful? *Psychology of Aesthetics, Creativity, and the Arts, 9*(1), 35–40.
Eidelman, S., & Crandall, C. S. (2012). Bias in favor of the status quo. *Social and Personality Psychology Compass, 6*, 270–281.
Erez, M., & Nouri, R. (2010). Creativity: The influence of cultural, social, and work contexts. *Management and Organization Review, 6*, 351–370.
Flavell, J. H. (1979). Metacognition and cognitive monitoring: A new area of cognitive developmental inquiry. *American Psychologist, 34*, 906–911.
Guilford, J. P. (1950). Creativity. *American Psychologist, 5*, 444–454.
Haselhuhn, M. P., Wong, E. M., & Ormiston, M. E. (2022). Investors respond negatively to executives' discussion of creativity. *Organizational Behavior and Human Decision Processes, 171*, 104155. doi: 10.1016/j.obhdp.2022.104155
Haught, C. (2015). The role of constraints in creative sentence production. *Creativity Research Journal, 27*, 160–166.
Kaufman, J. C. (2001). The Sylvia Plath effect: Mental illness in eminent creative writers. *Journal of Creative Behavior, 35*, 37–50.
Kaufman, J. C. (2016). *Creativity 101*. New York, NY: Springer.
Kaufman, J. C., Beghetto, R. A., & Watson, C. (2016). Creative metacognition and the importance of teaching kids when (not) to be creative. *Roeper Review, 35*, 155–165.
Kaufman, J. C., Bromley, M. L., & Cole, J. C. (2006). Insane, poetic, lovable: Creativity and endorsement of the "Mad Genius" stereotype. *Imagination, Cognition, and Personality, 26*, 149–161.
Keinänen, M., Sheridan, K., & Gardner, H. (2016). Opening up creativity: The lenses of axis and focus. In J. C. Kaufman & J. Baer (Eds.), *Creativity and reason in cognitive development* (2nd ed., pp. 261–281). New York, NY: Cambridge University Press.
Lan, L., & Kaufman, J. C. (2012). American and Chinese similarities and differences in defining and valuing creative products. *Journal of Creative Behavior, 46*, 285–306.

Leung, K., & Morris, M. W. (2011). Culture and creativity: A social psychological analysis. In D. DeCremer, J. K. Murnighan, & R. van Dick (Eds.), *Social psychology and organizations* (pp. 371–395). New York, NY: Routledge.

Mordden, E. (2016). *On Sondheim: An opinionated guide*. New York, NY: Oxford University Press.

Mueller, J. S., Goncalo, J. A., & Kamdar, D. (2011). Recognizing creative leadership: Can creative idea expression negatively relate to perceptions of leadership potential? *Journal of Experimental Social Psychology, 47,* 494–498.

Niu, W., & Kaufman, J. C. (2013). Creativity of Chinese and American cultures: A synthetic analysis. *Journal of Creative Behavior, 47,* 77–87.

Okamoto, S. (2001). *The man who saved Kabuki: Faubion Bowers and theatre censorship in occupied Japan*. Honolulu: University of Hawaii Press.

Scopelliti, I., Cillo, P., Busacca, B., & Mazursky, D. (2014). How do financial constraints affect creativity? *Journal of Product Innovation Management, 31,* 880–893.

Simonton, D. K. (2012). Taking the US Patent Office creativity criteria seriously: A quantitative three-criterion definition and its implications. *Creativity Research Journal, 24,* 97–106

Sternberg, R. J. (1985). Implicit theories of intelligence, creativity, and wisdom. *Journal of Personality and Social Psychology, 49,* 607–627.

Sternberg, R. J., & Lubart, T. I. (1995). *Defying the crowd*. New York, NY: Free Press.

Stokes, P. D. (2007). Using constraints to generate and sustain novelty. *Psychology of Aesthetics, Creativity, and the Arts, 1,* 107–113.

Viagas, R., & Farber, D. C. (2005). *The amazing story of The Fantasticks: America's longest-running play*. New York, NY: Lamplight Editions.

Westby, E. L., & Dawson, V. L. (1995). Creativity: Asset or burden in the classroom? *Creativity Research Journal, 8,* 1–10.

Chapter 3

Thinking on Your Feet
The Creative Process

Pippin (*Pippin*), Success
The Witch (*Into the Woods*), Suppress
Activity: Musical Theatre Idea Generation; Remote Theatrical Associations
Myth: Functional Fixedness and Sunken Costs

Most musicals have an "I Want" song, usually early in the show, when a lead character sings about their hopes. These songs set up their goals for the audience to quickly understand – think of "Somewhere Over the Rainbow" from *The Wizard of Oz*, "My Shot" from *Hamilton*, "Waiting for Life to Begin" from *Once on this Island*, or "What Baking Can Do" from *Waitress*. When we first meet Pippin, he is singing his "I Want" song, "Corner of the Sky." He dreams of finding his place in the world – his mission in life. He does not want to "waste [his] life on commonplace, ordinary pursuits," but instead find something "completely fulfilling.[1]"

Many of us also seek to experience that moment of insight where we realize our passion and find our metaphorical home. Pippin pursues that moment and tries on many different possible roles, from a war hero to a hedonistic Casanova to a people pleaser. Yet by the end, as the Leading Player urges him to immolate himself in a burst of glory, Pippin realizes that what he wants is the simple life: Having a wife and stepson, living in the country, and being a farmer. He has in some ways lived the opposite of a hero's journey, seeking fame and fortune yet finding happiness in the mundane. An alternate ending of the show has Pippin's son Theo begin singing "Corner of the Sky," suggesting that the cycle may begin anew (and, perhaps, end in a darker fashion for Theo).

Pippin ends up happy (even if, as he famously ends the show by saying, he is also trapped). He may not have a flashy or exciting life, but he is at peace. One way that he reached this goal is by staying the course, overcoming obstacles, and solving each problem that came his way. Compare Pippin's journey to that of the Witch in *Into the Woods*. We meet her as an old crone desperately seeking ingredients to a magic potion that will (we ultimately find out) restore her beauty. She bullies and bribes others to do the grunt work. The Witch actually has a number of riches in her life. She has a daughter who she cares about deeply (albeit in an unhealthy way) and magical powers that can even raise creatures from the dead. Act One

DOI: 10.4324/9781003389668-5

ends with her seemingly achieving her dreams; she gets the potion and becomes stunningly beautiful. Yet it comes with a price: She loses her powers. Further, her overprotective nature pushes her daughter Rapunzel away into the arms of a prince (and, eventually, into the path of a Giantess who tramples her to death). As chaos descends on the village, the Witch has no powers to help battle the Giantess and is left with a Machiavellian approach that doesn't work as well without magic to back her up. She ambiguously disappears, having lost her daughter, her powers, and ultimately her agency and will to exist. The last full song of the show, "Children will Listen," strikes a cautionary note about (among other things) making the right wishes.

Pippin ultimately made good choices and ends up happy. The Witch made poor choices and doesn't even exist by the time the curtain falls. In the real world, there are less flaming hoops designed to burn us alive and fewer magic beans to squander. Making good choices about your creativity, however, is a key part of your journey. At every point, you will encounter challenges, opportunities, and complications. In this chapter, we will talk about how you can use disparate aspects of creative problem-solving to keep advancing from role to role.

> Creativity Hurdle to Leap: As you consider your many creative possibilities, choose the one that will be best for your future self!

Creative Problem-Solving

Both Pippin and the Witch go on journeys to solve their problems, much as we all do (if a little less dramatically). Solving problems can be a complicated experience. In creativity research, there are many different models of problem-solving – so many that we're not going to even try to cover them all. Instead, we will boil them down to four stages that commonly reoccur throughout different theories.[2]

The first stage is problem-finding.[3] This step is often overlooked or misunderstood. We often think of problems as being relatively obvious – "I have an abscess in my jaw" or "I am really hungry." Yet, it is easy to misidentify the real problem. Maybe you are hungry because you are not getting proper nutrition (or you have a tapeworm), and you can eat all the snacks you want without solving your problem. Perhaps you are not getting callbacks at any of your auditions. You may think your problem is a lack of talent, but there are many other potential problems to be investigated first. Are you lacking confidence? How do you present yourself? Are you adequately prepared? Are you auditioning for the right kind of roles? In addition, some people may consider "I'm not getting audition callbacks" (or promotions) as the problem itself. Yet that is a symptom, not a problem. Taking Tylenol for a headache gets rid of the (painful) symptom; if you (or your partner) have a headache every night, there may be an underlying problem that needs to be addressed.

The ability to identify the right problem tends to be overlooked, yet it is a very strong predictor of eventual success.[4] For many of us, recognizing the problem to be solved is automatic. We may assume that we need to take a certain approach without even being aware we're doing so.[5] Yet those who are more creative are more likely to actively consider many different possible problems that may underlie the "symptoms.[6]" Choosing the wrong problem to solve – as the Witch did in trying to regain her beauty – can waste your time and cost you dearly. In the realm of the theatre, pursuing the wrong problem leads to unnecessary lessons, the wrong teacher, or setting your sights on poorly-chosen roles. How many performers have focused on improving their looks or regaining their youth in hopes of getting the lead role when the true issue is that their "type" is the comic relief or dance captain?

To begin a recurring example, let's say that you are in rehearsals to play Ado Annie in *Oklahoma!* You are consistently getting negative feedback from the director, the choreographer, and fellow cast members. What is the problem? It might be that you're doing great and everyone is jealous (that one is unlikely). It might be that you are terrible and should never act again (that one is also unlikely). Maybe the director wants you to imitate another actress and you do not see the role in that way. Maybe you were miscast. Maybe your skillset doesn't match the cast (e.g., your strength is singing and the cast tends to be actor-centric or better dancers)? Or perhaps your approach to the role doesn't jibe with the rest of the cast?

> Creativity Hurdle to Leap: Make sure you are solving the right problem before you dive in!

Let us say that after much consideration and discussion with trusted friends, you decide the problem is the last option. You decide that your take on Ado Annie is inconsistent with how the other actors are playing their roles. Your next step is idea generation. But before we examine this concept in detail, we're going to run you through the paces as an activity.

Activity: Musical Theatre Idea Generation

For each question, give yourself five minutes (or ten, if you want; we're not watching you) to generate as many different creative responses as you can.

1. *Think of any source material (book, movie, real-life person, etc.) that has not been used yet but could make an amazing musical. List as many as you can!*

2. *Take a moment and think of one mental or physical thing you would like to change about yourself – it could be the ability to play the piano or having better math skills or having a full head of hair or being able to sing a high C (or anything else).*

   What is it? _____

Now, again giving yourself about five minutes, what are all the different ways that this change would impact your career or your life? Use a piece of scratch paper and list as many as you can!

Idea Generation

Idea generation, as you likely have gathered, is seeking many different solutions to an open-ended question. It is a crucial step in problem-solving. Once you have found the underlying problem, your next move is to come up with as many solutions that are original yet appropriate for your problem. We don't mean each idea has to be shockingly new or a perfect fit, but you should aim for them to be a little different and at least related to the problem you are trying to solve. This process is also sometimes called divergent thinking, and it is a central part of creativity research.[7] It is also the basis of the most commonly used creativity tests.[8] Although we are not interested in assessing your levels of creativity, it may help to learn how these tests are scored.

The first score is for fluency, which is the total number of responses you have given. They only count if they are relevant to the question. For example, if your physical change was to be a foot taller and you said that it would help you memorize scripts faster, that doesn't really make sense or fit the question. It would not count toward your total.

A second way is to score for flexibility, or how many categories are represented by your various responses. So imagine if, for the first question, you wrote down *Star Wars, The Empire Strikes Back, Return of the Jedi, The Phantom Menace, Attack of the Clones, Revenge of the Sith, The Force Awakens*, and *The Last Jedi*. On one hand, these are technically eight different answers, and for fluency you would get "credit." On the other hand, they're all *Star Wars* movies. It's the same category. It's very different than if you put *Star Wars, Casablanca, Ghostbusters, Citizen Kane, Bridesmaids*, and *Friday the Thirteenth* – these are all quite different movies, representing different genres, styles, and eras.

Another way these tests can be scored is for originality, or how rare and unusual (while still being relevant) your responses are.[9] For example, many people likely put *Star Wars*, but very few put down *Midnight Madness* (an obscure 1970s comedy that is one of James's wife's favorite movies). It may be interesting to also consider your answers in this light.

Incidentally, if idea generation is done as a group with other people, it is quite similar to brainstorming. Brainstorming is people tossing out many different possible ideas or solutions with no one being critical or judgmental about any of the responses. If you regularly use brainstorming as a technique, make sure that (a) you have everyone write down their ideas first so introverts get to express themselves as well, and (b) have any supervisor or boss leave the room entirely before starting.[10]

> Creativity Hurdle to Leap: When you are brainstorming, try to think of many ideas, many varied ideas, and particularly original ideas!

Idea Evaluation

Back to the Ado Annie problem, there are many possible solutions. Maybe you should seek out additional rehearsals with the actors you interact with the most, such as Will, Ali Hakim, and Laurie. Maybe you should do research at the library to see what it was like to live in Oklahoma in 1906. Maybe you should hire an acting coach to work on your scenes with you. Maybe you should quit. Maybe you should watch a rehearsal with your understudy going on in the role to see the interactions from a broader perspective. Maybe (if possible) you can ask a trusted member of the cast for their honest feedback. Maybe you should have a friend read your lines for you into a recorder so you can hear another take. Maybe you should ask a cast member to switch roles and read lines with you over a cup of coffee. Maybe you should argue to the director that your approach is the correct one and the other cast members should match your performance.

These are all possible solutions, with some notably better than others. Maybe you've thought of another five or ten that we do not have listed. The third stage, idea evaluation, is when you sort through your ideas and pick the one that is both the most practical and the most likely to give you a successful outcome. This concept is also called convergent thinking.[11] Having good insight into which one of your ideas is the best choice to pursue is a more important ability than people realize. Brainstorming and generating many different ideas feel like creativity. Carefully evaluating each one and deciding which merits your energies is a little less sexy. Yet it is no less crucial toward successfully navigating your way through a challenge.[12] For Ado Annie, there are many possible solutions to pick. Let us say for the purpose of this discussion that you ask a cast member to switch roles and read lines with you over a cup of coffee (we are not arguing that this response is specifically the best).

The final stage is implementation – you try the solution and see what happens. So let's imagine that you and the actress who plays Gertie take an hour and you read Laurie and she reads Ado Annie. One possibility is that you hear how she approaches it and you modify your performance. At the next rehearsal, you click much better with the cast, and the creative team is happy. In this case, you have solved your problem – congratulations! Another possibility is that you modify your performance, yet at the next rehearsal things go even worse. In this situation, you go back to the beginning of the creative problem-solving process. Revisit even the problem-finding phase. You then continue experimenting until you figure out the solution (or you realize that this role, production, or creative vision may simply not be a good fit for you).

> Creativity Hurdle to Leap: It is important to be able to select the best idea for your situation!

Incubation

Of course, this concept of creative problem-solving is not the only one. There are other elements of the creative process that may prove very useful. For example, an early theory of problem-solving included the idea of incubation and insight.[13] Incubation is when you are working on a task and you get stuck, so you put it aside for a little bit. At some point, you get the needed insight to continue. All of us get stuck when we are creative – in theatre, it might happen when writing an 11 o'clock number, figuring out how to increase subscription sales, designing a usable prop that has to withstand extensive use, or how to adopt a specific accent for a role. It is tempting to just want to keep plugging away, and sometimes that is the best course (giving up quickly is rarely a path to success). If nothing is coming at all, however, it may be time to put this problem aside and work on something else.

When we stop actively working on the task that is challenging us, we enter the incubation phase. Our mind is still working on the problem in the background (kind of like your virus detector on your computer) while we engage in other activities. What is the best way to crack the code and gain insight? If you need your solution quickly, one study has shown that doing a similar activity will help reach insight.[14] For example, if you get stuck in composing a song, the best tactic would be to work on another song or simply fool around on the piano a little bit (it is, of course, important to avoid unconscious plagiarism). Indeed, one of Dana's tricks is to begin playing a piece with a similar feel as the song he is trying to write (sometimes one of his own songs). This method helps him get into the right frame of mind that he needs to write an original song. He feels he is embodying the spirit of what the song needs. If you worry you are fixated on a particular aspect, you might try thinking about the problem in a different context, such as going to a different room.[15]

Sometimes, we are working on a broader project without a pressing deadline. As a result, we are less in need of a quick fix than a deeper insight. For these situations, you may not need to actively work at it. There are times when life distractions are minimized and your brain may hit on the solution spontaneously.[16] If you think of times and places you gained sudden insights, many of them may be when your body is occupied, such as in the shower, driving, or taking a walk. Conversely, there are also times when letting go of conscious thoughts can help. As you are about to fall asleep or when meditating, your mind can wander freely and help the incubation process.[17] Use whichever pathway works best for you.

> Creativity Hurdle to Leap: When you are stuck, try working on a different task in the same domain – or simply letting it simmer!

Toward Insight

One theory of insight contains three ways that we can reach our solution: selective encoding, selective combination, and selective comparison.[18] What do these mean? Selective encoding is being able to separate relevant from irrelevant information. For example, one common puzzle is to ask: Mary's mom had five daughters. The oldest was named March, the second oldest was named April, the middle daughter was named May, and the youngest was named July. What was the fourth daughter's name?"

Take a moment to think and guess. We'll wait right here. Imagine the Jeopardy theme playing....

So what's your answer? Many people will say "June." This answer is wrong. Why? Because the irrelevant information – the names of the other daughters – was encoded as being important. The key is solving the problem is to focus on the relevant detail that it is Mary's mom we are talking about – which means the mother must have a daughter named Mary. Therefore, if four of the five daughters are named something else, the fifth daughter has to be named Mary.

How might this strategy be helpful for the theatrical life? Dana was working on the song "Look at Me" for *Witches of Eastwick* and wanted to include a key change to increase the intensity of the song to lead to an ultimate emotional release. However, the song was already in a high key and the three singers were already near the top of their range. Usually, key changes go higher to help heighten the excitement. However, if Dana had arranged the piece this way, the singers would have needed to shift to a more legitimate, operatic sound – thereby diluting the impact of the key change (and, perhaps, destroying their voices). Dana decided that having the key change shift higher was actually irrelevant; the relevant part was to have the key change occur in the first place. He, therefore, had the key change go down from D-flat to C, and the resulting effect achieved the same emotional lift for the audience.

Selective combination is being able to take seemingly unrelated bits of info and combine them together to reach a solution. For example, consider another fun problem:

> A man walks into a bar and asks the bartender for a glass of water. There is no one else in the bar and the two people have never met. The bartender promptly points a gun at the man. The man thanks the bartender (and is being genuine) and then leaves. What happened? Why did the man thank the bartender?

James, who teaches classes on creativity research, has given this problem to thousands of students and has heard almost as many different possible answers. Many people ask if the gun was a squirt gun. Some people ask if the bartender was using the gun to point to a water fountain. Others ask if the two people speak the same language, or if "glass of water" or "gun" were slang terms for different concepts. The correct answer – the only one that makes sense without having to stretch reality a little bit – is reached by being able to combine two parts of the problem together. Want to take a moment and try? We'll wait.

Okay, we just got back. Did you solve it? The answer is reached by considering what similar purpose may be served with either a glass of water or having a gun pointed at you. A glass of water might be requested out of thirst... or not. A gun might be aimed at someone to threaten, or simply to scare. What is it that can be fixed by either drinking a glass of water or being scared? Having the hiccups – which is, indeed, the solution. Incidentally, if you feel uncomfortable because there is only one right answer for this problem, that is a reasonable gut feeling. Creativity feels like it should have many different possible solutions for nearly anything, and that is often true. Insight is only one aspect of creativity.

Selective combination is often used in the theatre. *The Mystery of Edwin Drood*, instead of being a straightforward adaption of a lesser-known (and incomplete) Dickens' work, uses the setting of an English music hall to not only provide the tone of the show but also to resolve the lack of an ending. It is a show within a show, with the cast playing both the Dickens characters and the actors playing them. At the moment the "real" story ends, the cast goes into the audience to take a poll to determine the ending. Theoretically, every performance of a run of *Drood* may be a different show. It combines the style of an old English vaudeville-like performance with the dramatics of a Dickens story to create something unique.[19]

Finally, selective comparison is the ability to take old and new information and compare them to reach a new conclusion. An example might be rewatching a kids' movie that you enjoyed when you were younger and then noticing an "adult" joke that only makes sense upon your second viewing. For example, the 2015 Pixar film *Inside Out* may be the source of this phenomenon for future generations. The movie, which personifies emotions, has Fear worrying about a bear. Disgust reassures him that there are no bears in San Francisco. Anger then replies, "I saw a really hairy guy; he looked like a bear.[20]" We guess that most of our theatre-loving friends will not have trouble seeing the humor in this remark.

The old and new are often combined in theatre. Shakespeare, for example, has been musicalized countless times to varying effects. Two shows that brought the old (Shakespeare) and the new (then-present day) together were *West Side Story* (an adaptation of *Romeo and Juliet*) and *Your Own Thing* (an adaptation of *Twelfth Night*). It may surprise you to hear that *West Side Story* ran for 732 performances in its original Broadway run, whereas *Your Own Thing* – although running Off-Broadway, not on – lasted for 933. Of course, *West Side Story* continues to be revived and performed all around the world, whereas *Your Own Thing* is largely a relic.

Why was one successful and one largely forgotten? There are many reasons, of course. A cheap shot is to say that the team of Danny Apolinar, Hal Hester, and Donald Driver was not at the same level of Leonard Bernstein, Stephen Sondheim, and Arthur Laurents – but, then, what team is? It is also notable that although both shows used the current times for the setting, *Your Own Thing* also used a current style of music. It therefore quickly felt out-of-date and was retrospectively lumped together with

> Creativity Hurdle to Leap: Juggling old and new information can help you reach a creative insight!

many other shows that felt like *Hair* knock-offs. In contrast, *West Side Story* used present-day settings but with a traditional musical score. To further avoid feeling dated, it even made up its own slang. But, ultimately, the vagaries of what creative works last and which do not are a complex interaction of variables.[21]

Myth: Functional Fixedness and Sunken Costs

We've talked a lot about how we solve problems, gain insight, and reach solutions. Nothing is ever smooth, and there are a lot of goblins that sabotage our thinking without us even being aware of it. Some of them are obvious to spot. For example, a common fallacy is appeal to popularity, or "everyone's doing it." Even if you fall for that one, it's not going to be a shock to realize you were manipulated. Other ones, however, are trickier and can shake up our creative problem-solving abilities.

Functional fixedness is a common myth that people buy into without even realizing it. We can make assumptions about an object, a person, or a show and include these (often unwarranted) ideas in our thinking. These can lead to pursuing strategies that do not work.[22] For example, a common insight problem is to ask how you would use a candle, a match, and a box of thumbtacks to light up a room. You need both hands, and so you cannot hold the candle, yet if the candle is placed on the floor, it will fall over. We are often so fixed on the exact materials that we do not realize that the box that includes the thumbtacks is also an object. The correct answer is to dump out the thumbtacks, stick the box to the wall, place the candle in the box, and then use the match to light the candle.[23]

Functional fixedness can seep into our lives without us being aware. Dana noticed one day that he was smelling smoke at odd times. He eventually went to see the doctor, who was concerned, and sent Dana on a series of MRIs, EKGs, and other neurological tests. Dana faithfully recorded every time he smelled the mystery smoke, hoping to uncover whatever possible brain ailment might be at hand. Many doctor visits later, the answer turned out to be an upstairs neighbor... who was violating the terms of the lease and smoking in his apartment. Dana's smoke was actually smoke. Yet we are so conditioned that smelling phantom smells can be a sign of a stroke (or worse) that it is easy to miss the chain-smoking answer in front of our noses.

In theatre, functional fixedness can find its way into all facets. Casting has become a major issue as more and more shows are embracing colorblind casting – even shows based on historical figures, such as *Hamilton* and *1776*.[24] A set designer who insists on every location being built from scratch and lifelike to the point of functioning outlets and sinks as part of the set may be stuck and causing unneeded expense. A song that is written as a waltz does not need to be choreographed as waltz. In contrast, shows such as *Peter and the Starcatcher* and *You're a Good Man, Charlie Brown* can use basic objects to represent many different props and roles.

Functional fixedness is not the only mental block that can hold us back. Another all-too-common issue is the sunk cost fallacy. There are many times that we pursue bad ideas, from incompatible romantic partners to fixing up junk cars to accepting roles in mediocre shows. It is easy to spend a great deal of our emotion, energy, money, and time into such projects.[25] Once we have invested ourselves enough, it is hard to pull back. Imagine you bought a small apartment that you quickly discover is a money pit. You've spent countless hours handling everything from grout to ant infestations to broken appliances. At a certain point, there will come a time when it will cost more to make your apartment livable than it would to simply sell the apartment and accept your losses. However, most people become inclined to not choose the "sensible" road. So much money has already spent so much that it is very hard to admit that you have made a costly mistake. This principle also underlies why people stay in inert, loveless relationships years after the obvious expiration date.

The sunk cost fallacy applies to all aspects of theatre. Maybe you were commissioned to write a show and you've spent hundreds of hours on it and nothing is crystallizing. It is tempting to want to plough through the misery and finish the show, even if you know it will not be your best work (or even anything halfway decent). Similarly, perhaps you've been cast in a show and after a few weeks you realize the creative team does not have a vision and your performance will be unseen and unappreciated. It is incredibly hard to leave – not only, of course, because it means breaking a contract and letting down the team but also because it means acknowledging that you've wasted your time and chosen poorly. One key to know when to walk away is if whatever you put in the project going forward (regardless of any sunk costs) will still be more effort than will be worth the reward.

> Creativity Hurdle to Leap: Beware getting stuck, whether in your thinking or on a project!

Associative Thinking

We've talked about many dimensions of creative problem-solving, from recognizing the problem to generating and selecting ideas to gaining insight. Each of these will help you keep plugging away. We've talked about idea generation (or divergent thinking) as a way of coming up with possible solutions, often to open-ended questions or dilemmas. Associative thinking is another concept that can help both in real-life problems and as a way of getting the creative juices flowing.

Associative thinking is founded upon the idea that people who are more creative will be able to make more remote associations between different ideas.[26] For example, if we toss out the word "land," what comes to mind? Maybe you right away think of grass or dirt or some other manifestation of "land" meaning "ground." Or else you think of a word or name that is connected to "land" such as candy, Disney, or Lego. Possibly Woody Guthrie's "This Land is Your Land" comes to mind, or else gymnasts hitting a good landing, or *Knot's Landing*, or the idea of landing a plane. Maybe you go to rhymes and think of gland, bland, sand, grand, or manned. Dana would often hear from Sir Cameron Mackintosh about a scene, song, or arrangement not "landing" – in other words, it didn't work. Whatever emotional resonance or plot development was needed was not present.

For any word, there are obvious associations. Say "horse" and people will respond with neigh, stable, or rider. Say "cheese" and after people smile they will say Swiss, cheddar, or other types. Say "phone" and people will answer ring, call, cell, or other variants. It is when the less immediate or obvious responses come that our creative muscles are flexed. In the research literature, this concept is used for measurement, but it is equally helpful to enhance your imaginative thinking. Whenever there is a concept or idea that you want to develop, use the first few minutes to get the obvious responses out of the way.

> Creativity Hurdle to Leap: Aim to make remote associations between your ideas to maximize your creativity!

Activity: Remote Theatrical Associations

One way that remote associations are tested in creativity research is by presenting three words that are all connected by the same fourth word.[27] For example, if we give you the words "goat," "cottage," and "Swiss," the correct answer would be "cheese" – there is goat cheese, cottage cheese, and Swiss cheese. We thought it would be fun to create a brief theatrically-based version of the test. So, for example, we came up with "Man," "Sound of," and "Sheet." Any idea of what word connects all three and turns them into a concept, phrase, or title? In this case, the answer is "music" – "The Music Man," "Sound of Music," and "Sheet music." Try these next ten out and see if you can figure out these theatrical remote connections!

1	Spot	Ghost	In the Piazza
2	Leading	My Fair	Macbeth
3	Connection	High	Over the
4	Somewhere that's	Room	Adolph
5	Front of	Master of the	Manager
6	Stage	Trap	Love is an open
7	To do	Show	Trick
8	Piano	Hotel	Battement
9	Of the Pack	Band	Section
10	Hands	All That	Standard

Answers (no peeking until you're done trying!):

1 Light (Spotlight, Ghostlight, Light in the Piazza)
2 Lady (Leading lady, My Fair Lady, Lady Macbeth)
3 Rainbow (Rainbow Connection, Rainbow High, Over the Rainbow)
4 Green (Somewhere that's Green, Green Room, Adolph Green)
5 House (Front of house, Master of the House, House manager)
6 Door (Stage door, Trap door, Love is an Open Door)
7 Magic (Magic to do, Magic Show, Magic trick)
8 Grand (Grand piano, Grand Hotel, Grand Battement)
9 Leader (Leader of the Pack, Band leader, Section leader)
10 Jazz (Jazz Hands, All That Jazz, Jazz Standard)

How many did you get?

Using Associative Thinking

Dana has been using this associative thinking technique for years. Whenever he needs to write a piece of music for a particular situation, he first plays the "bad movie" version – the cheesy, obvious, cliché. By getting rid of those instant impulses, it serves to cleanse the palette. Dana can then write the more original melodies that are hidden within him. It's a way of dusting away the instant and routine responses to a prompt and making yourself dig deeper.

So, for example, let's say that you want to think of a new show for your company to do. In order to discover underappreciated musicals, you start with the idea of "musicals with historical figures." First you might think of the classics, such as *Annie Get Your Gun*, *Evita*, or *1776*. Then, perhaps, you might go to the modern era, such as *Hamilton*, *Ragtime*, *Floyd Collins*, *Parade*, or *Grey Gardens*. Next might be older shows by top songwriters, such as *Barnum*, *1600 Pennsylvania Avenue*, *Mack and Mabel*, or *Fiorello!* Even more remote ideas might include *Ben Franklin in Paris*, *Onward Victoria*, or *The First* (the Jackie Robinson musical).

Further, you can bounce from concept to concept. It is possible to start with one idea and then use remote associations to get many possible related directions. Next, one of those responses can be used to start the technique over again. So if we go back to the word "land" and look at all of the associations we had, we might then go to "Lego" and get a whole new list of associations, from obvious ("block") to more remote ("intense pain").

There is, of course, a right balance of remote associations. We talked about Ado Annie before; imagine a director is approaching a new production of *Oklahoma!* The obvious associations are ones you all know. Curly is the "aw shucks" hero; Laurey is the sassy and independent farm girl; Jud is the glowering outsider. More recently, directors have explored the complexity of the characters. Jud is often portrayed more sympathetically, for example, and Laurey can be seen to genuinely have some feelings for him. In one production, Jud was cast with an African American actor.[28]

This decision brought out layers of nuance in the show, with Curly's goading of him during "Pore Jud is Daid" seeming particularly insensitive (if not outright antagonistic and racist). Jud is often now seen as a three-dimensional antihero, with his humanity being clearly displayed. His death at the end is harder to gloss over and Curly comes off less as a knight in shining armor. Indeed, the 2019 Broadway revival makes Jud's death distinctly uncomfortable, and the frontier justice shown at the end comes off as much more disturbing. Such decisions made the 2019 revival a bit controversial; many people loved it and many hated it. Perhaps some felt this production made associations that were too remote. Remember, creativity has to be both new and task appropriate.[29] One can argue about that particular revival but on a broader level, it is easy to imagine a production going way too far. Imagine if a director decided to make Ali Hakim the true villain of the piece and the very end reveals that he actually killed Jud.... Most audiences would likely agree that would be too remote (and not appropriate).

> Creativity Hurdle to Leap: You can use the remote association technique for your everyday creative brainstorming (but don't go too far)!

Moving Forward

We have up until this point talked about core concepts in creativity. We have highlighted the importance of an original voice, staying appropriate for the task, and – just now – the nuance of the creative process. The process starts with identifying the right problem to solve, then generating possible ideas, and (ideally) choosing the best one to pursue. Throughout, there is incubation in search of the Aha! moment of insight.

In the next chapter, we will talk about the different pathways to creative success. We will introduce our SpotLight model, which outlines six categories of possible theatrical ambition, from being a student to a local play to a supporting actor to a lead to a star and all the way to being a legend. Where is your ideal place to wind up? Let's find out!

Notes

1 Hirson & Schwartz (1975, p. 13).
2 Sawyer (2012).
3 Abdulla, Paek, Cramond, & Runco (2020).
4 Reiter-Palmon & Robinson (2009).
5 Mumford, Reiter-Palmon, & Redmond (1994).
6 Getzels & Csikszentmihalyi (1976).
7 Runco & Acar (2019).
8 Torrance (1974, 2008).
9 Kim (2011).
10 Diehl & Stroebe (1987).

11 Guilford (1950).
12 Finke, Ward, & Smith (1992).
13 Wallas (1926).
14 Madjar, Shalley, & Herndon (2019).
15 Smith & Beda (2020).
16 Kounios & Beeman (2015).
17 Baird et al. (2012).
18 Davidson & Sternberg (1984).
19 Kaufman (2019).
20 Rivera & Docter (2015).
21 Csikszentmihalyi (1999).
22 Agogué et al. (2014).
23 Duncker & Lees (1945).
24 Clement (2016).
25 Arkes & Blumer (1985).
26 Mednick (1962).
27 Bowden & Jung-Beeman (2003).
28 Brodeur (2012).
29 Hennessey & Amabile (2010).

References

Abdulla, A. M., Paek, S. H., Cramond, B., & Runco, M. A. (2020). Problem finding and creativity: A meta-analytic review. *Psychology of Aesthetics, Creativity, and the Arts, 14*(1), 3–14.

Agogué, M., Poirel, N., Pineau, A., Houdé, O., & Cassotti, M. (2014). The impact of age and training on creativity: A design-theory approach to study fixation effects. *Thinking Skills and Creativity, 11*, 33–41.

Arkes, H. R., & Blumer, C. (1985). The psychology of sunk cost. *Organizational Behavior and Human Decision Processes, 35*, 124–140.

Baird, B., Smallwood, J., Mrazek, M. D., Kam, J. W., Franklin, M. S., & Schooler, J. W. (2012). Inspired by distraction: Mind wandering facilitates creative incubation. *Psychological Science, 23*, 1117–1122.

Bowden, E. M., & Jung-Beeman, M. (2003). One hundred forty-four compound remote associate problems: Short insight-like problems with one-word solutions. *Behavioral Research, Methods, Instruments, and Computers, 35*, 634–639.

Brodeur, N. (2012, February 21). 'Oklahoma' seen in a new light. *Seattle Times*. Retrieved from https://www.seattletimes.com/seattle-news/oklahoma-seen-in-a-new-light/

Clement, O. (2016, March 27). Diversifying 1776: "The present doesn't look like a bunch of White people." *Playbill*. Retrieved from http://www.playbill.com/article/diversifying-1776-the-present-doesnt-look-like-a-bunch-of-white-people

Csikszentmihalyi, M. (1999). Implications of a systems perspective for the study of creativity. In R. J. Sternberg (Ed.), *Handbook of creativity* (pp. 313–335). New York, NY: Cambridge University Press.

Davidson, J. E., & Sternberg, R. J. (1984). The role of insight in intellectual giftedness. *Gifted Child Quarterly, 28*, 58–64.

Diehl, M., & Stroebe, W. (1987). Productivity loss in brainstorming groups: Toward the solution of a riddle. *Journal of Personality and Social Psychology, 53*, 497–509.

Duncker, K., & Lees, L. S. (1945). On problem-solving. *Psychological monographs, 58,* i–113.

Finke, R. A., Ward, T. B., & Smith, S. M. (1992). *Creative cognition: Theory, research, and applications.* Cambridge: MIT Press.

Getzels, J. W., & Csikszentmihalyi, M. (1976). *The creative vision.* New York, NY: Wiley.

Guilford, J. P. (1950). Creativity. *American Psychologist, 5,* 444–454.

Hennessey, B. A., & Amabile, T. M. (2010). Creativity. *Annual Review of Psychology, 61,* 569–598.

Hirson, R. O., & Schwartz, S. (1975). *Pippin.* New York, NY: Avon books. https://www.seattletimes.com/seattle-news/oklahoma-seen-in-a-new-light/

Kaufman, J. C. (2019). The Mystery of Edwin Drood: A case study in creativity theories. *Estudios de Psicología, 40*(3), 526–539.

Kim, K. H. (2011). The APA 2009 Division 10 debate: Are the Torrance tests still relevant in the 21st century? *Psychology of Aesthetics, Creativity, and the Arts, 5,* 302–308.

Kounios, J., & Beeman, M. (2015). *The Eureka Factor: Aha moments, creative insight, and the brain.* New York, NY: Random House.

Madjar, N., Shalley, C. E., & Herndon, B. (2019). Taking time to incubate: The moderating role of 'what you do' and 'when you do it' on creative performance. *The Journal of Creative Behavior, 53,* 377–388.

Mednick, S. A. (1962). The associative basis of the creative process. *Psychological Review, 69,* 220–232.

Mumford, M. D., Reiter-Palmon, R., & Redmond, M. R. (1994). Problem construction and cognition: Applying problem representations in ill-defined domains. In M. A. Runco (Ed.), *Problem finding, problem solving, and creativity* (pp. 3–39). Westport, CT: Ablex Publishing.

Reiter-Palmon, R., & Robinson, E. J. (2009). Problem identification and construction: What do we know, what is the future? *Psychology of Aesthetics, Creativity, and the Arts, 3,* 43–47.

Rivera, J. (Producer), & Docter, P. (Director). (2015). *Inside Out* [Motion Picture]. United States: Walt Disney.

Runco, M. A., & Acar, S. (2019). Divergent thinking. In J. C. Kaufman & R. J. Sternberg (Eds.), *Cambridge handbook of creativity* (2nd Ed.) (pp. 224–254). New York: Cambridge University Press.

Sawyer, R. K. (2012). *Explaining creativity: The science of human innovation* (2nd ed.). New York, NY: Oxford University Press.

Smith, S. M., & Beda, Z. (2020). Old problems in new contexts: The context-dependent fixation hypothesis. *Journal of Experimental Psychology: General, 149,* 192–197.

Torrance, E. P. (1974). *Torrance tests of creative thinking. Directions manual and scoring guide, verbal test booklet B.* Bensenville, IL: Scholastic Testing Service.

Torrance, E. P. (2008). *The Torrance tests of creative thinking norms-technical manual figural (streamlined) forms A & B.* Bensenville, IL: Scholastic Testing Service.

Wallas, G. (1926). *The art of thought.* New York, NY: Harcourt, Brace, & World.

Chapter 4

Finding Your Light
Your Creative Aspirations

Jean Valjean (*Les Misérables*), Success
Gaston (*Beauty and the Beast*), Suppress
Myth: Success is Center Stage
Activity: The Twelve F-words

We make choices every day that impact our lives. We may eagerly seek out new situations or prefer the comfort of the known. We are all different people and even if we all share a love for musical theatre, there are still an unlimited number of ways that we will be our own unique creations. As the Cagelles sing in support of Albin in *La Cage Aux Folles*, we are what we are!

There are many different types of creativity. We have talked about how creativity requires being both new and task-appropriate and how it can encompass different processes and domains. In addition, it is also important to think about your levels of aspiration. Figuring out your best pathway is part of your creative journey.

Let us imagine that you are an actor with two offers on the table. The first is to be in the ensemble (Anatevkan #4) of a production of *Fiddler on the Roof* with a well-known comedian starring as Tevye. It would premiere out of town with the eventual goal of going to Broadway. The Yenta or Hodel may or may not keep their jobs when it hits the Big Apple. However, if you keep your head down, follow the lead of the dance captain (who is slavishly copying Robbins' original choreography), and react well to the star's mugging, then you have a good chance of following the show to New York.

The second offer you have is of a specialty cruise which features concerts of show music for many nights. The music director is an old college friend and has said it is fine for you to slip in some more obscure or even original songs into your repertoire. Along the four-week trek, you would have ample time to explore the Caribbean Islands. You could enjoy the local cuisine and sip Mai Tais while gazing at the ocean and working on your tan.

Your agent would have a rather firm opinion. Speaking purely objectively, the cruise is not an upward move. There are many wonderful reasons to do cruises, but career advancement is not one. Indeed, many people will omit such work from

DOI: 10.4324/9781003389668-6

professional resumes. These types of choices can be found in any career. What do you choose?

Many of the reasons or deciding factors that may be going through your mind may be focused on specific life circumstances. These may include considerations of personal mental health, career goals, family/work balance, and figuring out what will make you the most satisfied, all of which are topics we will be covering in future chapters. Instead, let us strictly focus on what is best for your creative pathway. One factor to consider is your level of career aspirations (theatrical or otherwise), and how aligned your current situation is with your goals. Another is the type of creative work that you want to do.

Theatrical (and Creative) Aspirations

Within creativity research, there is a distinction made between everyday creativity and eminent creativity.[1] Along with Ron Beghetto, James expanded on this dichotomy to propose a theory called the Four C Model of Creativity. It starts with mini-c, or personal creativity, which is meaningful to the creator but may be of little interest to anyone else.[2] You may have a flight of fancy where you imagine a bulldog dressed up as Millard Fillmore, and it may make you smile. However, it is entirely possible that no one else (particularly not the bulldog) would find this concept amusing, enjoyable, or creative. It still "counts." It's mini-c.

If your idea is articulated to other people and you receive feedback, guidance, and even mentorship, then you can advance to little-c, or everyday creativity. This type of creativity, which Ron and James like to call "county fair creativity," is what you might see at a good local fair. Handmade birdhouses, deep-fried sugar-filled oddities, fun caricatures of celebrities, and cross-stitched potholders may not change the world. They may, however, become part of your life (however briefly). Your creativity is enjoyed and appreciated by someone else. That's awesome.

Many people stay at little-c and are happy to stay there. We have already talked about the idea of creative domains (such as painting vs writing vs nuclear science). It is hard, if not downright impossible, to excel at many wildly different areas.[3] Most of us, if we work hard and put in years of deliberate practice, can then reach Pro-c or expert-level creativity.[4] The rise from Pro-c to Big-C, or creative genius, is harder to predict and typically can only be considered years after the creator's death. A mix of high quality, productivity, enthusiastic fans, hitting the right zeitgeist, and downright luck can lead to your creative work being remembered years after you are long gone.[5]

What does this theory have to do with you? To start, we've adapted it into the SpotLight Model of Creative Aspiration. We are offering this new version in part because this book is about musical theatre, and we are contractually obligated to discuss a Broadway show every three paragraphs and in part because we want to make these concepts clearly apply to the decisions you are making every day. Plus, we think it is pretty fun. Although our examples throughout will be theatre-focused, these principles apply to any creative area.

The ~~SpotLight~~ LightSpot SpotLight Model of Creative Aspiration

When James talks to organizations or schools about creativity and the Four C's, he will often discuss the need for people to figure out their creative aspiration. What is their ideal C-level (which sounds like it should be a sign outside of Death Valley)?

We have thus developed the SpotLight Model of Creative Aspiration. For this model, we're taking elements of the Four C's and adapting, renaming, and expanding them using a theatrical metaphor. We have separated the Four C's into six categories: Legend, Star, Lead, Supporter, Local, and Student. Actually, given that the categories start with L/S and not S/L, perhaps it should be the LightSpot model. Hmmmmm…

Wait – we've got it. We will start with the top and bottom first, since they represent very clear delineations. Legends, our Big-C category, only truly reach this level if their influence lasts for generations after their death. Students, our mini-c category, are a stepping stone that leads to a different ultimate pathway. People do not tend to aspire to being Students, and aspiring to be a Legend is self-defeating because it is ultimately beyond your control. Therefore, the model that is related to actual aspirations is Star, Lead, Supporter, and Local – or S/L, and SpotLight! Hence, the SpotLight Model of Creative Aspiration.

So we will preface our discussion with these bookends: The Big-C is the Legend – the person whose oeuvre will live on forever. Cole Porter. Ethel Merman. George Gershwin. August Wilson – For this brief sample, we stuck to people who are no longer with us; we could speculate on living legends all day. Any show we might be lucky enough to see that has the active involvement by a Legend will be something we would remember for the rest of our lives. James's Dad still talks about seeing the Philadelphia pre-Broadway tryout of *How to Succeed in Business Without Really Trying*, choreographed by an uncredited Bob Fosse.

The mini-c is the Student. Still learning and being shaped, the student has the potential to be anything. There are generally only a handful of reasons why we might specifically seek out student performances. Most common might be if we know someone in the cast or crew. Or, perhaps, a rare show is being put on; one of James's favorite obscure shows is *Birds of Paradise*, so he's caught two college productions of it. Maybe we might go if we really wanted to support local theatre or had nothing else to do. James will acknowledge that one of the greatest versions of *Fiddler on the Roof* he ever saw was a 20-minute first-grade production that starred his niece Nicole (now a successful Hollywood producer) as Yenta. The young actor playing Tevye was supposed to say, "You're just a simple tailor" to explain why Motel couldn't marry Tzeitel. Instead, he bellowed, "Motel, you're just a child!"

Which, in fairness, was true.

Onto the core of our model. The Star is the peak of what you can aspire to be in your lifetime. Some Stars become Legends and others do not. Consider Judy Garland versus Gertrude Lawrence. Both were divas who created amazing roles (Dorothy in *Wizard of Oz* and Anna in *The King of I*). Both died young (Garland was 47 and Lawrence was 54). In their lifetimes, both were clearly Stars. However, although Lawrence is certainly remembered, she is not part of the theatrical cultural zeitgeist the way that Garland remains.

So what is a Star? A Star is more than having talent (and, indeed, one could argue that talent is not even the biggest determinant of who becomes a Star). A Star is someone who if you meet at the stage door, your encounter – no matter how brief – becomes a story you will continue to tell. When James was a pre-teen, he met Maggie Smith after *Lettice and Lovage*. He told her how much he loved her in *The Prime of Miss Jean Brodie*, and she said (in a perfect Maggie Smith voice), "That was before your time, dear." It was one quick, pleasant exchange, and James remembers it like it was yesterday. Dana was on an airplane and noticed a striking woman across the aisle. When someone needed to pass by her, she lifted both legs directly up in the air in a perfect front dèvelopé devant. He looked at her, impressed, and realized it was Gwen Verdon. She met his eye, smiled, and then cocked an eyebrow. Without even a word, he had a Star story.

A Star can open a show and be the reason people choose to see it, despite poor reviews. Indeed, when a Star has a new show, it is noteworthy by that very fact. The next role that an Audra McDonald, Hugh Jackman, Bernadette Peters, or Patti LuPone tackles is interesting simply because of their participation. As Avery Sommers (Broadway's *Ain't Misbehavin'* and *Showboat*; National Tours of *Chicago* and *Best Little Whorehouse in Texas*) told us, "The barometer for me is the heat. It's what they do that draws you in." Sommers talked about how her Tony award-winning friend Andre DeShields has an energy that keeps an audience at the edge of their seats for an entire evening.

> She said "A master performer," has the ability to charm you and give you a sense that they are going to tell you something that you don't know and you are going to love it. It is as though they have something for you and you alone.

Contrast a Star with a Lead – A Lead can also take on a main role in a show and be absolutely wonderful. It is important to emphasize that Leads are not necessarily any less talented than Stars – they are only missing that certain *je ne sais quoi*. There are advantages to being a Lead (in addition to being able to walk the street unbothered). You can immerse yourself and disappear into a role in a way that may be impossible for a Star. There's almost a curse that comes with being a Star in that if you do your shtick, then you're just being yourself. If you try something new, it stands out and may not click with much of the audience. There are, of course, the occasional Stars who are also chameleons (Meryl Streep may be their patron saint), but it is rare.

Further, Leads can take on a supporting role without creating an imbalance. Kristin Chenoweth starred as Fran in the *Promises, Promises* Broadway revival – but can you imagine her playing Marge (the woman at the bar)? Both actresses who played Marge on Broadway (Marian Mercer and Katie Finneran) won the

Tony Award for Best Supporting Actress; it's a great role. But Chenoweth would upstage (even inadvertently) anyone playing Fran, which would not be beneficial for the production.

A Lead will rarely lack for work and be able to step into a show as a replacement for Dolly or Gaston or Curly or Eliza. If a Star is a replacement (unless it is much-hyped, such as Liza Minnelli in *Chicago* or *Victor/Victoria*), it can be seen as a career downturn. A Lead can go Off-Broadway or Regional for an independent or experimental role and not upstage the show. A Lead can do workshops and tryouts. They always run the risk of being replaced by a Star at the last minute (such as Ellen Foley, who James saw in San Diego, being replaced by Bernadette Peters in the original *Into the Woods*), but there is also the strong possibility that they will get to shape and create something brand new. Leads have long, rich careers, and they likely have many fans who consider them to be stars. There are worse things than not appealing to the masses.

A Supporter may occasionally get a lead on Broadway but will more likely be in a smaller role or the ensemble. Often their biggest strength is versatility – they can dance up a storm, sing beautifully, crack a joke, and deliver an important line. Supporters are usually easy and fun collaborators who get along well with others. They are great team members. Creators want them in the room. They bring a competence, a joy, and an energy to a project. Such Supporters are likely to be able to consistently find work on Broadway. In the pre-COVID 2018–2019 Broadway season, 863 different performers were on the Great White Way. Of this group, 206 had worked on Broadway for the last five consecutive years. Given that long-running shows such as *The Lion King, The Phantom of the Opera*, and *Wicked* also have the largest ensembles, our strong hunch is that most of the 206 well-employed actors are Supporters.[6] As of 2018, the absolute minimum for a Broadway actor who works the entire year is over $100,000, so regular work is not only fulfilling but also financially rewarding.[7]

Supporters can also tackle perhaps the widest variety of roles. They might be Victim Number Two in *Sweeney Todd* in a Broadway production, but they can play Sweeney in most LORT (League of Regional Theatres) or Equity-waiver theatres across the country. Indeed, it can be a perfectly viable career to get one ensemble credit on Broadway and then use that as a ticket to play lead roles in small theatres around the country. Supporters can also try on many different hats in the theatre world. They may direct or choreograph local productions. They may teach classes or mentor students. They may open dance schools or sing at local symphony concerts. A Supporter may also move higher on the trajectory into a Lead or even a Star; that is a natural progression. In contrast, a Lead who moves to Supporter (or "pulls a Cassie" in *A Chorus Line* parlance) is seen as regressing.

When a Supporter plays John Adams in a St. Louis performance of *1776*, who plays Stephen Hopkins or Josiah Bartlett? A Local. There are many ways that people can be a Local. Some may have day jobs and do theatre as a passion project. Others may support themselves with children's theatre or work backstage or in theatre education. Some Locals may join Equity and others may make a conscious decision to not join so they can still take roles with non-Equity troupes. Locals may devote their lives to the theatre, but they do not have to. Living in New York City is expensive and may preclude some basic life desires (such as owning a home or having a family or pets). Many Locals choose to live far away from New York; even those who may have been Supporters at one point may decide to move away and be a Local. Some Locals in other large cities, such as Washington DC, Chicago, or Los Angeles, may have careers that are virtually indistinguishable from Supporters. Others may live in smaller towns and be very happy living a life where theatre plays a major but not all-encompassing role.

What is best? It all depends on you. Would you rather be a small fish in a big pond or a big fish in a small pond? When James entered his Ph.D. program at Yale, he was suddenly in a very, very big pond. At the first meeting with the other psychology students starting their degrees, everyone was asked to introduce themselves and state their interests. James was first; he gave his name and said that he was interested in musical theatre. The next person gave her name and said that she was interested in examining how eye-tracking could give insight into people with autism. James suddenly realized that he completely misinterpreted the "state your interest" bit – Yale graduate students weren't supposed to have outside interests. On one hand, being at Yale brought an array of amazing opportunities. On the other hand, James was suddenly stupid again.

Sierra Boggess, who created the roles of Ariel in Broadway's *The Little Mermaid* and Christine Daae in West End's *Love Never Dies*, spoke to us about her appreciation for theatre in every location.

She told Dana "I did my first summer stock when I was in college," I got my equity card at the Little Theatre on the Square in Sullivan, Illinois, a town of a few thousand people. It's like heaven – everybody wants to be there. We're all building the sets and tearing them down and making the costumes. Everybody is there for the common goal of show biz. We have this weird calling where we need to be in front of people, no matter how big the house is. When I teach master classes, I talk about that. I see people getting hung up on the idea that if you're not on Broadway, you're not somebody. They think that if they haven't made it to New York then they're not as good. That's wrong. If you are passionate about performing, there are so many theatres and places to perform.

Creativity Hurdle to Leap: It is okay to be a Star, Lead, Supporter, or Local – or, at different times in your life, all of them. Find the best fit for you!

There are Stars, Leads, Supporters, and Locals in every domain. There are the lawyers whose cases become HBO movies and the lawyers who help their everyday clientele.

Professors can range from the Ivy Leagues to strong liberal arts universities to community colleges. A chef can aim to be sous-chef at a starred Michelin restaurant, a reality show winner, or to get to experiment daily at a local vegan café.

Activity: The Twelve F-Words

For this activity, we're going to see where you might fit into the SpotLight model using our twelve F-words. For each one, we'd like you to give two ratings. First, rate the importance of this F-word on a 1–4 scale. A one means you do not care at all (or, one might say, you don't give an F-word); a five means it is of great importance. Second, rate where you would put yourself right now. A one means you do not have this F-word in your life at the moment, and a five means that you have a great deal of it. We've briefly defined or specified some of the words that may have multiple meanings[2]:

	Value	Currently
Fame	_____	_____
Family	_____	_____
Finances	_____	_____
Finesse (i.e., skill, savvy)	_____	_____
Flexibility (i.e., in your career)	_____	_____
Flourishing (i.e., growth, development)	_____	_____
Fortitude (i.e., courage, strength)	_____	_____
Focus (i.e., concentration, expertise in an area)	_____	_____
Freedom (i.e., in your life)	_____	_____
Freshness (i.e., new situations and challenges)	_____	_____
Friends	_____	_____
Fun	_____	_____

For scoring, the most important thing is for you to reflect on where you are and where you want to be. What do these concepts mean to you, and where do they fall on the SpotLight model? We will provide our own thoughts, but if you disagree, listen to your gut. As an example, one F-word we deleted was Fulfillment – because presumably, choosing to continue to pursue a career, regardless of your level, means that you are fulfilled. In contrast, we kept the also subjective word of Fun because although all categories have fun, we would argue it is more likely when less is at stake.

Obviously, all categories can have differing levels of each F-word, but we are highlighting the concepts that we see as most specifically related to the SpotLight category.

Star:	Fame, Finances, Finesse, Fortitude
Lead:	Finances, Finesse, Flexibility, Fortitude, Focus
Supporter:	Flexibility, Flourishing, Focus, Freedom, Friends, Freshness, Fun
Local:	Family, Flourishing, Freedom, Friends, Fun

Again, there is no basic numerical scoring system here – it is a way to reflect on where are you, where you want to be, and what is the SpotLight category that will best help you get there. Maybe you are already there, which is fantastic. Maybe you can see that something very important to you may be difficult to maintain or achieve if you do not switch categories.

Understanding What You Can Control

It is also important to understand that some things are out of our control. It is often hard to switch categories. It is easier to move down the hierarchy – a Lead can move to Supporter or Local easier than a Local can move to Supporter, Lead, or Star. There are both obvious and less-obvious barriers to advancement. One big one, as we have alluded to, is geography. It is incredibly difficult to be a Local in New York City for more than a year or two; after that, you have either found a primary day job or you have moved out. When Jon tells Susan that she needs to stay in New York City to be a dancer in *tick, tick...BOOM!*, she responds, "I am a dancer. I'd still be a dancer if I lived in New England, but I'd have a dishwasher.[8]" Indeed, New York rates as one of America's least equal and most economically segregated metropolises.[9]

Conversely, if you live in Montana, it is going to be hard to escape the category of Local. This restriction does not mean that you cannot do amazing work – even, theoretically, Star-quality work. But you will not get many of the perks of being a Star, such as Fame or Finances. One reason is that big cities can offer support and connections for what is called the creative class – people who work in fields that require critical and creative thinking such as business, science, and the arts.[10] For example, cities with a high percentage of people in the creative class are more likely to embrace and reward tolerance, talent, and technology.[11] It is also interesting to note that two major markers of whether a city is considered to be attractive to the creative classes is if it has a large and flourishing community of LGBT and artistic people.[12]

Further, it is almost impossible to accurately understand your true potential in a more remote area. Let's say that you are living in Wyoming and regularly knocking it out of the park as Julie Jordan and Mama Rose and Mrs. Lovett and Laurey and Eliza Doolittle. If you were to move to New York and audition for Broadway shows, there are so many reasons why you might not even get in the door. Right away, the right type for a Julie Jordan would be unlikely to also be considered the right type to play a Mama Rose in a booming arts hub, even if the same person can play both roles in a local setting. Maybe the charisma and talent that made Wyoming critics rave is not the energy that will get callbacks in the Big Apple.

It is also possible that without a strong network of connections, your ability will not be enough. If you've impressed people with your audition, then the first questions asked when you leave the room will be, "Has anyone worked with them? Does anyone know someone who knows them?" Such questions aren't a matter of nepotism or intentional exclusion. Producers want to find someone they trust who can attest to your work ethic or whether you are a team player. Any major show costs a tremendous amount of money.

Casting someone who is selfish, unreliable, or doesn't deliver when everything is on the line can break the future of production. This process may result in making it even harder for newcomers to find success, but it is hard to fault producers who are averse to unnecessary risks. This type of personal vouching happens everywhere and in every talent-based industry, including any large corporation.

Certainly, your goal should be to strive to achieve the best category possible for you. But it is also possible you are stuck in a specific category with no reasonable way to advance. Maybe you have four young children and need a guaranteed steady income. Or your parents are ill and you need to be their primary guardian. Or your partner can't leave their job and so you are restricted to a particular location that is not conducive to a big break. Or perhaps you want to be a Star but you simply don't have that shine.

The inability to adjust your aspirations to reality can be harmful. James had a dear friend, "Doug," who wanted to be a Star in his industry (not theatre). Yet Doug was clearly a Lead and only received Lead (or Supporter) opportunities. Doug was quite successful, yet the only people who knew that he was not living his dream life were James and Doug's father. Doug ended up breaking off all contact with both of them, continuing to be miserable, despite seemingly being highly accomplished by most people's standards. It is natural to feel upset, sad, or even devastated when your hopes and goals do not come true. There are many ways of handling these times in a healthy way. One is to make the life choices that allow you to be resilient and carry one. Another is to keep persisting and trying when it is possible. A third is to recognize that there are still positive, joyful, and fulfilling directions that are still there for you. Indeed, there may be a time when, a la *Merrily We Roll Along*, you realize that what you thought was a failure could be the best thing that could have happened. Accepting that some variables are out of your control – and adjusting your aspirations – can be the first step to being satisfied with what you have. Sometimes, this is the right decision.

Consider an alternate fate that could have happened for our Suppress model, Gaston from *Beauty and the Beast*. Gaston might be the hero of a musical from an earlier day; he falls for the bookish girl, is determined to win her love, and is willing to fight a monster to win her. Unfortunately for Gaston, he's in the wrong show (and does not understand the concept of consent). Gaston woos Belle and continues to pursue her even after she makes it clear that she is not interested. Particularly relevant here is that Gaston is surrounded by (at least) three adoring women who are madly in love with him. He could accept that variables out of his control are preventing him from winning Belle's love, yet is unable to do so (perhaps residual effects from eating four dozen eggs every day as a boy). Instead, Gaston obsessively continues to chase after Belle. He schemes to lock her father up in an insane asylum and then leads the town in an uprising to kill the Beast. He embraces the dark side and ends up dead.

Consider an alternate telling of the story. Gaston falls in love with Belle but realizes they are not meant to be together. He pursues Silly Girl #2 (let's call her Joan),

> Creativity Hurdle to Leap: Accept things that are out of your control. It is okay to be realistic with your aspirations!

who is already infatuated. Gaston and Joan get married in a big celebration, surrounded by decorative antlers, with LeFou as his best man. They live happily ever after and have seven strapping boys, oblivious to Belle rotting away in the Beast's castle. It is a fine line between not daring to dream big versus accepting that reality sometimes does not align with our deepest desires.

Myth: Success Is Center Stage

It's natural to want to be a Legend. Those performers who are brave enough to go on stage and sing and dance and act have at least a small part of themselves that loves the limelight. That's okay. Most people do not go into theatre aiming to be a professional Shark, Iowa City resident, one of the King of Siam's wives, third talking spoon, rejected Chorus Line dancer, or anonymous citizen of Anatevka.

There are a huge number of talented folks who have a list of credits a mile long, whether it is filled with Broadway shows or dinner theatre. It is a testament to the stigma of not being a Star that we hesitated to reach out to interview one of the many people we know who have survived and thrived as a working actor for decades. We worried it would be seen as condescending or embarrassing, when our intentions were the exact opposite. Even to list the people we considered as perfect examples felt a little risky. It illustrates how deeply engrained this myth is in a theatre fan's psyche.

One of the goals of the Spotlight Model was to show the cyclical nature and wide continuum that exists for success. There are sacrifices needed to be a Star that may be beyond what you are willing to do. There are benefits to being a Local that may ultimately make up for time spent away from center stage.

All of these categories are fulfilling in different ways. It is similar to how someone who is married may envy the freedom of a single person – who may, in turn, envy the security and stability of marriage. Sondheim expresses these feelings beautifully in *Company* in "Sorry-Grateful," and *A Chorus Line*'s "What I Did for Love" taps into the same emotions.

If you're not in the place you want to be, are you sorry you got involved in theatre in the first place? Even if your relationship with theatre is bittersweet or unfulfilled, we hope your answer is "no." All of these ideas are largely true regardless of your field, as long as you are pursuing a career that you chose.

There is always something more that we will want to accomplish. That is human nature. We guarantee you that Lin-Manuel Miranda, who is arguably about as successful as it is possible to be on this planet, has goals and plans and aspirations. Some of them will never happen. If we look at the greatest theatrical geniuses of the last century, every one of them had heartbreak, unexpected failures, bad reviews, lost opportunities, and crushed dreams.

We are not saying to find joy in schadenfreude. Rather, your emotional career journey is no less valid or real that the journeys of Leonard Bernstein or Dorothy Fields or August Wilson. Someone's experience as a Local or a Supporter is legitimate. They do not need to be a Star or to shine in New York City or the West End in order to be part of the continuing story of theatre. Yes, center stage is one destination – but so are rigging the lights, manning the ticket booth, directing the high school play, or playing Benvolio in a South Dakotan production of *Romeo and Juliet* in a church basement. It's all good if it makes you feel good and brings joy to others.

> Creativity Hurdle to Leap: If you are happy in your current creative role (in a show or in life), find ways to appreciate it. Don't pursue stardom for the wrong reasons!

Creative Styles and Types of Creations

Creative styles are separate from creative ability. Creative styles represent your preference for how and what you create. An example of creative styles is the distinction between trying to be New and trying to be Different.[13] People who want to be creative in the New style want to contribute in ways that are New and not what has been done before.

Perhaps they want to redirect their field or shift the boundaries or conceptions of their field.[14] They want to make radical changes and major innovations.[15] In contrast, people who want to be creative in the Different styles are interested in adapting and reshaping existing work. They want to make incremental contributions that stretch forward their fields. They often are focused on ways to optimize strengths and overcome specific constraints.[16]

The Propulsion Theory delves deeper into the New-Different continuum.[17] We won't go into all of the categories but will highlight some that may speak to what excites you about theater. For example, under the Different umbrella, people can replicate past work. The goal is to reproduce as close as possible the original creation. Such productions, which are usually Local, will often use the original cast album (or filmed production, if available) as a training device and try to recreate the original choreography. Replications are great in allowing an audience in modern-day El Paso to see what *How to Succeed in Business Without Really Trying* might have looked like in its original run. However, many theatrical artists may feel unsatisfied going from replication to replication. If you're playing the title role of *Sweeney Todd*, capturing every nuance of how Len Cariou or George Hearn inhabited the role may feel like a fun challenge or it may feel like a dull technical exercise.

Another Different type of production is a redefinition. These are when you take a show people know and find an interesting way of reinterpreting it. Some shows do not allow such modifications; the licensors hold tight rein and make it clear that the original choreography, setting, gender roles, and other dimensions must be kept consistent. Shows that have more latitude may enable a director to reimagine the show. Shakespeare's plays are a wonderful jumping-off point; many modern directors set them in different time periods and play with costumes and casting. The text is held sacred, but the context offers another layer.

Consider the 2013 revival of *Pippin*, which incorporated circus performers and acts to enhance the chaotic energy of the show. There is also the 2018 West End revival of *Company* which came to Broadway in 2021 in which they used judicious gender swapping of many characters (including the title role) to touch on slightly different themes from the original. The idea of Bobbie having a biological clock, for example, adds layers to the show.

Two types of New interpretations are synthesis and reinitiation. Synthesis is taking two distinct genres or stories or fields and merging them together to create something original. Tommy Tune has quoted Sondheim as saying "Old plus old equals new,"[18] and this dictum holds quite true in this instance. Consider Julie Taymor, the first woman to win a Tony Award for best director. She integrated the story of *The Lion King* with an elaborate style of masks and puppets that she learned in her travels to Indonesia and other countries.[19] This synthesis gave her a strikingly New style which captivated the theatre world.

Reinitiations take a strikingly unique perspective, often pushing the field in a new direction. Early on, the idea of a musical having an actual story (*Showboat*) or of using dance to advance characterization and the plot (*Oklahoma!*) were reinitiative concepts. In more recent years, interactive theatre, in which the audience plays a central role, has also changed the domain itself. We earlier discussed how the viewers' help select the killer in *Drood*; audiences also play their own roles in such shows as *Tony and Tina's Wedding*. Social media will likely change the landscape even further.

> Creativity Hurdle to Leap: People have distinct styles and approaches to creativity. One is not inherently better than another.

Creative Pathways

Jean Valjean, our Success model for this chapter, undertakes a number of transformations in *Les Misérables*. When the musical opens, he is a prisoner mired in hard labor, serving an overlong sentence for stealing a loaf of bread and then repeatedly trying to escape. Upon release, he gamely applies for many jobs, never being hired because he is an ex-convict. He realizes he is never going to be gainfully employed and decides to return to crime for survival, taking advantage of a local bishop's good will. When the bishop lies to the police and does not let him be arrested, Valjean has a moment of truth. He decides to make amends through his life and deeds. He hides his past in the service of his greater journey such that when we next see him he is a wealthy business owner and small town mayor. Still pursued by the determined

Inspector Javert, Valjean sacrifices his current position and lifestyle to save an innocent man from being wrongfully convicted for Valjean's past escape. On the run, he devotes himself to raising a young girl, Cosette. We again fast forward through a few years to find Valjean again prosperous using a new identity. When Cosette's suitor Marius joins a student rebellion, Valjean goes to fight for the doomed cause. Valjean saves Marius's life, only to be finally caught in the sewers by Javert. Valjean pleads for time to get Marius to the hospital, and Javert acquiesces.

It is at this point we can contrast the two leads. At every turn, Valjean not only continues to redeem himself but also to constantly reinvent himself. He is a businessman, politician, father, and soldier who uses his physical strength, wits, and will to help others. Javert is not a bad person, but he is rigid and fixed. When he lets Valjean go (albeit with a promise that Valjean will return to be punished), he cannot resolve his behavior with his belief system. In Javert's world of absolutes, people cannot change or be redeemed. Javert, seeing no other way of living, commits suicide. Valjean returns to Cosette and eventually dies knowing he has made amends and contributed to the world in a meaningful way.

Valjean finds many different pathways to happiness and success. He does not choose the easiest routes, simply the morally correct ones. We are not trying to equate our actor's choice at the beginning of the chapter (between playing in the *Fiddler on the Roof* ensemble or performing on a cruise ship) with Valjean's decisions on how to juggle his promise to a dying mother with his determination to not let injustice win. However, the same attributes that enabled Valjean to succeed can help you. There are so many different potential creative pathways. They can be choosing between steady work or aiming for stardom. They can be how you decide on the work-life balance that is best for you. They can be in the way that you want to manifest your creativity. It is all part of understanding the best choice for your career (and life) and being able to find satisfaction in a wide variety of scenarios and opportunities.

All of this advice is, of course, easier said than done. In real life, it can be hard to tell whether you are feeling excited because of your potential opportunities or anxious over the lack of control you may be experiencing. Both reactions increase arousal levels and figuring out if the emotions are positive or negative is not always intuitive. A creative life is filled with choices, emotions, and the curious blend of inactivity and sudden high stakes (which is sometimes called "hurry up and wait"). It is easy to not only embrace the unknowns and surprises but also to associate them with the highs and lows that can subsequently result. It is a fine line between taking appropriate risks and allowing yourself to care passionately about your work versus living in a roller coaster and feeling like you are not in control of your own life.

Moving Forward

To briefly review, our SpotLight model outlines six categories of possible theatrical ambition, from being a Student to a Local to a Supporter to a Lead to a Star and all the way to being a Legend. Each level has its own plusses and minuses; the key is to find your desired place. Moving on, we will continue talking about creativity, but with more of a focus on you and your particular patterns and strengths. As we switch from understanding creativity to understanding yourself, we'll talk about a number of key issues. What aspects of yourself are most linked to creativity? How can your personality, motivation, and mood spur your creativity? How can you know your creative self? Let us find out.

Notes

1 Csikszentmihalyi (1998).
2 Beghetto & Kaufman (2007).
3 Baer (2015).
4 Kaufman & Beghetto (2009).
5 Simonton (2011).
6 Brady & Fierberg (2019).
7 Culwell-Block (2018).
8 Larson (2001, p. 14).
9 Florida (2017).
10 Florida (2012).
11 Florida (2019).
12 Florida & Gates (2001).
13 Reiter-Palmon & Kaufman (2018).
14 Sternberg (1999) and Sternberg & Kaufman (2012).
15 Gilson & Madjar (2011) and Kirton (1976).
16 Scholar & Higgins (2013) and Stokes (2007).
17 Sternberg, Kaufman, & Pretz (2001, 2002).
18 Nargi (2008).
19 Burns (1988).

References

Baer, J. (2015). *Domain specificity of creativity*. San Diego: Academic Press.
Beghetto, R. A., & Kaufman, J. C. (2007). Toward a broader conception of creativity: A case for "mini-c" creativity. *Psychology of Aesthetics, Creativity, and the Arts*, *1*, 13–79.
Brady, M., & Fierberg, R. (2019, July 11). How do ensemble actors fare in the current Broadway landscape? *Playbill*. Retrieved from http://www.playbill.com/article/how-do-ensemble-actors-fare-in-the-current-broadway-landscape
Burns, B. (1988). Julie Taymor: Breaking the mold. *Theatre Crafts*, *22*, 48–53.
Csikszentmihalyi, M. (1998). Reflections on the field. *Roeper Review*, *21*, 80–81.
Culwell-Block, L. (2018, April 16). How much money do Broadway actors make? *Playbill*. Retrieved from http://www.playbill.com/article/how-much-money-do-broadway-actors-make
Florida, R. (2012). *The rise of the creative class revisited*, New York, NY: Basic Books.
Florida, R. (2017). *The new urban crisis*. New York, NY: Basic Books.
Florida, R. (2019). The creative city. In J. C. Kaufman & R. J. Sternberg (Eds.), *Cambridge handbook of creativity* (pp. 623–639). New York, NY: Cambridge University Press.
Florida, R., & Gates, G. (2001). *Technology and tolerance: The importance of diversity to high-technology growth*. Washington, DC: The Brookings Institution Center on Urban and Metropolitan Policy.

Gilson, L. L., & Madjar, N. (2011). *Radical and incremental creativity: Antecedents and Handbook of Creativity* (pp. 623–639). New York, NY: Cambridge University Press.

Kaufman, J. C., & Beghetto, R. A. (2009). Beyond big and little: The four C model of creativity. *Review of General Psychology, 13*, 1–12.

Kaufman, J. C., & Rowe, D. P. (in progress). *The creating your spotlight workbook.* Retrived from https://creatingyourspotlight.com/

Kirton, M. (1976). Adaptors and innovators: A description and measure. *Journal of Applied Psychology, 61*, 622–629.

Larson, J. (2001). *tick, tick... BOOM!* New York, NY: Applause.

Nargi, J. (2008, April 14). Tommy Tune: Steps in time. *Broadwayworld.com.* Retrieved from https://www.broadwayworld.com/boston/article/Tommy-Tune-Steps-in-Time-20080414 processes. *The Psychology of Aesthetics, Creativity, and the Arts, 5*, 21–28.

Reiter-Palmon, R., & Kaufman, J. C. (2018). Creative styles in the workplace: New and different. In R. Reiter Palmon, V. Kennel, & J. C. Kaufman (Eds.), *Individual creativity in the workplace* (pp. 191–202). San Diego, CA: Academic Press.

Scholer, A. A., & Higgins, E. T. (2013). Dodging monsters and dancing with dreams: Success and failure at different levels of approach and avoidance. *Emotion Review, 5*, 254–258.

Simonton, D. K. (2011). Creativity and discovery as blind variation and selective retention: Multiple-variant definitions and blind-sighted integration. *Psychology of Aesthetics, Creativity, and the Arts, 5*, 222–228.

Sternberg, R. J. (1999). A propulsion model of types of creative contributions. *Review of General Psychology, 3*, 83–100.

Sternberg, R. J., & Kaufman, J. C. (2012). When your race is almost run, but you feel you're not yet done: Application of the propulsion theory of creative contributions to late-career challenges. *Journal of Creative Behavior, 46*, 66–76.

Sternberg, R. J., Kaufman, J. C., & Pretz, J. E. (2001). The propulsion model of creative contributions applied to the arts and letters. *Journal of Creative Behavior, 35*, 75–101.

Sternberg, R. J., Kaufman, J. C., & Pretz, J. E. (2002). *The creativity conundrum*. Philadelphia, PA: Psychology Press.

Stokes, P. D. (2007). Using constraints to generate and sustain novelty. *Psychology of Aesthetics, Creativity, and the Arts, 1*, 107–113.

Part II

Your Creative Tools

Chapter 5

Keeping It Fresh
Staying Open to New Things

Alexander Hamilton (*Hamilton*), Success
The Jets and the Sharks (*West Side Story*), Suppress
Myth: Not One Big Break
Activity: Increasing Openness with Random Random Random;
Too Perfect: Does Your Attitude Need Adjusting?

Tracy Turnblad is not your typical American teenager. From the moment she opens *Hairspray* with her vibrant "Good Morning, Baltimore," her exuberance is contagious; indeed, her generous spirit has her wanting to lift others up to be as joyful as she is. She wants to do new things, such as appearing on the Corny Collins show, and she is open to learning new dances from other cultures. She is tolerant, accepting, and filled with wonder. Tracy in many ways is a perfect model of someone who is open – open to new experiences, ideas, cultures, and opinions. Someone who is open is primed to be creative.

In this chapter, we're going to cover the role of individual personality, life experiences, and group dynamics in creative success. Some readers may think of the Myers–Briggs, which is a personality test that categorizes each person on four global dimensions such as Thinking (T) versus Feeling (F). The scores lead people to happily catalog themselves with four letters (such as, "I'm an INTJ!") Unfortunately, the evidence that the Myers–Briggs actually works is pretty weak.[1] One key issue is that personality traits are not an on/off switch; they're more like a dimmer switch. You aren't either "Introverted" or "Extraverted" – you are somewhere in the middle, likely leaning in one direction. So there may be two people who would both be labeled as introverts on the Myers–Briggs, but one might score 1 out of 10 and the other might score 4 out of 10. Lumping them together, but placing a person who scores 6 out of 10 in the extravert category, is a little silly.

Researchers who study personality tend to instead use the Big Five. These are five broad factors that underlie our personality, which impacts our behavior, feelings, and thoughts. It is generally agreed that these five factors are Emotional Stability, Openness, Agreeableness, Extraversion, and Conscientiousness.[2] Although the other factors correspond to creativity in different ways depending on the

DOI: 10.4324/9781003389668-8

domain or situation, Openness is a pretty constant predictor of creativity regardless of circumstance.[3]

This consistent finding shouldn't be surprising. Think of the people you would want to work with in a theatre company (or in any group). You would want an actor willing to try a few different ways of delivering a punchline to see which one works best. You want a costume designer who will try constructing a breakaway costume (even if she's never done it before) so that the actor can make a series of quick changes. Similarly, you want the set designer who can move from representational to evocative to realistic styles, depending on the production. Who wouldn't choose the choreographer who can work within the performers' specific skills and tricks – or perceived limitations – to make them look their best?

We spoke to multiple Tony nominee Marc Kudisch (*Thoroughly Modern Millie, Assassins*, and so much more), who told us he thinks that creative success "is not going to happen in the way that you may envision it in your mind, as a story for one person. You have to be open to the day-to-day of what might be introduced into the pot."

One way that Openness is studied is by splitting it into Openness to Experience and Openness to Intellect.[4] Openness to Experience is wanting to try new things, whether eating new foods or traveling and experiencing other cultures or simply finding a new way to walk home. People high on Openness to Experience can appreciate the beauty of nature and often enjoy the arts a great deal. They will also be more likely to take sensible risks (we don't mean boxing with kangaroos or jumping out of airplanes without a parachute). Indeed, a willingness to defy the crowd, the *zeitgeist*, and even yourself is an important component of being creative at higher levels.[5] Openness to Intellect is more about wanting to learn new things, understanding different perspectives, and enjoying having your beliefs challenged.

People high on Openness to Intellect would like going to museums or reading about the latest scientific discoveries or having philosophical debates. People who are particularly high on Openness to Experience are more likely to gravitate to being creative in the arts, whereas people who are particularly high on Openness to Intellect are more likely to pursue being creative in more science-related areas.[6]

Alexander Hamilton of *Hamilton*, our Success model for this chapter, displays a great deal of openness both to experience and intellect throughout the show. He sings in "Right Hand Man" that he has initially stuck to his plan to be a hero on the battlefield. Hamilton does not want to be anyone's secretary or assistant. Yet when George Washington meets with him and explains how dire the situation is and how much he is needed in the role, Hamilton agrees to be his aide. Our titular character recognizes he needs to shake up his original idea of wanting to show his leadership in action and instead help out in whatever way maximizes his talents. As a result, he accepts and jumps into his new role wholeheartedly. Hamilton brainstorms plans for getting Congress to offer more supplies, reaches out to his contacts and friends, and devises ideas for using spies. Further, he recognizes that working for Washington is an opportunity worth switching up his original ideas, whereas earlier opportunities did not warrant rethinking his strategy. Hamilton saw in this new role a challenge worthy of his time, energy, and expertise.

It is not just the real and fictional Hamilton who uses Openness to reach new heights. People who will try new experiences often can find multiple paths to success. Consider Craig Lucas. He started as an actor – and a mighty accomplished one, appearing in the original Broadway casts of *Rex, Shenandoah,* and *Sweeney Todd.* He co-authored a clever (and early) take on the jukebox musical, *Marry Me a Little,* using cut or lesser-known Sondheim songs to tell the story of two lonely, single people. It has been continually revived, yet its ultimate impact was when Sondheim advised Lucas that his truest talents were in writing, as opposed to acting or singing.[7] Although Lucas's achievements already exceeded the dreams of most aspiring actors, he was open to change. His subsequent work as a playwright and librettist brought him Tony nominations for *Prelude to a Kiss* and *Light in the Piazza*; he has also written films (including *Longtime Companion*), operas, and adaptations.

We will discuss later in the book the fine art of knowing when to exit. Lucas's story is different. He left on top to pursue even better things. Although he stopped acting because of his writing success, others have become multi-hyphenates. Bruce Norris (*Clybourne Park*) and Tracey Letts (*August: Osage County*) both wrote Pulitzer Prize-winning plays while continuing to act, as did John Cariani after writing the smash hit *Almost, Maine.* Emerald Fennell has regularly switched from acting in such shows as *The Crown*, writing and directing award-winning films such as *Promising Young Woman*, and writing the libretto for Andrew Lloyd Webber and David Zippel's *Bad Cinderella.*

Creativity Hurdle to Leap: Make sure to stay open to new experiences and ideas!

Activity: Increasing Openness with Random Random Random

To start off, we're going to do a variant of one of Dana's coaching exercises, Random Random Random. Go to Google (or your preferred search engine) and type in three (or four) words: Your birth state, your favorite color, and the first word of your favorite Broadway musical (not counting "the" or "a"). Go to the third hit and click on it. Then find the third paragraph, go to the third line, and keep reading until you get an adjective or noun (if you find one that is uninspiring, feel free to use the next one). James ended up with "styling," whereas Dana got "house."

Use a little associative thinking (as we talked about in Chapter 5). Start with your word and keep generating concepts or ideas that you see as connected. Just word vomit until you get something that triggers a potential adventure that is either brand new to you or something you have not done for many years. For example, James went from styling to hairstyling and realized he has not been to a hair salon since he began going bald. One new experience he could pursue is going to get his hair done (or perhaps, even better, getting pampered at a spa). Dana went from house to log cabin to tent to RV, which landed him on the concept of camping. Dana has had his fill of camping from childhood experiences but thought about the idea of getting away from home. Dana lives in New York, which made him consider a "staycation" – going with his spouse to a nice hotel in New York and enjoying the city the way a tourist would.

Now you try!

Your word:_____

Your associations:_____

Your new experience to try:_____

Openness, Cultures, and Diversity

Part of being open to new experiences or ideas is being open to different cultures and types of people. Exposure to other cultures is related to creativity in a number of different ways. First, simply being given information about other countries can enhance creativity.[8] Being exposed to other cultures can not only increase your ability to generate ideas but also show how receptive you are in listening other's ideas.[9]

However, these findings do not mean that the key to creativity is simply buying a ticket to another country. If you are already high on Openness, that's great. If you are low on Openness, however, traveling abroad can have a negative impact on creativity.[10] Why? If you've traveled to other countries, particularly tourist spots, you'll notice a lot of people who seek out experiences and companions from their own culture. How many American students on a semester abroad spend it with other Americans, eating at the foreign McDonalds and getting drunk? Obviously, there are many, many people who want to immerse themselves in a new culture. But simply being there – much as in life – isn't enough. Similarly, people who spend more time abroad[11] or who have more multicultural understanding[12] will reap many more creative benefits from their travel.[13]

Many amazing musicals benefit from weaving in ideas, concepts, and styles from other cultures. Sondheim's *Pacific Overtures* uses many Japanese traditions, such as men in women's roles and the use of percussion to accent spoken words. These conventions make it stand out not only from Sondheim's oeuvre but also from most Western musicals. When Lin-Manuel Miranda wrote *In the Heights*, he used his love of hip-hop, rap, and salsa music to infuse energy and innovation into what would become his first hit musical. This same blend of styles and cultural influences would also be present in *Hamilton*.

In addition to having experience with other cultures, there is also a lot of evidence that working with people from different cultures or backgrounds can improve everyone's creativity. For example, groups made up of people from different cultures,[14] statuses,[15] life experiences,[16] and ethnicities[17] tend to produce more creative results than more homogenized groups. Simply having members with more multicultural experiences can improve group creativity.[18]

Our examples of Suppress for this chapter are the Jets and the Sharks of *West Side Story*. As much as our differences can nurture and inspire collaborative creativity, people need to be open for these benefits to happen. Although Tony and Maria are able to set aside their cultural backgrounds to pursue a type of creativity, the other members of the warring gangs are not (perhaps because they are not experiencing the same intense hormonal yearnings of the lead couple). We open the show with Bernardo beating up A-Rab in retaliation for stink-bombing his father's store. This exchange is but one of many fights between the Jets (described in the libretto as "an anthology of what is called 'American'"[19]) and the Sharks (who are from Puerto Rico).

Both the Jets and the Sharks are closed in their own ways, which results in the "us against them" mentality that causes the tragic subsequent events. The Sharks, like their namesake, are perceived by the Jets as the "other." They are seen as being different, encroaching on the Jets' territory, and dangerous. Again, like their namesake, the Sharks may have been misunderstood and seen as threatening when no harm may have been intended. However, when we begin the show, both sides are actively fighting. Further, the Sharks reveal themselves as not being fully open to their new country in the number "America" (not to minimize the prejudice they encountered upon their arrival).

The one time the gangs align together is to keep the local cops (Krupke and Schrank) in the dark about their activities. Otherwise, any chance for a mutually beneficial relationship (even if not a friendship) is absent. It is not until the violence and loss in the second act that the two gangs can reach any common ground. In what is either a hope for the future or a token gesture, Tony's body is picked up by two Jets and two Sharks, and Baby John (a Jet) helps Maria (a Shark) put on her shawl.

If the gang members had been open to new ideas and different cultures, then it is possible their creativity would have increased. Even if we see their main area of creativity as being crime or juvenile delinquency,[20] one would imagine that if the gangs joined forces, they would have found new ways of outwitting police and generally disrupting the peace. Teaming together could have allowed them to have wreaked more havoc (or, ideally, pursued more benevolent means of expression). Granted, it would be a much different show, perhaps having Act One closing with Shrank frantically calling in the FBI to stop this new multicultural crime wave.

> Creativity Hurdle to Leap: Working with people from different backgrounds or cultures can foster team creativity – if you let it!

Myth: Not One Big Break

Openness is not the only personality factor to impact creativity. Another is Conscientiousness. For example, picture Tommy Albright in *Brigadoon*. He's made the wrong decision – he left Brigadoon, he went back to New York, and he's stuck in his old life with his unpleasant fiancé and realizes he is trapped. He knows the doors to Brigadoon are figuratively and literally closed, and yet he cannot give up. He and his friend Jeff go back to Highlands and search for the hidden opening and – against all odds – his love wakes up Mr. Lundie, who lets him back into Brigadoon and into Fiona's waiting arms. Granted, his friend Jeff will probably be tried for his murder, but that's not what we're going to talk about right now.

We're not saying that if you missed your big opportunity, then you can turn back time or change a producer's mind. Rather, we're arguing that there is no one big break. There is not just one shot. Indeed, we'd like to think that even if Tommy had been locked out of Brigadoon, he would've had the persistence and industriousness to look for another true love.

There is no one make-or-break opportunity. We are not saying that there are not wonderful moments that align luck and talent that can help someone "make it," of course. There are many classic stories, such as Shirley MacLaine going on for Carol Haney in *The Pajama Game*. As the legend goes, she impressed a Hollywood producer and (at a separate performance) director Alfred Hitchcock; she was cast in *The Trouble with Harry* and a legendary movie career began.[21] Of course, such breaks do happen. Our point is that even if you miss such a break, your dreams should not be over.

There can be benefits to not becoming an overnight sensation right away. As Tony winner Randy Graff told Dana,

> I tell students that it's better that it doesn't happen right away. They want it to happen overnight because they see that happening on reality shows. But it's better when it doesn't. God bless you if you're ready and it happens overnight. I was working and it happened little by little and baby step by baby step. I wasn't terrified because I was ready for it. I encourage kids to just keep showing up and be patient. One thing does lead to another and you may not get one role, but they'll remember you for another role and that's just how it works. Show up and do your best.

Indeed, it can be wonderful to set goals for yourself, such as getting your Equity card or making your Broadway debut by a certain age. But life has its own ebb and flow (or, to give it a musical theatre twist, its own Ebb and Kander). All of us have the power to redesign who we are and change ourselves. You can limit yourself by holding on to early dreams. These passions may have impacted who you are and may have driven you to achieve a great deal. But if you are not careful, the same dreams that once opened up possibilities can also constrict your growth.

Look down at your phone. The odds are that it's a reasonably recent version of a smartphone; it's able to take pictures and videos, surf the internet, and play games. You may have a sentimental attachment to an old flip phone; perhaps you even keep one in a nostalgia box. But trying to abide by the goals you set for yourself when you were twelve is like trying to use your old flip phone and expecting it to be able to run current apps. It's just not going to work.

Another one of the Big Five personality factors is Conscientiousness. It broadly refers to how well you are disciplined, persistent, honest, rule-oriented, and organized.[22] It is generally considered to be a good thing; indeed, it is the personality factor most associated with success in school[23] and work.[24] On the other hand, it can also be associated with people who are a bit buttoned down; the kind of folks who like all their ducks in a row. Conscientiousness is associated with higher creativity in science and business but with lower creativity in the arts.[25] Sometimes, it is split into two sub-factors, orderliness and industriousness.[26] So some of being Conscientious is being organized and dependable and some is being a hard worker and achievement-focused.

Both aspects of conscientiousness are needed to some degree in the arts. No casting director is going to rehire someone who's consistently late for rehearsals or is slacking off, unless it's a superstar whose name can sell tickets. But what the management might put up with for an established headliner is not what they will accept from you. Unless you are Idina Menzel reading this book, in which case you're all set.

Of course, superstars are often the most likely to work hard. Often people who are seen as being lucky when they succeed are simply doing much more preparation than anyone else. Two-time Tony winning director/choreographer Jerry Mitchell remembers being the first person to enter the dance studio and the last to leave.

> Jerry told us, "I don't actually believe in luck," I don't think there is luck; I think there is opportunity and I think there is being prepared. When you're prepared and there's a knock at the door, you're going to have a very good day – or a lucky day, as some people might say. But if you are unprepared and that comes, it's not going to turn out lucky…. Opportunity is always present; the question is, are you ready for the opportunity when it presents itself?

It is important to note that being Conscientious is not enough. There are thousands of people who would be happy to show up ten minutes early and bust their heinies off for a chance to understudy an ensemble role in the least popular show on Broadway. But we've discussed that bit of magic that helps you "make it" in other chapters (and will continue to do so). Here, we focus on the dimensions of Conscientiousness that will help you in your career.

Two ideas related to being Conscientious are perfectionism and persistence. Perfectionism can be either good or bad.[27] Good perfectionism is when you have high standards but allow yourself to make the occasional mistake. Bad perfectionism is when you are so scared of making mistakes that you become paralyzed – you are afraid of doing anything, you criticize yourself too much, and you end up not advancing your career because you don't risk trying out and making yourself vulnerable. The fear of failure ends up overwhelming the desire to create. Good perfectionism is related to being more accomplished and creative,[28] whereas bad perfectionism either isn't related or can actually make you less successful.[29]

It is easy to take rejection very personally, as Broadway and television star André Ward (*Moulin Rouge!* and *Pose*) told us. However, he has changed:

> I think the best advice I ever got was someone said to me, André, if you are as prepared as you can be and you've done the best that you can do, and you go out for a job and you get it, then that was your job to have. If you don't get it, then it wasn't your job to have. Because if it's yours, there's nothing you can do wrong. And if it's not yours, there's nothing you can do right.

When it comes to bad perfectionism, consider Sweeney Todd, who was born Benjamin Barker. Barker was a barber who was sent to Australia on a trumped-up charge (or so he claimed), so the local judge could have his way with the barber's wife. When Barker escaped, caught a ride with Anthony back to London, and renamed himself Sweeney Todd, he had two choices – one pathway would be to seek out his wife and daughter and try to resume a semblance of a life. Conversely, he could seek his bloody revenge. It is true that Todd went back to his old stomping grounds hoping to find Lucy and Johanna, but he was mighty quick to stop when Mrs. Lovett told him that Lucy was dead. Imagine if you were told that the love of your life was dead – wouldn't you want to confirm it, go to their grave, and find out more information? If you knew your child lived and was under the care of a madman, wouldn't you try to rescue him or her?

Instead, Sweeney switched immediately to option two and began setting long-range traps for the judge and his beadle. This decision may represent one of the most unfortunate examples of bad perfectionism: I can't have things how I want them, so I will abandon everything, destroy it, and salt the earth. We've all had these impulses, but acting on them doesn't just close doors; it completely burns bridges and removes all of your options. It is not a coincidence that Sweeney Todd does not have the happiest of endings.

Persistence is another component of Conscientiousness. Think about Tommy in *Brigadoon*. If he was like Sweeney Todd, he would have realized his mistake in New York as he listened to his shallow fiancé and then simply locked himself in his apartment and drank himself to death. There's a reason that the musical didn't end that way; hearing Jeff say a few words at Tommy's funeral while Fiona wails from far away and doesn't have quite the same impact as the tearful embrace in front of Mr. Lundie.

We tend to underestimate how important persistence is to our creative success.[30] Indeed, persistence and good perfectionism can combine to represent the aspects of Conscientiousness that help us reach our

> Creativity Hurdle to Leap: Being conscientious, persistent, and unafraid of making mistakes are underrated paths to creative success!

creative goals. The key is to distinguish persistence from simply hanging on to something after its expiration date and good perfectionism from bad.

Activity: Too Perfect: Does Your Attitude Need Adjusting?

We've made up this questionnaire to see where you are with good perfectionism/ persistence vs bad perfectionism/self-punishment – try it and see![31]

For the following questions, respond using the following options (and we chose a four-point scale to force you to choose a side):

1 = Absolutely Not
2 = Not Especially
3 = Yes, Slightly
4 = Absolutely Yes

1   I worry a lot about all of the mistakes I am making. _____
2   I make sure I am on time for any audition or rehearsal. _____
3   I think my childhood self would be disappointed with who I am now. _____
4   I don't mind hard work. _____
5   Everything needs to be "just right" or I get upset. _____
6   I push myself to do better. _____
7   I am my own worst critic. _____
8   I take advice and direction well. _____
9   I will pursue an idea over and over again, even if it is clear it's not going to work. _____
10 I set high standards for myself. _____
11 I let other people's mistakes impact my ability to be happy and succeed. _____
12 I don't give up right away. _____
13 I have trouble staying on track. _____
14 I keep my word to people. _____

For these items, we kept it simple; odd is "attitude change time" and even is "good attitude" – as you tally things up, start with zero and subtract the odd-numbered scores and add the even-numbered scores. If you have a negative number, start thinking about shaking things up, especially if it is lower than negative five. If you have a positive number, you're likely on the right track (especially if it's higher than five), although shaking things a little can often help in most situations.

Toward a Creative Personality

We've discussed the role that Conscientiousness plays in creativity. In addition, Extraversion is often helpful for performers,[32] whereas Emotional Stability can help actors handle stage fright.[33] However, we've reserved the bulk of our discussion for Openness. This trait is at the heart of having a creative personality.

There are many pathways to become more open. We've talked about the core split of experiences versus ideas and about how being exposed to other cultures can help in being more open. These are not the only important concepts related to Openness (and, by extension, creativity). Some of the pathways are ones that are familiar to anyone who loves theatre. For example, one is having a high aesthetic sense (a healthy appreciation of the arts).[34] In addition, being open to fantasy, another such component,[35] is essential to suspend your disbelief in the dark. In real life, people tend to not sing and dance. We accept that musical numbers represent moments of great emotion or importance. When a character in a show experiences a feeling so intense that words are insufficient, they sing. When even songs cannot convey their passion, characters dance.

Other aspects of Openness may be less obvious but make sense. Valuing your feelings, embracing the unconventional, and having many interests all contribute.[36] Another concept is being able to tolerate ambiguity[37] – in other words, being okay living with uncertainty. In an everyday sense, not knowing what will happen next can be hard. Can you handle the uncertainty of having tentative plans for the weekend that might fall through? Can you leave a new present wrapped? These are small steps compared to the giant leaps awaiting you in a life in the theatre.

If you pursue theatre, then tolerating ambiguity will become part of your daily routine. Will you get a callback? Will your show be produced? How long will your show run? The theatre, like many industries, is a contingency workforce. If you're working as an actor, then you're an actor. Dancers are dancers when they are hired to dance. If you're a writer, whether or not your show is produced (and how many times) can be the difference between seeking out a day job and being able to devote yourself to the next show.

It is a life filled with uncertainty, and the ability to cope with ambiguous situations is key. Performers move from gig to gig, waiting to find out if they have a job or if the cast list has been posted without their names present. There is an element of ghosting in many professions, but people in the arts encounter such situations regularly. You can feel a true connection or even be actively courted by a producer, agent, manager, or casting director, only to somehow become the "unflavor of the week" and be met with a wall of radio silence. Imagine opening up the *New York Times* and finding out – for the first time – that your show is closing and you need to figure out how to pay for next month's rent.

Openness increases in children and teenagers, peaking at ages 18–22 years old. It begins to decrease in adulthood, reaching its nadir when people are in their 60s.[38] Indeed, if you want to become truly depressed, your ability to problem solve and handle new things peaks at around 25 and goes into sharp, rapid decline immediately by your 30s.[39] What if we want to maintain or even increase our Openness (we won't go into raising intelligence for many reasons)? Well, to continue the negativity of this paragraph, getting married tends to reduce someone's Openness – and getting divorced or separated increases Openness in males.[40]

According to science, one way to increase Openness is to take hallucinogenic drugs[41] – but we don't necessarily recommend this pathway. What are the less risky ways? One is related to motivation. If you have what is called a promotion focus, then you are motivated to seek success (as opposed to avoiding failure). In other words, you are more likely to want to approach something as opposed to avoid it.[42] People with this promotion focus are more likely to seek out new experiences and, therefore, are higher on Openness.[43] As we've mentioned, exposure to other cultures and countries can also increase your Openness.[44] Another study had older adults practice their reasoning abilities (including doing crossword and Sudoku puzzles) and found that their Openness increased when the program was complete.[45]

Beyond what science has officially studied, there are many things you can do based on the theoretical construct of Openness. One is to understand the difference between traits and states.[46] Traits are tendencies over time – like Openness. Being a happy person, for example, is a trait; so is enjoying fruit and preferring to sleep late. States are how you feel in the moment. You might be a chocolate-lover (trait) who does not want chocolate right now (state) because you have an upset stomach. You might be a happy person (trait) who is currently sad (state) because your pet rat died or you stubbed your toe. This distinction is important; even the most well-balanced and emotionally healthy person can get upset over a bad review.

Therefore, even if you might be lower on Openness as a trait that you would like, there are many solutions. You can still take advantage of moments where your state allows you to engage in new behaviors. So, for example, even if you naturally do not seek new experiences, you can start small. You might try finding a new way to go from work to your home. Similarly, you can try a brand new restaurant or recipe (or order a new dish at a favorite restaurant or tweak a tried-and-true recipe).

It's easier said than done, but try looking at things from a new perspective. Take your favorite movie or show and imagine the story as it would be told by a minor character (Tom Stoppard's alternate take on *Hamlet* was the classic *Rosencrantz and Guildenstern are Dead*, but we're not expecting that). Try going to a new museum exhibit or attending a public lecture. Although it has become more and more difficult these days, perhaps try to have a conversation about the state of the world with someone who has a different point of view (perhaps do this activity in a public place with many witnesses).

We value knowledge and expertise – and, indeed, those are the cornerstones of creativity. However, it is easy to lose your curiosity if you already think you know the answer. People tend to rely on their general knowledge instead of their imagination if it is easier.[47] These days, with so many sharply divided opinions, it is easy to create an echo chamber of people who agree with you on everything. Such narrowness is not the way to grow. Although there is wisdom in keeping a steady course, it is also important to leave enough of a window in your brain (or heart) open to let some new notions in.

> Creativity Hurdle to Leap: Fight the trend, and become *more* open as you age!

Moving Forward

We've talked about the importance of being open – to experiences, ideas, and cultures. Many of you are probably already open to new things or you wouldn't have bought this book. What drives us to seek out new people, places, knowledge, and life events? One component is as simple as enjoying it. We are thrilled at the thought of a night in a dark theatre not because of what we will profit or acquire, but because it is a rush. We feel joy and excitement at the prospect of discovery. Other personal traits that can help creative success include being conscientious, persistent, curious, and tolerant of uncertainty. Some things that may seem helpful, such as being a perfectionist, can actually be barriers. In the next chapter, we're going to explore that bubbling drive to follow your interests, passions, and values as you create.

Notes

1. Stein & Swan (2018).
2. DeYoung (2015).
3. Feist (1998) and Jauk, Benedek, & Neubauer (2014).
4. DeYoung (2014).
5. Sternberg (2018).
6. Kaufman (2013) and Nusbaum & Silvia (2011).
7. Klawitter (2005).
8. Leung, Maddux, Galinsky, & Chiu (2008).
9. Leung & Chiu (2010).
10. Leung & Chiu (2008).
11. Maddux & Galinsky (2009).
12. Maddux, Adam, & Galinsky (2010).
13. Maddux, Lu, Affinito, & Galinsky (2021).
14. Chua (2018).
15. Choi (2007).
16. Pluut & Curşeu (2013).
17. Milliken & Martins (1996).
18. Tadmor, Satterstrom, Jang, & Polzer (2012).
19. Bernstein, Laurents, & Sondheim (1958, p. 11).
20. Cropley, Kaufman, & Cropley (2008) and Kapoor & Kaufman (2022).
21. Fassler (2017).
22. Conrad & Patry (2012).
23. Poropat (2009).
24. Brown, Lent, Telander, & Tramayne (2011).
25. Feist (1998)
26. DeYoung, Quilty, & Peterson (2007).
27. Frost, Marten, Lahart, & Rosenblate (1990) and Hamachek (1978).
28. Frost, Marten, Lahart, & Rosenblate (1990) and Wigert, Reiter-Palmon, Kaufman, & Silvia (2012).
29. Goulet-Pelletier, Gaudreau, & Cousineau (2022).
30. Lucas & Nordgren (2015)
31. Kaufman & Rowe (Creating Your Spotlight workbook, in progress).
32. Kogan (2002).
33. Goodman & Kaufman (2014).

34 Tinio (2013).
35 Costa & McCrae (1992).
36 McCrae (1987).
37 Zenasni, Besançon, & Lubart (2008).
38 Roberts, Walton, & Viechtbauer (2006).
39 Kaufman (2000, 2001).
40 Specht, Egloff, & Schmukle (2011).
41 MacLean, Johnson, & Griffiths (2011).
42 Higgins (2006).
43 Gasper & Middlewood (2014).
44 Leung & Chiu (2010).
45 Jackson et al. (2012).
46 Van Allen & Zelenski (2018).
47 Ward et al. (2002) and Ward & Sifonis (1997).

References

Bernstein, L., Laurents, A., & Sondheim, S. (1958). *West side story*. New York, NY: Random House.
Brown, S. D., Lent, R. W., Telander, K., & Tramayne, S. (2011). Social cognitive career theory, conscientiousness, and work performance: A meta-analytic path analysis. *Journal of Vocational Behavior, 79*, 81–90.
Choi, J. N. (2007). Group composition and employee creative behavior in a Korean electronics company: Distinct effects of relational demography and group diversity. *Journal of Occupational and Organizational Psychology, 80*, 213–234.
Chua, R. Y. (2018). Innovating at cultural crossroads: How multicultural social networks promote idea flow and creativity. *Journal of Management, 44*, 1119–1146.
Conrad, N., & Patry, M. W. (2012). Conscientiousness and academic performance: A mediational analysis. *International Journal for the Scholarship of Teaching and Learning, 6*, 1–13.
Costa, P. T., & McCrae, R. R. (1992). *NEO PI–R: Professional manual*. Odessa, FL: Psychological Assessment Resources.
Cropley, D. H., Kaufman, J. C., & Cropley, A. J. (2008). Malevolent creativity: A functional model of creativity in terrorism and crime. *Creativity Research Journal, 20*, 105–115.
DeYoung, C. G. (2014). Openness/Intellect: A dimension of personality reflecting cognitive exploration. In M. L. Cooper & R. J. Larsen (Eds.), *APA handbook of personality and social psychology: Personality processes and individual differences* (vol. 4, pp. 369–399). Washington, DC: American Psychological Association.
DeYoung, C. G. (2015). Cybernetic Big Five Theory. *Journal of Research in Personality, 56*, 33–58.
DeYoung, C. G., Quilty, L. C., & Peterson, J. B. (2007). Between facets and domains: 10 aspects of the Big-Five. *Journal of Personality and Social Psychology, 93*, 880–896.
Fassler, R. (2017, June 29). At this performance the role of…. *Medium*. Retrieved from https://medium.com/@ronfassler/at-this-performance-the-role-of-d006dbd778a1
Feist, G. J. (1998). A meta-analysis of personality in scientific and artistic creativity. *Personality and Social Psychology Review, 2*, 290–309.
Frost, R., Marten, P., Lahart, C., & Rosenblate, R. (1990). The dimensions of perfectionism. *Cognitive Therapy and Research, 14*, 449–468.

Gasper, K., & Middlewood, B. L. (2014). Approaching novel thoughts: Understanding why elation and boredom promote associative thought more than distress and relaxation. *Journal of Experimental Social Psychology, 52*, 50–57.

Goodman, G., & Kaufman, J. C. (2014). Gremlins in my head: Predicting stage fright in elite actors. *Empirical Studies of the Arts, 32*, 133–148.

Goulet-Pelletier, J. C., Gaudreau, P., & Cousineau, D. (2022). Is perfectionism a killer of creative thinking? A test of the model of excellencism and perfectionism. *British Journal of Psychology, 113*(1), 176–207.

Hamachek, D. (1978). Psychodynamics of normal and neurotic perfectionism. *Psychology: A Journal of Human Behavior, 15*, 27–33.

Higgins, E. T. (2006). Value from hedonic experience and engagement. *Psychological Review, 113*, 439–460.

Jackson, J. J., Hill, P. L., Payne, B. R., Roberts, B. W., & Stine-Morrow, E. A. (2012). Can an old dog learn (and want to experience) new tricks? Cognitive training increases openness to experience in older adults. *Psychology and Aging, 27*, 286–292.

Jauk, E., Benedek, M., & Neubauer, A. C. (2014). The road to creative achievement: A latent variable model of ability and personality predictors. *European Journal of Personality, 28*, 95–105.

Kapoor, H., & Kaufman, J. C. (2022). The evil within: The AMORAL model of dark creativity. *Theory & Psychology, 32*, 467–490.

Kaufman, A. S. (2000). Seven questions about the WAIS-III regarding differences in abilities across the 16 to 89 year life span. *School Psychology Quarterly, 15*, 3–29.

Kaufman, A. S. (2001). WAIS-III IQs, Horn's theory, and generational changes from young adulthood to old age. *Intelligence, 29*, 131–167.

Kaufman, J. C., & Rowe, D. P. (in progress). *The creating your spotlight workbook*. Retrived from https://creatingyourspotlight.com/

Kaufman, S. B. (2013). Opening up openness to experience: A four-factor model and relations to creative achievement in the arts and sciences. *Journal of Creative Behavior, 47*, 233–255.

Klawitter, G. (2005, November 1). Craig Lucas: Playwright with a movie in him. *The Gay & Lesbian Review*. Retrieved from https://glreview.org/article/article-1099/

Kogan, N. (2002). Performing arts: A psychological perspective. *Creativity Research Journal, 14*, 1–16.

Leung, A. K-y., & Chiu, C-y. (2008). Interactive effects of multicultural experiences and openness to experience on creative potential. *Creativity Research Journal, 20*, 376–382.

Leung, A. K.-y., & Chiu, C.-y. (2010). Multicultural experiences, idea receptiveness, and creativity. *Journal of Cross-Cultural Psychology, 41*, 1–19.

Leung, A. K-y., Maddux, W. W., Galinsky, A. D., & Chiu, C. (2008). Multicultural experience enhances creativity: The when and how. *American Psychologist, 63*, 169–181.

Lucas, B. J., & Nordgren, L. F. (2015). People underestimate the value of persistence for creative performance. *Journal of Personality and Social Psychology, 109*, 232–243.

MacLean, K. A., Johnson, M. W., & Griffiths, R. R. (2011). Mystical experiences occasioned by the hallucinogen psilocybin lead to increases in the personality domain of Openness. *Journal of Psychopharmacology, 25*, 1453–1461.

Maddux, W. W., Adam, H., & Galinsky, A. D. (2010). When in Rome… Learn why the Romans do what they do: How multicultural learning experiences facilitate creativity. *Personality and Social Psychology Bulletin, 36*, 731–741.

Maddux, W. W., & Galinsky, A. D. (2009). Cultural borders and mental barriers: The relationship between living abroad and creativity. *Journal of Personality and Social Psychology*, *96*, 1047–1061.

Maddux, W. W., Lu, J. G., Affinito, S. J., & Galinsky, A. D. (2021). Multicultural experiences: A systematic review and new theoretical framework. *Academy of Management Annals*, *15*(2), 345–376.

McCrae, R. R. (1987). Creativity, divergent thinking, and openness to experience. *Journal of Personality and Social Psychology*, *52*, 1258–1265.

Milliken, F. J., & Martins, L. L. (1996). Searching for common threads: Understanding the multiple effects of diversity in organizational groups. *Academy of Management Review*, *21*, 402–433.

Nusbaum, E. C., & Silvia, P. J. (2011). Are openness and intellect distinct aspects of openness performance. *Psychological Bulletin*, *135*, 322–338.

Pluut, H., & Curşeu, P. L. (2013). The role of diversity of life experiences in fostering collaborative creativity in demographically diverse student groups. *Thinking Skills and Creativity*, *9*, 16–23.

Poropat, A. E. (2009). A meta-analysis of the five-factor model of personality and academic promote idea flow and creativity. *Journal of Management*, *44*, 1119–1146.

Roberts, B. W., Walton, K. E., & Viechtbauer, W. (2006). Patterns of mean-level change in personality traits across the life course: A meta-analysis of longitudinal studies. *Psychological Bulletin*, *132*, 1–25.

Specht, J., Egloff, B., & Schmukle, S. C. (2011). Stability and change of personality across the life course: The impact of age and major life events on mean-level and rank-order stability of the Big Five. *Journal of Personality and Social Psychology*, *101*, 862–882

Stein, R., & Swan, A. B. (2018). Deeply confusing: Conflating difficulty with deep revelation on personality assessment. *Social Psychological and Personality Science*. doi: 1948550618766409.

Sternberg, R. J. (2018). A triangular theory of creativity. *Psychology of Aesthetics, Creativity, and the Arts*, *12*, 50–67.

Tadmor, C. T., Satterstrom, P., Jang, S., & Polzer, J. T. (2012). Beyond individual creativity: The superadditive benefits of multicultural experience for collective creativity in culturally diverse teams. *Journal of Cross-Cultural Psychology*, *43*, 384–392.

Tinio, P. L. (2013). From artistic creation to aesthetic reception: The mirror model of art. *Psychology of Aesthetics, Creativity, and the Arts*, *7*, 265–275.

Van Allen, Z. M., & Zelenski, J. M. (2018). Testing trait-state isomorphism in a new domain: An exploratory manipulation of openness to experience. *Frontiers in Psychology*, *9*, 1964.

Ward, T. B., & Sifonis, C. M. (1997). Task demands and generative thinking: What changes and what remains the same? *Journal of Creative Behavior*, *31*, 245–259.

Ward, T. B., Patterson, M. J., Sifonis, C. M., Dodds, R. A., & Saunders, K. N. (2002). The role of graded category structure in imaginative thought. *Memory & Cognition*, *30*, 199–216.

Wigert, B., Reiter-Palmon, R., Kaufman, J. C., & Silvia, P. J. (2012). Perfectionism: The good, the bad, and the creative. *Journal of Research in Personality*, *46*, 775–779.

Zenasni, F., Besançon, M., & Lubart, T. (2008). Creativity and tolerance of ambiguity: An empirical study. *Journal of Creative Behavior*, *42*, 61–73.

Chapter 6

What's Your Motivation?
Passion and Balance

> Maria von Trapp (*The Sound of Music*), Success
> Eva Peron (*Evita*), Suppress
> Myth: Reward Yourself – You've Earned It!
> Activity: The Driving Range: Enjoyment, Success, and Growth

There are things we like to do. Whether it is eating ice cream or playing with your dog or watching an exciting movie or riding your bike through Central Park on a beautiful afternoon, everyone has an activity that is pure pleasure. Consider Jeff Blumenkrantz, renowned as both a performer (*Candide, How to Succeed in Business Without Really Trying, Sweeney Todd*, and so much more) and composer (Fred Ebb award winner and Tony nominee for *Urban Cowboy*). In Dana's *Take it From the Top* podcast, Blumenkrantz talks about his passion for music. His mother had a closet filled with theatre scores and vocal selections, and he would spend hours going through the music books and playing them on the piano.

> He told Dana "I was self-immersed," Nobody was making me; nobody was suggesting I do it or telling me to do it. I was doing it because that's what I wanted to do. It was truly different from when you hear people say, 'Oh, I started my kids on piano lessons but they never want to play.' For me it was the opposite. I'm sure my mother thought, 'will somebody make that kid stop playing?'

That passion that Blumenkrantz felt – which we hope many of our readers have also experienced – is a core part of the creative process.

There are other things that need to be done, but many people do not enjoy. These may include cleaning your toilets, waking up early, driving in heavy traffic, doing your homework, or completing bureaucratic paperwork (we are sure there are some people who love cleaning toilets, and we encourage them to contact us for a chance to enhance their skills). Despite lacking a passion for these less-enjoyable things, we still do them. We file our taxes. We wash our dishes. Most likely, your first job was not terribly fun, whether it was delivering papers or working at a fast food

DOI: 10.4324/9781003389668-9

restaurant or any retail or service work. Yet there was a reason for pursuing these early jobs, and most likely it was the paycheck.

Joy and a paycheck (or, for those still in school, joy and good grades) are not necessarily in opposition, but they do represent different end goals. In psychology, these broad concepts are called intrinsic and extrinsic motivation.[1] Intrinsic motivation is performing an activity because it gives pleasure or provides meaning. Extrinsic motivation is doing something for an outside reason. It could be for money – but there are many possible extrinsic motivators. These may include applause, recognition, validation, status, awards, or good grades.

Finding Flow

Auntie Mame Dennis is a woman of passion. When we first meet the titular character of *Mame*, she is singing of how every day is a celebration. There is a reason to revel in each minute, regardless of circumstance. She embraces every new adventure, whether it is becoming the guardian of her nephew, throwing a speakeasy party, appearing in a musical, transforming herself into a Southern aristocrat, or saving the world from normalcy. Mame is driven by happiness, desire, excitement, and change. She lives her life in near-perpetual intrinsic motivation. She does what she wants and finds a way to do it.

All of us may not have so many disparate sources of pleasure as Mame, but we all have things we love and enjoy. It is not surprising that when you enjoy something, you are more likely to do it (and to continue to do it).[2] It will also probably not be a shock that when you are passionate about what you are doing, other matters being equal, you will be more creative.[3] The research is more complex, of course, but this basic connection is an essential starting place. Mame infuses each activity with joy, which leads her to be quite creative. She becomes the first female equestrian to go on a fox hunt and bring the fox back alive, celebrates Christmas on cue, gives elaborate fashion makeovers, and writes her memoirs.

What makes us intrinsically motivated? What makes us develop an interest and then passion for a topic? Maybe you get that excited feeling about theatre – whether it is in the form of acting, writing, directing, working behind the scenes, or attending shows. Or else you feel this way about cooking, designing scientific experiments, outlining a marketing plan, or tinkering with a broken appliance. If we could answer these questions specifically and accurately, we'd have our own billion-dollar franchise. However, we can offer some tips.

One way that people can experience pleasure in creating is through Flow. Flow (sometimes called being "in the zone") is when you are so involved in what you are doing that you lose track of time and space and nothing exists except you and the current moment.[4] People can achieve Flow in other circumstances (most notably athletics), but creativity is a prime example. Above all else, being in Flow is fun. It is a magical rush that makes you feel completely alive. We enter Flow when we are challenging ourselves. You will not enter this state when doing something that is well below your skill level or attempting something so difficult that you are overwhelmed. Ideally, it is something attainable but still a stretch. For example, when Dana learned Chopin's *Fantaisie-Impromptu Opus 66 in C-sharp minor* in high school, it was both thrilling and terrifying. At first, it was daunting, requiring each hand to play conflicting rhythms. Dana did not enter Flow at this point. Yet as Dana practiced, slowly and painstakingly for months, his ability and familiarity with the piece grew. As he improved, playing the piece sent him soaring, metaphorically hang-gliding through the air. Dana had entered Flow and was able to subsequently recognize how his hard work led to this glorious state. He was hooked.

What else can help you feel intrinsically motivated? Let us consider our Success model for this chapter, Maria Rainer (soon to be von Trapp). For the purpose of this example, we will be using the movie of *The Sound of Music* instead of the Broadway version (for the purists out there, we humbly apologize). As you likely remember, the show begins with Maria training to be a nun. The Mother Abbess (correctly) doubts Maria's ability to adjust to the lifestyle and sends the young novice to be a governess for the seven children of Captain Georg von Trapp. After a few initial growing pains, Maria loves the job and taking care of the children. She shows genuine passion and intrinsic motivation in her interactions; even more, she also demonstrates prosocial motivation.[5] She is driven by the need to help other people. Self-focused intrinsic motivation seeks fulfillment and passion; in contrast, other-focused intrinsic motivation aims at guidance.

Maria gets enjoyment from teaching the children. When there is a scary thunderstorm, she models how to stay positive during tense times by singing about her favorite things. The song gives details of pleasant but simple experiences and objects and how she is able to get joy (even during scary moments) by remembering and reflecting on them. The poise she is teaching them comes in handy when they must sing "So Long, Farewell" before a largely-Nazi audience before they all make their escape. Even though she is driven into the Captain's arms, Maria goes back to the Abbey when she believes this choice is best for the children. Intrinsic motivation can come not only from following your own passion but from listening to intense feelings for other people. If your life is like a movie musical, it will all work out okay in the end, anyway.

> Creativity Hurdle to Leap: Nurture goals that offer passion and enjoyment!

The Importance (and Risks) of Intrinsic Motivation

It is perfectly okay to have intrinsic motivation sprout from your own personal needs. For example, two fundamental human needs are to feel competent and to feel capable of independence. Activities that make us feel competent increase intrinsic motivation.[6] Receiving positive feedback on our efforts can enhance intrinsic motivation (although negative feedback can diminish such motivation[7]). However, in order for such input to be effective, we must feel as though our performance was due to our own efforts.[8] In other words, if you are in a show playing a tree and all you do is stand and not move, with all the other cast members doing the exciting parts, even extensive and heartfelt praise for your role in the show may not be inspiring.

Sometimes the need to feel like we are not only competent but also responsible for our performance can lead to embarrassment. One memorable scene in *Mame* has the main character accepting a walk-on part that is basically being a living piece of scenery. The star of the show is her best friend, Vera Charles, playing an astronomer, whereas Mame plays the moon. Mame's need to "earn" her place in the show leads her toward ostentatious behavior that results in a disastrous collapsing of the moon. She unintentionally upstages her friend and destroys the show – not out of a need for attention but out of the need to be both competent and independent. As Dana tells his students, there are times to "don't just do something – sit there."

This story illustrates the potential harm in intrinsic motivation, albeit an excessive and unlikely case. There are more common ways in which relying too heavily on intrinsic motivation can be self-sabotaging. At its absurd extreme, someone motivated purely by intrinsic forces would be a hedonist (which, indeed, is a label some have applied to Mame[9]). Further, anyone only operating on intrinsic motivation would never get anything finished. There are always parts of any project that are not fun. A writer continually revising a show in response to critical feedback, an actress accepting a less-interesting ensemble part so she can understudy a juicier role, someone taking an unpaid internship in a tech department, or an aspiring professional serving as a personal assistant (a go-fer) to a director are not making these decisions because the associated actions are overwhelmingly fun. But they are necessary to survive and thrive in the theatre – or any career. For example, in academia, such rites of passage include boring research assistant work, graduate studies that may need to conform to your advisor's agenda, years of stagnant postdocs, and service on many university committees. Consider the comparable steps needed to reach your own career or creative goal.

Similarly, there are aspects of any creative endeavor that are needed to finish up a project that will not be fun. Dana loves creating new music. Writing a song that has never existed is magical. It is a small moment of giving life and allowing something to become. Sondheim has famously dubbed this experience as "finishing the hat.[10]" Composing does not end when the song has been first drafted. Along the way, Dana will: (1) adjust the melody to better fit the lyrics; (2) create an initial lead sheet with only the core melody, lyrics, and chord symbols; (3) record a simple version of the harmony; (4) flesh out the piano accompaniment to include countermelodies; (5) draft the vocal arrangements; (6) use music manuscript software to notate the score so someone new to the song could perform it; (7) record himself singing a basic demo that conveys the song's tone and energy; (8) create orchestral tracks using a digital audio workstation; (9) rehearse professional singers to record a polished demo; (10) share this initial vision with potential producers and creative teams; and then (11–2,000) revise the song throughout this process and beyond based on feedback, critics, production needs, and changing times. Indeed, Dana is still revising, revamping, and collaborating on *The Fix* – more than 25 years after the show's premiere.

It is important to emphasize that not every venture needs such a level of commitment. We have already discussed in the last chapter that perfectionism can be harmful for your creativity. Sometimes, an idea may burst out of you but not go anywhere. That is okay. Creativity is meaningful for its own sake. A moment of insight or feeling that does not evolve into a final form still has value[11]. However, those rare ideas that show the potential to blossom and become a unique entity in their own right do require more commitment. Like Dana, you need to plow through the mundanity of the tasks that do not inspire intrinsic motivation.

It is not always easy to do. Dana's list is comprised of many duties that are not as compelling as capturing the initial melodies that formed in his head. Certainly, there is much fulfillment and gratification and feelings of accomplishment. Still needing to work on older shows means they are still relevant and being produced. But many of these tasks are tedious and detail-oriented. There are so many moving and growing parts, at times similar to the ripples following a stone skipped across a river, that keeping track of them can feel impossible at times.

Ideally, Dana would get to experience the thrill of writing original music without the requisite subsequent steps. Yet there is a certain responsibility in creating something new, on the same dimension of having a plant, pet, or even a child. You want to see your best ideas to fruition and have them thrive in the world. If you only follow your passion, you will have hundreds of small sparks but no blazing fire that continues to burn for potentially years and years. Paying attention to an idea's subsequent needs allows it to be manufactured, produced, published, sold, and shared. Without caring and feeding for the product of your Flow moment, it will fail to thrive. There were many times throughout the writing process of this book that we missed the excitement of the initial brainstorming and exploration. However, we knew that we would need to show up with the same rigor to find the most up-to-date references, most evocative anecdotes, and most illustrative metaphors. Otherwise, the final book would not capture that element of what Dana would call the "special sauce" in those early moments. As much fun as the honeymoon phase of a creative endeavor is, it is important to not overlook the deeper satisfaction of a finished product that makes you proud.

> Creativity Hurdle to Leap: Recognize the value of and need for the boring parts!

The Importance (and Risks) of Extrinsic Motivation

Often, extrinsic motivation gets a bad rap. If you meet someone who says they're only doing theatre (or anything) for the money, it'll probably rub you the wrong way (and, perhaps, question their sanity). We make certain judgments and assumptions. It is true that under some circumstances, working for the paycheck is harmful and can reduce your creativity.[12] Similarly, some argue that knowing you are going to be evaluated can make you feel less creative[13] or less competent.[14] This issue can be particularly relevant to theatre, given it is one long series of evaluations – first in the audition, then from the director, audiences, critics, and even posterity.

Small acts of kindness can make such daunting evaluations bearable. Consider Randy Graff's journey to create the role of Fantine in the original Broadway cast of *Les Misérables*. She had performed many shows on and off-Broadway, but Fantine was her breakout role which won her a Tony nomination (she would later win for *City of Angels*). Randy told Dana about her experience at her callback:

> Everybody wanted to be in *Les Misérables*. The stakes were so high and everybody was so nervous. I went in and there were 13 people behind the table. I started singing 'I dreamed a dream' and I started cracking on every high note. I stopped and I said, 'I'm sorry. I'm very nervous.' And [director] Trevor Nunn, such a gentleman, came up to me from behind the table, put his arm around me, and said, 'That's okay. We know that you can sing; we heard you sing in your first audition. I don't care if you crack. I just want to see you have a nervous breakdown.' He cared about the acting. So I took my shoes off, I got down on the floor, and I started singing. I was cracking but I was acting. I was connecting to the lyrics. A month later, I got the call that I got the part.

Sometimes evaluations can be difficult because of the prestige of the people offering feedback. When Dana wrote the overture for *Witches of Eastwick*, it was barely over a minute long. Although it was initially well-received, there was concern that it was too short (most overtures are three to five minutes). Dana was told to write an alternate version that was more traditional, which would be turned in to the late, great Bill Brohn to orchestrate so that Sir Cameron Mackintosh could hear both versions between shows and decide which one to use. Before Dana began work, he was told that the next day's performance would have a visitor – a certain Stephen Sondheim. Dana furiously composed two new overtures that were more traditional in both timing and sound. As Mackintosh conferred with Sondheim in the back of the theatre, Dana paced back and forth around the orchestra, waiting for the verdict. The decision was to stick with the original, which Sondheim liked – whereas he felt the two more traditional ones were less compelling. The brief version stayed – and has been widely praised and included on compilations.[15]

Another potential trigger for extrinsic motivation is the presence of rewards. They can be harmful to one's passion for a task, but the possible damage is downplayed if the creators have experience with[16] or a passion for such work,[17] or if someone has a positive creative self-image.[18] Indeed, rewards under these circumstances may even boost performance. For example, if you are a classically-trained actor who has extensive experience with Shakespeare and O'Neill and Moliere, getting a lucrative contract to be in a Broadway production of *The Crucible* will not be harmful. In fact, it will probably be helpful – you would feel like your skills are known and appreciated; thus, you can feel free to use your expertise and skills to wow the audiences every night. However, if you end up being offered a role in the ensemble of *42nd Street*, then the all-singing, all-dancing requirements may be daunting. In this scenario, the prospect of the paycheck and applause may become pressures instead of motivators.

Studies have shown that if a reward is specifically tied to *creative* work (and not simply completing a task), it can also be beneficial.[19] If you are hired as a rehearsal pianist, where your job is to not be noticed, then you are being paid to be there and do a specific job. If you decide to do a jazz improvisation in the middle of playing "Oh, what a beautiful morning," then your creativity will actually distract from the task. In a sense, you are being hired to be competent but not creative.

Obviously, people need to make a living. Being a rehearsal pianist is a perfectly noble way to use a specific and valued set of skills. However, if you see your creativity as primarily being able to riff and play with an established melody, then too many standard assignments may lead to frustration and even a loss of that initial excitement you felt. Similarly, imagine that your job is to help scientists prepare the paperwork to apply for copyrights and patents. If your true passion is thinking of new inventions, some degree of offering input may be helpful. But if you turn what should be a straightforward, hour-long meeting to fill out forms into a four-hour idea fest that is not wanted or helpful, neither you nor your employers will be happy.

It is, however, just as important to note that an exclusive focus on extrinsic motivation is rarely good. Most musical theatre characters who are motivated by an extrinsic reward end up changing by the end of the show. Whether it is Veronica Sawyer's desire to be popular in *Heathers*, Harold Hill's greed in *The Music Man*, Elle Woods's journey to Harvard to get back together with her ex-boyfriend in *Legally Blonde*, or William Barfée seeking to win the spelling bee (and the prize money) in *The 25th Annual Putnam County Spelling Bee*, most lead characters will have a moment of insight that has them shift their values (at least a bit) and see the light. If a character is extrinsically motivated and does not have a change of heart, they will likely meet a poor end. J. Pierrepoint Finch in *How to Succeed in Business Without Really Trying* is an exception – but that is also satire.

Consider our Suppress model, Eva Peron from *Evita* (the character, not the historical figure). After a poor and neglected childhood, she was determined to advance her social status by any means necessarily. Rather than pursuing a specific career, she chose whatever would be in her best long-term interests – whether that was being a groupie, actress, or the wife of the president of Argentina. Indeed, even as her health began failing, she proposed running as vice president as part of her husband's presidential ticket. On some measures, Eva was a success. She went from nothing to being one of the most powerful women in the world. However, was she ultimately fulfilled? In her last song in the musical, "Lament," she questions her life choices. She makes some curious logical leaps, assuming that her quest for fame in some way was responsible for her early death from cancer. Yet if this false dichotomy is read more as a metaphor, then it is not that she truly thinks that she is dying young because of her ambition but rather that she finally recognizes the ultimate cost of her continued pursuit of status (whether that is not leading an authentic life, not having a family, or not contributing to the world can be left up to the viewer's discretion). Despite Eva's dynamic presence throughout the play, she both enters and exits as a corpse.

Extrinsic motivation may be detrimental for your passion (and even your creativity), but it can be used in the service of good. Our interpretation of *Evita* – indeed, Webber and Rice's interpretation of Eva Peron's life – is still just one point of view. We asked Madalena Alberto, the acclaimed West End star who received raves for her titular performance in the 2014 revival of *Evita*, to reflect on the complex character.

Alberto told us, "Since she is a real-life character, and the accounts on her life and intentions are contradictory," I had to choose an angle to see how I could do her justice. For that, I looked at what I might have had in common with her – her childhood dreams and her vulnerabilities. Of course there was a lot of ambition and resentment towards the middle classes due mainly to her childhood, but in my view, all she wanted was to be an actress! She loved Hollywood movies and the glamour of its stars. So at 15 her mom took her to Buenos Aires (which is probably a more accurate account than the one depicted in the musical). Whether she made her way through life – in order to survive and fulfil her dreams – by using men is also for debate; they would have used her all the same.

[Eva] made it as a stage actress and got gigs as a radio actress where she impersonated big powerful women characters; that might have also inspired her. I don't think she ever had the ambition to go into politics, but when the opportunity arose she definitely took it. I actually met someone related to the man who took her to the ball where she met Peron. She was having an affair with him and left him for Peron! Once they were together I do think there was a partnership; they depended on each other in many ways, especially because of the way she was perceived by the lower classes. They worshiped her, saw in her the Cinderella story. Whether there was embezzlement and other shady things going on… we are talking about South America in the 1950s! We need to put it into a historical context. I truly believe she did what she thought was of most benefit to the people, to the point that even she started believing in the myth around her – to the point of exhaustion, where she would only sleep four hours and spent the rest of the time working and seeking out the poor.

'Lament' was my favorite song; it was the moment I could exorcise what had happened in the previous two hours. It was a moment of reflection where she comes to terms with her story. That it was her choice. For a long time, she refused to accept she was as ill as she was and continued on her mission. For me, her death is tragic because it comes down to one thing: The need to be loved. By her people, by her father, by God.

Alberto's insights offer a nuanced examination of Evita – a character still driven by extrinsic forces, but one whose ultimate goals are benevolent. Eva's desire to achieve and be loved became dominant to the point that she ignored her physical health. Whether you see Evita as a fundamentally selfish character or as a tragic hero who worked herself to death, she was someone whose external needs (whether for love, power, charity, or personal gain) likely led her to an early grave.

> Creativity Hurdle to Leap: Know when to play for love and when to play for money and don't let either one completely dominate you!

Myth: Reward Yourself – You've Earned It!

Whether your vice is food, drink, sex, or binging Netflix, there is no harm in the occasional indulgence as long you have it under control and nobody (including yourself) gets hurt. Our point here is not to make our readers feel like they must be Puritans.

There is a mentality – often one that begins in school[20] – that good papers get gold stars and a finished assignment or an outstanding report card entitles you to a hot fudge sundae. Often, this way of thinking continues to college and adulthood. Weekends are times to party, and getting an unpleasant task completed warrants an extra glass of wine. Certainly, there are times when it is absolutely fine to think this way. If you've spent an hour cleaning your apartment and organizing your closets, then go ahead and finish that carton of ice cream.

There is a reason why this process continues; it is so easy to overlook good work we have done. We are much more likely to focus on the blown audition than the one where we blow away the director. However, rewards are different from celebrations. We can recognize that we have done good work and enjoy that feeling without tying these accomplishments to specific activities that we like to do.

The real danger is when you reward yourself for standard behavior. Going to an audition, having a good voice lesson, even getting cast in a role – these are all solid markers that your career is progressing. However, if you want a life in the theatre, these represent part of the routine. It is similar to a scientist applying for a grant or a writer submitting a story or an accountant finishing a difficult client's tax returns. Ideally, your passion for what you are doing and what you want to do will carry you through the sawdust work of repeated auditions, rehearsals, and negative critical responses. No academic enjoys revising a paper in response to harsh reviews, but that is the price of wanting to get your work out in the world.

If you need that outside boost to keep yourself functioning in your career – whether it lies in theatre or teaching or being a plumber – then you have not found a perfect fit. Every field has drudgework, just as every field has internally rewarding moments. Recognizing the pleasure you get from doing the job itself is essential. The idea that every step on the ladder deserves a special reward is an attitude left

> Creativity Hurdle to Leap: Don't be too quick to reward yourself for a job mediocrely done!

over from school. People who use outside rewards as a motivator to do tasks that are standard for the job are going to find before too long that they've lost their initial spark and passion. Soon you'll be solely focused on the reward, and it will take bigger and better rewards to keep you going.

Activity: The Driving Range: Enjoyment, Success, and Growth

For this activity, we would like you to start by thinking of past projects. If you are in theatre, they might be shows you have worked on in any capacity, from ensemble to writer to tech to stage manager to star. These shows might span from high school to regional theatre (or even Broadway!). Or you can pick any project from school or work or everyday life. Anything that has used your creative talents in some way qualifies, whether a correct diagnosis or finished landscape or finalized marketing campaign. In the pages that follow, we provide space to list up to 12 projects. If you cannot think of 12 different projects, do not worry; just complete however many you can.

The first step is to name the project. It might be "Playing Sarah in Guys and Dolls in High School" or "Directing a ten-minute play at a local festival" or "Making a bookshelf from scratch." Next, you will see three rows underneath each project that ask you to evaluate your experience. All ratings will be on a six-point scale going from low to high (we are using six points instead of four to allow a larger spread of what motivates you). First, we ask you to rate your enjoyment of the project, by which we mean the fun and excitement you experienced during the process of the project itself. Next, we ask you to rate the success of the project. Here we are referring to the final product. If it was a show, how was it received and reviewed? If it was a non-theatrical product, what were people's reactions? Was it a new and useful creation? Finally, we ask you to rate your own growth from the project. Growth could be personal (such as learning how to interact with a difficult collaborator) or professional (such as trying a new acting method or design style).

Now that you have done this first part, we would like you to think about your intrinsic and extrinsic motivation *going into* each project. By intrinsic motivation, we mean your inherent interest and personal investment in the project. By extrinsic motivation, we are talking about your perceived prospect of reward (whether financial or career advancement) and potential evaluation. Of course, your motivation will change throughout the duration of a project, but we are most interested in how you felt at the beginning. It is important to note that intrinsic and extrinsic motivation are not necessarily in opposition to each other. You may have felt intense passion for a project while simultaneously anticipating an enticing payoff.

100 Your Creative Tools

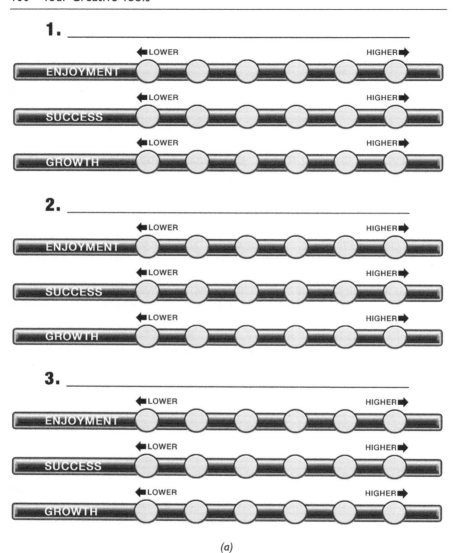

(a)

Figure 6.1 Driving Range Activity, (a) Part One/Page One

What's Your Motivation?: Passion and Balance 101

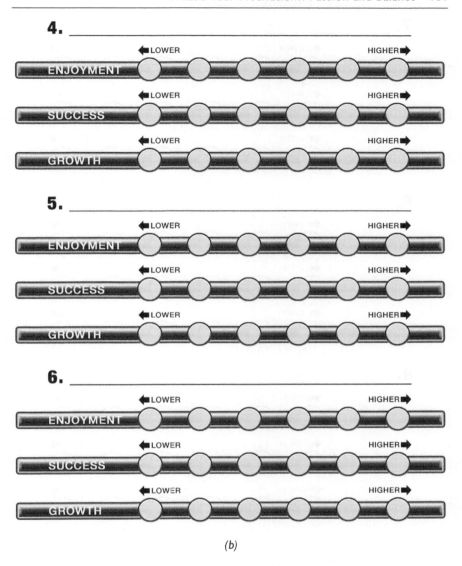

(b)

Figure 6.1 Driving Range Activity, (b) Part One/Page Two

102 Your Creative Tools

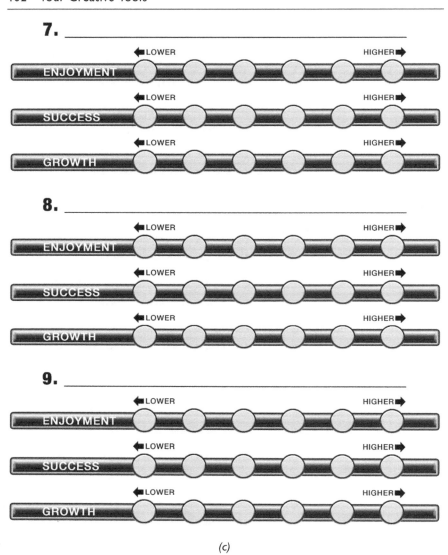

Figure 6.1 Driving Range Activity, (c) Part One/Page Three

What's Your Motivation?: Passion and Balance 103

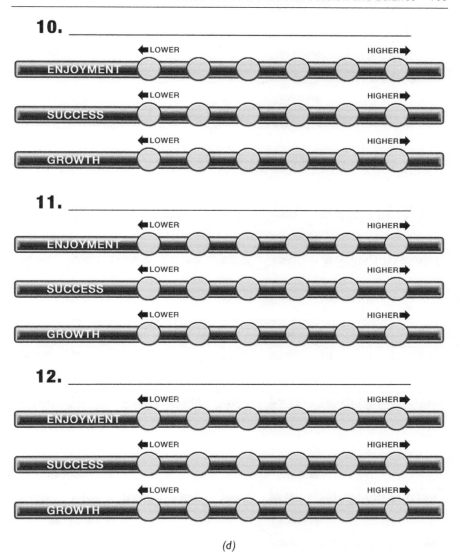

(d)

Figure 6.1 Driving Range Activity, (d) Part One/Page Four. © Kaufman and Rowe (Creating Your Spotlight workbook, in progress)

104 Your Creative Tools

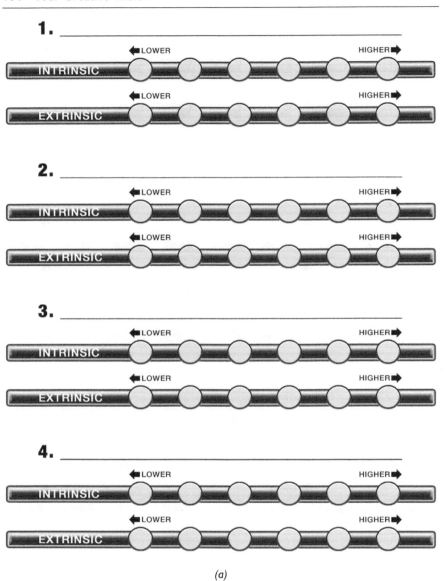

(a)

Figure 6.2 Driving Range Activity, (a) Part Two/Page One

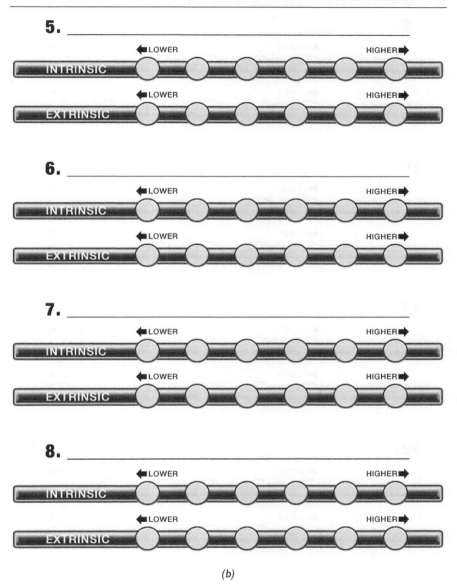

Figure 6.2 Driving Range Activity, (b) Part Two/Page Two

106 Your Creative Tools

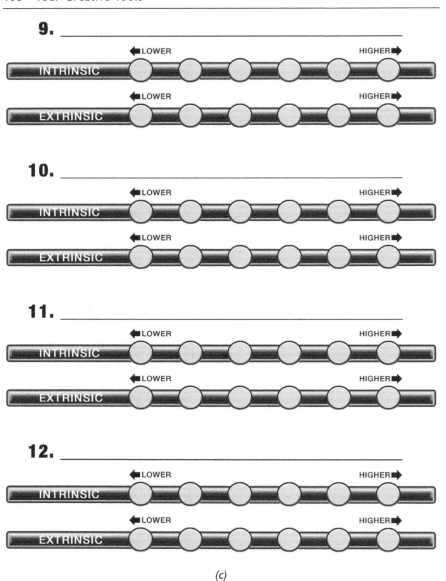

(c)

Figure 6.2 Driving Range Activity, (c) Part Two/Page Three. © Kaufman and Rowe (Creating Your Spotlight workbook, in progress)

After completing both parts of this activity, we will attempt to work with you to see how the variables that drive you match up with the best possible outcomes. When you look at the projects that you scored high on enjoyment, what were your motivation scores like? Based on the research, we would guess that your intrinsic scores would be high, but everyone is an individual; no one system or concept applies equally to everyone. It is very possible that your enjoyment develops throughout a project regardless of the reasons you started. Similarly, how did your motivation scores correspond with projects that were low on enjoyment?

For your success scores, again, look at your highs and lows. What types of motivation have been most associated with better final products? Perhaps instead of focusing on the difference between intrinsic and extrinsic, it might be that your successful outcomes are connected to higher levels of any type of motivation, whereas scoring lower on both motivations may not lead to the same positive results.

Finally, examine your growth scores. Again, although past research suggests that higher intrinsic motivation should relate to growth,[21] there is no magical formula. Indeed, we can define growth in many different ways. Growth could mean developing a specific talent, becoming a better person, gaining an interpersonal skill, or feeling like you are part of a cohesive group. Examine the patterns for your growth (and, of course, patterns may not emerge for every dimension). Do you grow most when you are high in both types of motivation? High in one but low on the other?

No answer is the correct one. It is all about self-insight. Whatever match results in your best work – however *you* define what is best, whether it is enjoyment, success, or growth – is the one you may wish to pursue. If external rewards ensure a good experience, make sure that they are in place. If you need to feel a strong investment in the project in order to reap the most benefits, ensure those feelings are there.

Choices vs Constraints

We've discussed how it is easy to trigger extrinsic motivation at the expense of intrinsic motivation. However, is it possible to stimulate *intrinsic* motivation? You can't make someone care about a particular topic. If you have a friend who hates musical theatre (heaven forbid!), there are some steps you can try. For example, you can make sure they are exposed to the best possible shows, whether that is taking them to a local, high-quality production of a lesser-known gem or introducing them to classic Broadway shows preserved on film. Capitalizing on their existing interests is another way to go. If they love baseball, maybe try *Damn Yankees*. If they are an American history buff, *Hamilton* is the obvious place to start, but don't forget *1776, Fiorello!, Ragtime, Parade, The Scottsboro Boys*, or *Assassins*. If they are obsessed with trains, give them a ticket to *Starlight Express* and bid your friendship farewell.

It is equally important that once you (or anyone else) have found your passion (even if it is not musical theatre), you can hold onto that initial spark. One way is to ensure you have a choice about how to pursue it. Being able to have a voice in what you work on is essential in holding onto your intrinsic motivation,[22] although it is more important for Western cultures than Eastern cultures.[23] Knowing the scenarios that excite you is important, too; do you like collaborating? Do you need real-world relevance? Is seeing how your creativity can help other people the way to keep you inspired?

These basic principles extend beyond your own motivation. For example, this element of choice is also a key part of maintaining student interest in the classroom. Teachers can help preserve students' intrinsic motivation by allowing them to integrate course content with their own choice of topics (e.g., mathematics can be taught using either baseball statistics or cross-stitch sewing patterns). Similarly, there may be several alternate assignments that offer students different ways to show and demonstrate their knowledge.[24]

How does this principle play out in theatre? When Dana and John Dempsey wrote *Witches of Eastwick*, they wrote a series of songs for Act Two that were lyrically on point but did not work as well musically. The second number in the act demanded a large-scale production number. Sir Cameron Mackintosh suggested that they try a song similar to "We Go Together" from *Grease*. The disconnect between Dana's initial interpretation of his vision of the show and of Sir Mackintosh's suggestion limited his choices; indeed, it created a certain amount of writer's block.

However, it is here that we can distinguish between choice and constraints. Having no choice is not good. Having so much choice that there are no parameters can be equally paralyzing – consider the fear of the blank page. Too many constraints can stymie creativity.[25] However, as we discussed earlier, having a basic constraint or two can actually inspire creativity.[26] Dana eventually realized that Sir Mackintosh did not mean "write a song exactly like *Grease*," but instead wanted a song with an infectious, celebratory tone. The key for Dana was to realize that the issue was not a lack of choice but rather operating under a constraint. He could write an energetic, compelling song in his own way. Once Dana had this insight, his creativity increased and he was able to write "Dance with the Devil," which is consistently seen as a high point of the show.

> Creativity Hurdle to Leap: Pursue the freedom to have choices but embrace the possibilities presented by constraints!

Beyond Motivation

Intrinsic versus extrinsic motivation is a well-established, straightforward split. There are related dimensions that may offer additional insight. For example, motivation is strongly related to goals. Although you already understand the idea of having a goal, in psychology it is a little more nuanced. There are two types of goals, learning and performance.[27] Learning goals are when you want to grow and improve your ability at a task. Even if the resulting product is not what you intended, you may feel a project is a success because you refined your craft and expanded your breadth of abilities. Performance goals are when you are primarily focused on the final product or outcome.[28]

Dana played in the pit orchestra for a professional regional theatre production of a well-known show (we have modified details to keep people anonymous). The director was a rising star who, indeed, would go on to become a star. Dana noticed that different cast members demonstrated different types of goals. One actor clearly had learning goals. She wanted to improve her acting and learn from the director. Two performers had performance goals, but they varied a little. The first wanted to give a great performance and impress the director, even if it came at the expense of stealing other actors' spotlights. The second was insecure about his own abilities and felt that he didn't belong in the cast. As a result, his full focus was on his final performance; he wanted to prove that he was capable. In this case, the first actor wanted to showcase his abilities, whereas the second actor was worried about looking incompetent.[29] On opening night, it was hard to tell which actor had which type of goal.

However, we have the luxury of time and perspective. The learning goal performer continued to excel and push herself and has been on Broadway several times. The actor with performance goals who wanted to show off his talents stayed in the business for another decade. He went to New York but had no notable success, then returned home and had some regional highlights. However, once he realized he wouldn't be a star, he gave up his dream of performing and opened a local acting studio. The cast member with performance goals who was worried about being ineffectual kept struggling with insecurity. Even when cast as the lead in a future show, he still doubted his abilities and felt that he didn't belong. He left theatre soon after. Out of all the possible approaches, the performance goal of people who are worried about looking bad will most often end poorly.[30] They can easily end up becoming a victim of their own narrative, forever worried about being good enough. Such performers can spend so much mental energy on this concern that they do not have the resources left over to shine.

Obviously, things are not this clear-cut all the time. Sometimes scene-stealers or very insecure performers become stars. Sometimes people who challenge themselves stay in regional theatre ensemble roles. But the consistent difference is what the actor gets out of the performance. Having a learning goal means that even if the show gets bad reviews or sells poorly, you know that you've done your best and that you've grown as a performer. Further, your goals can change for the task or role. Some shows will challenge you and offer an opportunity to learn and stretch. Other shows may be roles that you've played hundreds of times. You want to do your best, but you may have performance goals because it's more important that the audience and critics appreciate the show in this instance. You've already learned and mastered the role; even if you keep your eyes out for improvement areas, you want the show to succeed and may be more focused on the outcome.

110   Your Creative Tools

Related to goals and motivation is the concept of mindset.[31] Mindset is how you view your own abilities. Some people, for example, have a fixed mindset, which means that they see talent (or creativity or intelligence) as being a specific quantity. Other people have a growth mindset. They see their abilities as more stretchy. One way to think about it is to consider a time when you gave a project your all. You tried as hard as you possibly could, used every last ounce of skill, and still failed. Is your impulse more to say, "I need to improve," or "I guess I can't do it"? People with a fixed mindset would be more inclined to think that either they have Broadway-level talent, or they do not. People with a growth mindset would be more likely to believe that even if they had limited initial talent, they can keep trying and eventually reach Broadway level. It's about which narrative you have created for yourself and your possible career trajectory.

Before we give our inspiring example, we need to make sure we are not overselling it. Most people have a blend of fixed and growth mindsets. A growth mindset does mean that you are necessarily persistent or hard-working or open-minded or positive. It is not a golden ticket. It has been represented in the popular press as being much more important than it actually is, to the point that the original theorist has pushed back.[32] In the creativity research world, a fixed mindset about your creative abilities does have some negative associations and a growth mindset has some positive associations,[33] but they are just that: associations. We aren't Harold Hill here (say that five times fast) trying to sell you that a growth mindset is the ticket to creative success. That said, do consider the parallel trajectories we will now describe.

If someone is succeeding, the mindset doesn't matter. If two actors are regularly getting cast in Broadway shows, one may have a fixed mindset and the other may have a growth mindset and it probably won't make much of a difference. Both actors have the luxury of their mental storylines matching up with reality. However, let's say that both fall out of favor. Maybe one has lost her voice or another has aged out of handsome leading man roles or anything else.

The actor with the fixed mindset is more likely to think, "Okay, this is it. I've had a good run, but I've peaked. I got to be in these four Broadway shows, and that was great, but that's my story." That actor easily might end up leaving the business altogether.[34] As we will discuss later, such a decision is not always bad. However, giving up at the first signs of failure can be self-defeating.

In contrast, consider an actor with a growth mindset. Even upon multiple setbacks, she is still willing and ready to persist, reinvent, and maximize her abilities. Consider the story of Rachel Bay Jones. She was cast in her first Broadway show, 1989's *Meet Me in St. Louis*, at the young age of 19. However, finding more New York work became harder. She did tours and regional theatre, devoted

> Creativity Hurdle to Leap: Continue to master and develop your gifts. If you don't reach your ultimate destination, consider new approaches and uses of your abilities to find another pathway there!

time to family life, and recorded a CD. Yet she never gave up, even as decades passed from her Broadway debut. As Bay Jones told us as we worked on this book, she kept chipping away and returning to New York. Being cast in *Hair* in 2009 was the turning point; she then understudied Patti LuPone in *Women on the Verge on a Nervous Breakdown*[35] and had a star turn in *Pippin*. She then was in the original cast of *Dear Evan Hansen* and won Tony, Emmy, and Grammy Awards.[36]

Moving Forward

You can be motivated intrinsically (enjoyment and growth) or extrinsically (fame and fortune). Feeling the passion and flow is amazing and often linked with more creativity, but achieving goals in both theatre and life also requires doing the boring parts. Having the right dangling carrots can help one plug through the revisions, the troubleshooting process, gathering of resources, and other aspects of creativity that may not appeal to everyone.

However, it takes more than the best kinds of motivations, goals, and mindsets to be at your best. Your beliefs also matter, whether it is what you believe about yourself, your creativity, or your abilities. Are you an accurate judge of your talent? Do you know when to tap into your creative reserves and when to hold off? In the next chapter, we will explore your creative self and how you think can impact what you do.

Notes

1. Deci & Ryan (1985).
2. Lepper, Greene, & Nisbett (1973).
3. Amabile (1996) and Ruscio, Whitney, & Amabile (1998).
4. Csikszentmihalyi (1990, 1996).
5. Forgeard (2022) and Forgeard & Mecklenburg (2013).
6. Amabile & Pratt (2016).
7. Fong, Patall, Vasquez, & Strautberg (2019).
8. Hennessey (2019) and Ryan & Deci (2000).
9. Jones (2003).
10. Sondheim & Lapine (1991).
11. Beghetto & Kaufman (2007).
12. Amabile, Hennessey, & Grossman (1986).
13. Amabile (1996).
14. King & Gurland (2007).
15. Rowe (2000).
16. Eisenberger, Haskins, & Gambleton (1999).
17. Eisenberger & Rhoades (2001).
18. Malik, Butt, & Choi (2015).
19. Byron & Khazanchi (2012).
20. Beghetto, Kaufman, & Baer (2014).
21. Clinkenbeard (2012).
22. Cordova & Lepper (1996).
23. Iyengar & Lepper (1999).
24. Beghetto & Kaufman (2013, 2014).

25 Medeiros, Partlow, & Mumford (2014).
26 Haught-Tromp (2017).
27 Barron & Harackiewicz (2001) and To, Fisher, Ashkanasy, & Rowe (2012).
28 Midgely (2014).
29 Porath & Bateman (2006).
30 Cellar et al. (2011).
31 Dweck (2000).
32 Dweck (2016).
33 Karwowski (2014).
34 Miele, Finn, & Molden (2011).
35 Gans (2013).
36 Wilker (2017).

References

Amabile, T. M. (1996). *Creativity in context: Update to "The Social Psychology of Creativity."* Boulder, CO: Westview Press.

Amabile, T. M., Hennessey, B. A., & Grossman, B. S. (1986). Social influences on creativity: The effects of contracted-for reward. *Journal of Personality and Social Psychology, 50*, 14–23.

Amabile, T. M., & Pratt, M. G. (2016). The dynamic componential model of creativity and innovation in organizations: Making progress, making meaning. *Research in Organizational Behavior, 36*, 157–183.

Barron, K. E., & Harackiewicz, J. M. (2001). Achievement goals and optimal motivation: Testing multiple goal models. *Journal of Personality and Social Psychology, 80*, 706.

Beghetto, R. A., & Kaufman, J. C. (2007). Toward a broader conception of creativity: A case for "mini-c" creativity. *Psychology of Aesthetics, Creativity, and the Arts, 1*, 13–79.

Beghetto, R. A., & Kaufman, J. C. (2013). Fundamentals of creativity. *Educational Leadership, 70*, 10–15.

Beghetto, R. A., & Kaufman, J. C. (2014). Classroom contexts for creativity. *High Ability Studies, 25*, 53–69.

Beghetto, R. A., Kaufman, J. C., & Baer, J. (2014). *Teaching for creativity in the common core classroom.* New York, NY: Teachers College Press

Byron, K., & Khazanchi, S. (2012). Rewards and creative performance: A meta-analytic test of theoretically derived hypotheses. *Psychological Bulletin, 138*, 809–830.

Cellar, D. F., Stuhlmacher, A. F., Young, S. K., Fisher, D. M., Adair, C. K., Haynes, S., & Riester, D. (2011). Trait goal orientation, self-regulation, and performance: A meta-analysis. *Journal of Business and Psychology, 26*, 467–483.

Clinkenbeard, P. R. (2012). Motivation and gifted students: Implications of theory and research. *Psychology in the Schools, 49*, 622–630.

Cordova, D. I., & Lepper, M. R. (1996). Intrinsic motivation and the process of learning: Beneficial effects of contextualization, personalization, and choice. *Journal of Educational Psychology, 88*, 715.

Csikszentmihalyi, M. (1990). *Flow: The psychology of optimal experience.* New York, NY: Harper & Row.

Csikszentmihalyi, M. (1996). *Creativity: Flow and the psychology of discovery and invention.* New York: HarperCollins.

Deci, E. L., & Ryan, R. M. (1985). *Intrinsic motivation and self-determination in human behavior.* New York, NY: Plenum.

Dweck, C. S. (2000). *Self-theories: Their role in motivation, personality and development*. Philadelphia, PA: Taylor & Francis.

Dweck, C. (2016). What having a "growth mindset" actually means. *Harvard Business Review*, *13*, 213–226.

Eisenberger, R., Haskins, F., & Gambleton, P. (1999). Promised reward and creativity: Effects of prior experience. *Journal of Experimental Social Psychology*, *35*, 308–325.

Eisenberger, R., & Rhoades, L. (2001). Incremental effects of reward on creativity. *Journal of Personality and Social Psychology*, *81*, 728–741.

Fong, C. J., Patall, E. A., Vasquez, A. C., & Strautberg, S. (2019). A meta-analysis of negative feedback on intrinsic motivation. *Educational Psychology Review*, *31*, 121–162.

Forgeard, M. (2022). Prosocial motivation and creativity in the arts and sciences: Qualitative and quantitative evidence. *Psychology of Aesthetics, Creativity, and the Arts*. doi: 10.1037/aca0000435.supp

Forgeard, M. J. C., & Mecklenburg, A. C. (2013). The two dimensions of motivation and a reciprocal model of the creative process. *Review of General Psychology*, *17*, 255–266.

Gans, A. (2013, September 20). Diva talk: Chatting with Pippin star Rachel Bay Jones. *Playbill*. Retrieved from http://www.playbill.com/article/diva-talk-chatting-with-pippin-star-rachel-bay-jones-com-209775

Haught-Tromp, C. (2017). The Green Eggs and Ham hypothesis: How constraints facilitate creativity. *Psychology of Aesthetics, Creativity, and the Arts*, *11*, 10–17.

Hennessey, B. A. (2019). Motivation and creativity. In J. C. Kaufman & R. J. Sternberg (Eds.), *Cambridge handbook of creativity* (2nd ed., pp. 374–395). New York, NY: Cambridge University Press.

Iyengar, S. S., & Lepper, M. R. (1999). Rethinking the value of choice: A cultural perspective on intrinsic motivation. *Journal of Personality and Social Psychology*, *76*, 349–366.

Jones, K. (2003, July 11). *Mame will play Minneapolis in August 2004 prior to Broadway; Who'll play Auntie?* Playbill.com. Retrieved from http://www.playbill.com/article/mame-will-play-minneapolis-in-august-2004-prior-to-broadway-wholl-play-auntie-com-114237

Karwowski, M. (2014). Creative mindset: Measurement, correlates, consequences. *Psychology of Aesthetics, Creativity, and the Arts*, *8*, 62–70.

King, L. A., & Gurland, S. T. (2007). Creativity and experience of a creative task: Person and environment effects. *Journal of Research in Personality*, *41*, 1252–1259.

Lepper, M. R., Greene, D., & Nisbett, R. E. (1973). Undermining children's intrinsic interest with extrinsic reward: A test of the "overjustification" hypothesis. *Journal of Personality and Social Psychology*, *28*, 129–137.

Malik, M. A. R., Butt, A. N., & Choi, J. N. (2015). Rewards and employee creative performance: Moderating effects of creative self-efficacy, reward importance, and locus of control. *Journal of Organizational Behavior*, *36*, 59–74.

Medeiros, K. E., Partlow, P. J., & Mumford, M. D. (2014). Not too much, not too little: The influence of constraints on creative problem solving. *Psychology of Aesthetics, Creativity, and the Arts*, *8*, 198–210.

Midgley, C. (2014). *Goals, goal structures, and patterns of adaptive learning*. New York: Routledge.

Miele, D. B., Finn, B., & Molden, D. C. (2011). Does easily learned mean easily remembered? It depends on your beliefs about intelligence. *Psychological Science*, *22*, 320–324.

Porath, C. L., & Bateman, T. S. (2006). Self-regulation: From goal orientation to job performance. *Journal of Applied Psychology*, *91*, 185–192.

Rowe, D. P. (2000). *Overture*. [recorded by the Theatre Royal Drury Lane Orchestra] on *Beginners Please!* [Compact Disc]. London: First Night Records.

Ruscio, J., Whitney, D. M., & Amabile, T. M. (1998). Looking inside the fishbowl of creativity: Verbal and behavioral predictors of creative performance. *Creativity Research Journal, 11,* 243–263.

Ryan, R. M., & Deci, E. L. (2000). Self-determination theory and the facilitation of intrinsic motivation, social development, and well-being. *American Psychologist, 55,* 68–78.

Sondheim, S., & Lapine, J. (1991). *Sunday in the park with George*. New York, NY: Applause.

To, M. L., Fisher, C. D., Ashkanasy, N. M., & Rowe, P. A. (2012). Within-person relationships between mood and creativity. *Journal of Applied Psychology, 97,* 519–612.

Wilker, D. (2017, May 11). Tony awards: Rachel Bay Jones' 'Dear Evan Hansen' nomination caps three-Bdecade quest. *Hollywood Reporter*. Retrieved from https://www.hollywoodreporter.com/

Chapter 7

Showing Them What You've Got

The Creative Self

Louise/Gypsy Rose Lee (*Gypsy*), Success
Sally Bowles (*Cabaret*), Suppress
Myth: Effortless Creativity
Activity: Using 1950s Musicals to Distinguish Self-Beliefs, Self-Efficacy, and Metacognition; Test Your Creative Metacognition

It may have struck you that when we discussed motivation, we did not address one of the memorably driven characters in musical theatre history: *Cabaret*'s Sally Bowles. We first see her through Cliff Bradshaw's eyes singing a racy nightclub number in 1930s Berlin (whether you are hearing "Don't Tell Mama" or "Mein Herr" will depend on how you first saw the show, filmed or live). Over the course of the musical, she falls in love with Cliff, witnesses the rapid rise of Nazism, and becomes pregnant. Cliff asks her to leave Germany and come with him to America so they can become a family, although this route would mean setting aside her ambitions. Sally is thus presented with a pivotal choice about what she wants in life: Does she choose love and family or continue to pursue stardom? She ultimately decides to hold on to her dreams of fame and success. She has an abortion, lets Cliff leave without her, and continues to perform at the cabaret.

Her final number ("Cabaret") is often misunderstood (particularly when heard out of context) as a triumphant celebration of living life to its fullest. It is more a song of denial and desperation, with Sally unwilling or unable to acknowledge the growing fascist movement, her poor life choices, and – most relevant for our purposes – her lack of superstar talent. Indeed, one of the few missteps in the film version is that Liza Minelli is too good. We can imagine Liza's Sally Bowles becoming a star, in which case Sally may have made the right decision! If you listen to the original cast recordings, the original Broadway Sally (Jill Haworth), the original West End Sally (Judi Dench), and the Broadway revival Sally (the late Natasha Richardson) all sound like mediocre singers who would clearly not have the right stuff for stardom. If the audience, in seeing Liza Minelli belt out a winning "Cabaret," thinks that she has the goods to make it, then it becomes a different story. Sally Bowles is no longer a cautionary tale, but rather an inspirational one.

DOI: 10.4324/9781003389668-10

116   Your Creative Tools

Our goal in this chapter is not to teach you how to identify growing Nazi movements (a sadly still-relevant ability in some parts of America). Instead, we want to walk you through your beliefs about your own creative talents. We want to help you articulate your areas of strength and places where you may need to improve. We will veer a bit into some topics that may seem irrelevant to your creativity, such as evaluation and analysis. But being a successful creator (in or out of the theatrical world) means thinking in many different ways. It is important to have many good ideas, but as we have noted, it is also essential to be able to select the best ones.

Your Creative Self

Often when we think about being creative, we think of the final product or the process itself. Less common is to think of the role that creativity plays in our everyday lives. Our creative selves can encompass many different meanings: our beliefs about both creativity in general and our own abilities, how much creativity is part of our identities, our feelings on how creative we can be, and our accuracy in assessing our own talents.[1]

Everyone has explicit and implicit beliefs. An explicit belief is one you can easily articulate, such as "I hate Doug," or "I enjoy eating cake," or "I want to help people in need." Questions about your explicit beliefs should be easy to answer; these are things that you should be able to talk about in a straightforward way. Implicit beliefs are ideas or feelings we have without necessarily realizing we have them. Sometimes they can be harmful (people may be racist or sexist without being aware), but sometimes they are neutral. Maybe, for example, your best friend in high school was named Adam, you work with a different person named Adam who you like a lot, and one of your neighbors is named Adam and often comes round with a fresh plate of scones whenever he has been baking. It is possible, then, that you could meet someone new named Adam and instinctually like the guy without knowing why. You have been unconsciously trained to like people named Adam.

The same concept holds for creativity. Most people do not actively think about the nature of creativity (except for James and his wacky friends). A common implicit belief, for example, is called the "art bias," and it is thinking that creativity is more likely to be found in the arts than in other areas (such as science or business).[2] It is important to note, by the way, that this thought is a myth; it is possible to be creative in any domain you can imagine.[3] Like the art bias, many implicit beliefs about creativity can be harmful. People may think that only geniuses are creative or else that creativity is born and not developed; they may then use these beliefs as excuses to give up.[4] It is much easier to accept failure if we tell ourselves we never had a chance in the first place.

We also have beliefs about our own creativity. Some of them are general ("I am creative"), and some of them are very specific ("My triple pirouette is worthy of a prima ballerina"). Our creative self-beliefs can lead us to actively pursue opportunities or worry whether we have what it takes. Similarly, we all have many different aspects to our personal identities. We might see ourselves as "physically fit and strong" or "nurturing and kind" or "smart and witty." Others would include "creative" as a key descriptor.

These can extend to our professional identities as well. If you work in business or sales, what are the stereotypes you are faced with when you meet people at a social gathering? How about if you work for a non-profit? What about if you are a kindergarten teacher, a corporate lawyer, a nurse, a firefighter, or an accountant? If you are a dentist, like Orin Scrivello, D.D.S. from *Little Shop of Horrors*, how many jokes have you heard about whether you enjoy seeing people suffer?

Indeed, think of how many theatrical archetypes there are for actors. Someone might be the romantic ingénue? The quirky best friend? The wise father? There are many possible personas – awkward, energetic, laser-sharp wit, dangerous, sexy, neurotic? There are benefits and detriments to such categories. On one hand, an actor runs the risk of being stereotyped for a certain type of a role; on the other hand, they're still getting work. One of us knows a casting director who, when casting any role that is a "type," will only call in actors who are the best-known leaders of that category (such as "kindly old man" or "bawdy matron"). If that actor auditions well and continues to impress, then the director is more likely to call them in for a related (even if not identical) type of part. Anyone starting out as an actor has the added burden of being unknown. One way of being known (if superficially) is to fit a known category. We are not saying that this practice is fair, but any actor will always be judged and anything that can give someone an edge should be embraced. Consider Mordecai Brown, who as a young boy lost some fingers to a feed chopper and subsequently became known as "Three Finger Brown." In part because of his childhood injury, he became a superstar baseball pitcher who could throw one of the greatest curveballs of all time.[5] We need to take advantage of any boost we can.

Implicit creativity beliefs can be very powerful even if you are unaware of them. If you play the piano, you may be very conscious that your hands are on the small side. What you may not realize is that you are avoiding certain pieces (such as Rachmaninov's works) or even considering a different instrument because you are worried your hands are not big enough to play well. When you consider there have been several successful pianists who had damaged hands or even were missing fingers,[6] however, your implicit beliefs about what is required to be a good pianist may be actively holding you back.

In addition to your implicit thoughts about creativity, there is also the concept of creative self-efficacy. Self-efficacy itself is your belief that you are able to accomplish a particular goal.[7] You can have high self-efficacy for anything, whether it is building a deck, cooking chicken cordon bleu, or running a half-marathon. Self-efficacy is what (literally) drives the little engine that could. It keeps plugging away and thinking it can – and it eventually succeeds. We tend to like people with self-efficacy; there's a reason there's no children's book called "The little engine that was found crashed on the side of the road." The difference between self-efficacy and self-confidence is that someone with high self-confidence will tend to assume they will do well at *anything*, whereas someone with high self-efficacy is considering a very specific task and determining if it is in their wheelhouse.

Creative self-efficacy is your belief that you can do a specific creative task.[8] It is not how you see your creativity in general. It is possible, for example, that when the choreographer is teaching the Act One finale, you may be like Mike in *A Chorus Line* and instantly think "I can do that!" When you are taught the closing production number, however, you may think "Even if I was possessed by the spirit of Bob Fosse, I could not pull that off."

Certainly, having high creative self-efficacy is important. If you go into auditions or interviews thinking that you are going to fail, you are not setting yourself up for success – and you don't need us to tell you

> Creativity Hurdle to Leap: Make sure you explore your beliefs about creativity, even the ones you may not know you have!

that. However, there is something more important than creative self-efficacy. We will discuss this concept in the next section.

Knowing Your Strengths and Weaknesses

It is important to have self-efficacy. But it is even more important to be reasonably accurate. If you are convinced that you are able to juggle flaming chainsaws, your self-efficacy is admirable – but if you end up both burning and slicing up your audience, it's all a moot point. Here is where metacognition comes in. Metacognition is knowing what you know.[9] In other words, do you have a deep understanding of your own knowledge, ability, and – especially – creativity[10]? Or are you out of touch in either direction, being either too over-confident or too under-confident? Think about yourself and your knowledge of musical theatre. Are you a casual fan? Or are you one of those true-blue musical theatre nerds who not only have heard of *Rachael Lily Rosenbloom (And Don't You Ever Forget It)* but can also tell us that composer/co-write Paul Jabara was also responsible for the songs "Last Dance" and "It's Raining Men"?

Activity: Using 1950s Musicals to Distinguish Self-Beliefs, Self-Efficacy, and Metacognition

Let's illustrate the difference between self-beliefs, self-efficacy, and metacognition – and with 1950s musicals[11]!

First, we want you to give a rating for the following question: How much do you know about the stars, history, and songs of 1950s musicals?

1	2	3	4	5	6	7
Nothing	A little		Some		A lot	Everything

Showing Them What You've Got: The Creative Self   119

Your rating: _____ Let's call this rating "A"

Now we're telling you that we're going to ask you ten fill-in-the-blank questions about 1950s musicals. A word of warning: Some of them are tough.
Out of these ten questions, how many do you think you will answer correctly?
Your response: _____ Let's call this rating "B"

Okay, are you ready? Let's go!

1. Which actress won *four* Tony awards (for acting) in the 1950s?

   _____

2. This musical was based on the novel of the same name; however, the novel was originally titled *Grant Avenue*. This original title ended up as the name of a song in the show. What is it?

   _____

3. Vincente Minelli had already directed such classical musical films as *Meet Me in St. Louis* and *The Pirate*. He would go on to direct such musical movies as *Bells are Ringing* and *On a Clear Day You Can See Forever*. The 1950s, however, was his decade to truly shine. In addition to non-musicals such as *The Bad and the Beautiful*, *Lust for Life*, and *Tea and Sympathy*, he directed five movie musicals, all of which are well-remembered today. Name one:

   _____

4. *New Faces of 1952* was a musical revue perhaps best known today for discovering so many talented people. Although some, such as Eartha Kitt and Carol Lawrence, were performers, two other legends made their debuts behind the scenes. One zany comedian wrote many of the sketches in the show, whereas the other, who would go on to write musicals based on Jewish culture, wrote lyrics to some of the songs. Name either one:

   _____

5. Two of the biggest Broadway musical hits of the 1950s, both firmly about working-class heroes, were written by the same composer and lyricist team. Tragically, one died in 1955 at the age of 29. His partner continued writing but never reached the same heights. Name either one of the duo or one of the hit musicals:

   _____

120   Your Creative Tools

6. A classic play with a mythology-inspired title was long considered impossible to turn into a musical. Not only was it a Broadway smash but it introduced to Broadway one of the most beloved theatrical actresses ever. She would achieve her greatest success not on stage but on film – but, notably, not the film of this musical. Name the show or name her:

_____

7. This Tony-winning Broadway musical, later adapted into an Oscar-winning movie, has the rare distinction of its opening number, set on a moving vehicle, being sung completely a cappella. What is the show?

_____

8. This songwriting team had several Broadway shows in the 1940s which adapted music from classical composers as the score. Their big hit was in 1953. Name either the show, the songwriters, or the classical composer whose work was the inspiration for their hit show.

_____

9. This 1951 Broadway classic, which has been frequently revived, listed the male lead as a "featured actor" who received second billing on all advertisements and posters. In later productions (many of which starred the same actor), the male lead nearly always appears above the title. Name the show or the follically-challenged actor:

_____

10. In *Paint Your Wagon's* hit song "They Call the Wind Maria," what are the names given to the rain and fire? Name one:

_____

Okay! Now that you've taken the quiz: Out of those ten questions, how many do you think you answered correctly?
    Your response: _____ Let's call this rating C

Here are the answers – tally up how many you answered correctly:
1   Gwen Verdon
2   *Flower Drum Song*
3   Any of the following: *An American in Paris, The Band Wagon, Brigadoon, Kismet,* or *Gigi*
4   Either of the following: Mel Brooks or Sheldon Harnick

5 Any of the following: Lyricist Jerry Ross and composer Richard Adler or their musicals *The Pajama Game* and *Damn Yankees*
6 Either of the following: *My Fair Lady* (adapted from *Pygmalion*) or Julie Andrews
7 *The Music Man* (the song in question is "Rock Island")
8 Any of the following: *Kismet*, by Robert Wright and George Forrest, based on the music of Alexander Borodin
9 Either of the following: *The King and I* or Yul Brynner
10 Either of the following: The rain is "Tess" or the fire is "Joe"

Subtract the response you put for "C" from the actual number of correct answers (so if you thought you would get 5 right and you only got 3 right, your score would be 2). What's that number? _____ We'll call it D.

So what does this all mean?

Your number for A is your self-confidence or self-beliefs about how much you know about musical theatre in the 1950s.

Your number for B is your self-efficacy for how much you know about musical theatre in the 1950s. What's the difference? A, your self-confidence, is more general. B is about a specific, upcoming task. You may have high self-confidence about auditioning in general, for example, but lower self-efficacy about auditioning for a particular director or for, let's say, a musical with a lot of dance routines.

Your number for C is your prediction for your score. Hopefully, your C score is closer to your final score than your B number. Why? Because after taking the quiz itself, you have better insight into your knowledge base.

Your number for D represents your metacognition. The closer this number is to zero, the more in touch you are with your performance (at least on this particular quiz). If the number is positive, you overestimated your abilities. If the number is negative, you underestimated your abilities. The most important aspect, however, is how high the number is, regardless of whether it is positive or negative.

Why? The closer you are to zero, the more accurate you are about your knowledge base. It is clear to see the potential damage of consistently overestimating yourself. An actor with an unreasonable sense of their own prospects might try out for roles they have no chance of getting. They waste their time and the producers' time. It's good to have self-confidence, but anyone who has a distorted sense of what they bring to the table risks pursuing opportunities they are not qualified for and potentially missing out on good matches.

However, underestimating yourself is not great, either. Do not be fooled by the excitement of outperforming your expectations. If you think you need more practice or training that you do not actually need, you're spending time on a task (whether dance rehearsal or singing lessons) that you could be spending on other activities – from training areas in which you really do need to improve to simply having fun and enjoying life. In addition, you also run the risk of talking yourself out of trying for a job that you might get. You're letting yourself be driven by doubt and risk low self-esteem. Certainly, if you are estimating yourself as being poor at a skill and you truly are terrible, then it may be justified low self-esteem. But don't saddle yourself with negative feelings that are not only painful but inaccurate.

Creative Metacognition

You have metacognition for almost anything you can imagine – cooking, cleaning a toilet, or gardening. Creative metacognition expands on these principles. Part of is, indeed, correctly identifying your strengths and weaknesses, just as we illustrated with the quiz. Except with creative metacognition, it is not your knowledge being analyzed but your creative (perhaps artistic) talent. After the first preview of a show concludes in front of an audience, your thoughts in that split second between the curtain and the audience response is a window into your creative metacognition. How well can you predict what will happen? Do you envision a standing ovation and then get scattered applause?

One example of poor creative metacognition found online is an actress auditioning for a college show and, as she finished, hearing "Thank you, Jenny," from the creative team. The young actress smiled then said, "Great – but my name isn't Jenny." The team said they were well aware of that, and they were thanking the audition pianist. Needless to say, Not-Jenny did not get the part.[12]

Creative metacognition does not just occur for the person being evaluated. Consider theatre critics; their reviews do not need to agree with how the audience reacts, but they have to understand what a general crowd will think. Good critics know their audience and can both give their honest appraisal but also make sure the readers get the information they need. For example, a critic in New York City reviewing a show by Michael John LaChiusa or Ricky Ian Gordon is anticipating a very different level of audience sophistication than a critic in Butte, Montana. Both critics may love the show, but the Montana critic may feel the need to caution audiences that it is a difficult or unmelodic score where people may not leave humming the tunes. Similarly, the NYC critic would never consider needing to warn the readers that a show has adult themes and situations.

A good example of a well-known theatre person with outstanding creative metacognition (although perhaps a bit too harsh on herself) was Mary Rodgers. She enjoyed a great deal of success in theatre and other artistic domains – her musical *Once Upon a Mattress* is still a community theatre staple and her young adult novel *Freaky Friday* has been adapted into its own musical as well. However, as the daughter of the legendary Richard Rodgers and the mother of Tony-winning composer Adam Guettel, she was aware of the limit of gifts. She was quoted as saying, "I had a pleasant talent but not an incredible talent. I was not my father or my son. And you have to abandon all kinds of things.[13]"

It is in exploring our interpretation of her quote that we can delve a little deeper into the personal benefits of high creative metacognition. If you feel as though your talents transcend mere mortals and offer a true legacy to the world, you are more likely to make extensive sacrifices and give up core life staples such as romantic relationships, friendships, stability, and security. The choice to give up so much in pursuit of success, akin to selling one's soul to the Devil, is often called the Faustian bargain.[14] However, if you know you are "merely" good (or even exceptional) but not at the truly great level, then you may think twice. It is very possible to be successful at a wide range of levels and still have a life, whereas it is much harder to strive for genius while juggling the trappings of domesticity.

In Dana's first year at Indiana University, he actively pursued advanced study in vocal performance. Before the last step, he had a heart-to-heart talk with his professor, the late Jean Deis. Dana asked for an honest appraisal of whether he had what it took to make it as a singer. His professor responded, "You'll work." Dana persisted – he had visions of being the next Pavarotti. Could that be possible? he asked. The response, again, was "You'll work – you'll have a career. But it's never going to be world-class. Your voice has a big sound but it is not big enough." Dana decided, instead, to focus on both voice and piano and to go on to (initially) become a vocal coach for opera singers. James had a similar experience in his creative writing class and with Dr. T. Coraghessan Boyle, who read countless stories and attempted novels and gave detailed feedback which was usually "This is good, but not great." Like Dana, James decided to pursue a career elsewhere (although he kept writing plays).

There is a danger in a mentor being too completely honest. Consider in *Everybody's Talking About Jamie*, when Jamie tells his teacher, Miss Hedge, that he wants to be a performer. She tells him,

> Join the queue, love, with all the footballers, the movie stars, and the Sheffield's next top model…Let's be real. I wish I could tell you that you were all gonna achieve your dreams. But I'd be lying to you if I did…That'd be cruel. Did you think me being here today teaching you was my first choice?[15]

If the feedback is too harsh (even if it is to avoid being cruel, as Miss Hedge claims), there is a risk that the student may experience such a deep feeling of shame that it may kill the creative impulse entirely.[16] Indeed, both Dana and James struggled a bit with the less-desired prognosis, but ultimately it helped them find their true strengths and maximize their potential.

Creative metacognition goes beyond whether you decide to go on a particular career path. It helps infuse your choices and your reflections on these choices. Denis O'Hare is best known for his Emmy-nominated work on such hit television shows as *American Horror Story, This is Us*, and *True Blood*. O'Hare has also starred on the stage in such musicals as *Assassins* and *Sweet Charity*; he won a Tony Award for *Take Me Out*. Dana interviewed him for *Take It From the Top*.

> O'Hare told Dana, "I think people have a romantic idea of what they should be playing," A lot of young actors want to play Hamlet. But that may not be the part they were meant to play – maybe they should be playing Malvolio, or Caliban. It's all about perception and what we think we need to be seen as. That being said, to be honest, I've definitely auditioned for roles and not gotten the part and then seen the product and thought, 'Eh, I could have done that probably as well, but not better.' Or I've thought, 'You know what? I couldn't have done that. I couldn't have touched what he did. That's a great job.' Or 'I definitely could've done that better. That's my part up there. I was robbed.'

Having strong creative metacognition, as O'Hare does, allows an actor to grow and mature.

One thing to be aware of is that there is an interaction between your level of ability and your metacognition. People who are better at a task tend to also be more accurate at gauging their performance.[17] In other words, if you're a great dancer, you are likely to recognize that you are great. If you are a terrible dancer, you may well still think you are great. What does this phenomenon mean for you? If you are not cast in a role you think you deserved, try to get a feeling from other people whether or not you actually deserved it. It may be hard to get an accurate reading and you should proceed with caution. Some colleagues cannot wait to tell you the many ways in which your audition failed. Meanwhile, friends and family tend to tell us what they think we want to hear. Most people who love us are less likely to say that we sucked. However, try to encourage honesty (albeit polite honesty). If you are the only person who thinks you were robbed, then perhaps you need to work on your metacognition.

Another concept of creative metacognition is the idea of knowing when to display your creativity.[18] Obviously, if you are pursuing a career in the theatre or another artistic field, you will be using your creativity a great deal. However, there are times to show off what you can do and times to blend in. For example, one actor received a callback to a show Dana wrote. When the group was dispersed, this actor chose to do a series of backflips out of the room. The director recognized that this behavior was not indicative of a team player; he instantly found this actor's resume and tore it up. There are times to stand out with your individuality and times to not be the tall poppy that gets cut down.

An analogy that James likes using is the difference between Batman and Superman. We live in a world where we tend to associate creativity with a Batman-like approach. Bruce Wayne is a normal guy who has all these tools to make him a superhero. He has the batcave, the batmobile, the batbelt, and the batweapons. Similarly, we often can think that we need every available boost to be more creative. But some of us are more like Superman. Our minds are always moving and thinking of new ideas, just like Superman had natural powers (like superspeed, superjumping, and supersight). However, in the real world, Superman is too exhausting and would zap your energy as you try to avoid his superbreath and make sure you are wearing lead undergarments. In order to be effective, Superman has to create Clark Kent, a "normal" guy who blends in. Then, at the right time, Clark can disappear for a moment and become the Superman that the world needs. But nonstop Superman – like the backflipping actor – is simply too much. Actors who are always "on" are not only tiring but they are rarely the best ones (Daniel Day-Lewis excepted).

Let us now ponder our Success model for this chapter, Gypsy Rose Lee. We will be using the musical *Gypsy* as our source of knowledge (as opposed to sorting out the truth of the actual Gypsy Rose Lee's life). As a young girl (then known as Louise), she was always second-best to her sister June in their vaudeville act. It was June who first demonstrated true insight into their abilities when she told Louise, "It's a terrible act and I hate it…. I hate singing those same awful songs, doing those same awful dances, wearing those same awful costumes…[19]" By the second act, Louise reached the same conclusion about her solo show: "...I've tried as hard as I could. The act is rotten and I'm rotten in it."[20] When Louise and her mother end up in a burlesque venue, Louise is hesitant to strip – not out of shame but out of fear she has no talent. The three friendly strippers (Mazeppa, Electra, and Tessie) show Louise that all it takes is a basic gimmick to be successful. Louise – soon to use the name Gypsy Rose Lee – agrees to strip. She is initially nervous, but she realizes she has a natural rapport and instinct for the business and begins to enjoy it. Gypsy Rose becomes a hit, yet her mother still tries to retain control over her. Gypsy Rose recognizes exactly what is happening, telling her mother, "I am not a kid anymore. From now on, even if I flop, I flop on my own.[21]" She does reach a general understanding with her mother at the end, but as equals.

Gypsy Rose demonstrates both aspects of creative metacognition. She understands her strengths as well as her weaknesses. Throughout the show, she goes from being a dormouse underneath her mother to being someone who can assert herself and knows the right time to take charge and show off what she can do. It is rare that the true protagonist plays second (or third) banana to other characters for most of the show. Louise/Gypsy Rose uses her insight and intuition to genuinely claim the spotlight at the end.

> Creativity Hurdle to Leap: Understand your own creative strengths and weaknesses and know when to use them!

Myth: Effortless Creativity

Remember from last chapter the idea of Flow, in which you lose track of time and place when you are truly "in the zone" creatively. This feeling – and the general joy that comes from creation – can lead some people to feel like creativity only works if it comes naturally. Creativity that takes conscious effort and hard work is not as good as the creativity that just magically happens. Unfortunately, the idea of effortless creativity is a myth. There are many reasons, some of which we will discuss in more depth later on. For now, we want to continue our focus on the self.

If you believe that the best creativity is effortless, you're setting yourself up to be blocked. There are countless times that the planets aren't aligned and you can sit at a desk or practice on a stage or play on a piano and nothing comes. Indeed, that may describe 90% of your working hours. What to do? Dana believes in the concept of Imperfect Action. Even if your ideas are pedestrian or arbitrary, put it on the page! It always has the chance of taking flight with enough thought or deliberation. James has a similar strategy when writing his academic papers. If nothing is coming, he writes the title and authors on the first page, the word "abstract" (and nothing else) on the second page, and then retypes the title on the third page. All of a sudden, he is on page three, and that sure feels like progress is being made.

The best way to break a block is often related to the insight you gain from creative metacognition. What are your true strengths? What have been your great ideas? Revisiting past successes is a great way to get back into the mindset that will give you new ideas. This connection is because context is a huge part of how we remember. A classic psychology study had deep sea divers learn vocabulary words either underwater or on land; they were then asked to recall the words in either the same or the alternate environment. The divers remembered notably more words when the testing location matched the place where they learned (i.e., if they learned the words underwater, they did better when tested underwater).[22]

In terms of recapturing creativity, replicating the context can take many forms. Whether you are simply rereading your past work, enacting past performances, playing past compositions, or any similar variation, you are still physically and mentally engaged. Your mind is going back to a place where it was being creative. You can get connected to those same feelings and experiences. You may remember moments when you successfully created. Of course, rote recall and active creation are different things; sometimes this strategy will work and sometimes it will not. Either way, it is better than staring at a blank page or stage.

Another way is to use your creative metacognition. Which tricks or strategies worked best in the past? Where, when, and under what circumstances was your best work created? Sometimes it may be using a particular piano or notebook or pair of lucky tights that may help put you in the mood (no, not *that* mood).

Just as we cautioned against passively waiting for the muse to strike in the first chapter, you cannot rely on creativity pouring forth from you effortlessly. If it happens, great! Be there to catch it. But make sure you have your own strategies to fight off the times when the ideas are not flowing.

> Creativity Hurdle to Leap: Don't wait for the muse to strike – creativity takes hard work!

Let's do another activity specifically aimed at creative metacognition. You will need friends who know your work for this one.

Activity: Test Your Creative Metacognition

What we would like to have you do is first answer these questions as honestly as you can.

1 What is your theatrical "superpower"? What is it about you is that it makes you stand out – to an audience, producer, casting director, colleague, or critic?

2 What is your theatrical "kryptonite"? What do you need to improve on to get the absolute most out of your abilities?

3 What makes you a good team player? Regardless of your role in a show, what is it about you that would make people want to hire you over and over again?

4 Which person has your aspirational career trajectory? In other words, what well-known person has a similar affect and strengths as you?

Now that you have answered these, we would like you to ask some friends to answer the same questions (except about you).

Ideally, we'd like you to send it to (a) a good friend who will reflect your best self, (b) a peer who will be bluntly honest, and (c) someone who knows you well but is not in your field – as well as anyone else whose opinions you value.

Now that you have all of their responses, compare them to your own. Were you too harsh? Too soft? Were you accurate? Is your image of yourself the same as how other people see you?

We've spent a long time on what you think about your abilities and creativity. Your perceptions and beliefs can be very powerful. If you overlook some of your talents, then having them won't help you. If you put all of your energy into an area where you may be less gifted, you risk wasting a lot of time and resources. Knowing when you are in your element and when you should yield to someone else's expertise is a crucial factor in success. Wanting to be good at something isn't the same as actually having talent. Similarly, being cautious because you don't want to seem arrogant or self-obsessed isn't a positive trait if you are hiding your talents from the world. There is a thin line to walk that lets you get the most out of your abilities and shine while still being a team player and thinking of what's best for the show (or project).

Moving Forward

The way we think about our own creativity matters. This concept can include both self-beliefs ("I think I can") and insights into our own personal strengths and weaknesses. Ideally, we can develop our creative metacognition and recognize what types of creative expression are the best fit for our abilities and talents.

We're nearing the end of this second section. We've discussed how creativity interacts with your personality, motivation, and your self-beliefs. But what about your emotions? How does your mood impact your creativity – or vice versa? How can you maximize your creativity in a way that also will put you on solid emotional ground? Let's find out!

Notes

1. Karwowski & Kaufman (2017) and Kaufman (2019).
2. Glăveanu (2014).
3. Kaufman, Glăveanu, & Baer (2017).
4. Plucker, Beghetto, & Dow (2004).
5. James (2003).
6. Sforzini (2011).
7. Bandura (1997).
8. Beghetto (2006) and Tierney & Farmer (2002).
9. Flavell (1979).
10. Karwowski, Czerwonka, & Kaufman (2020) and Silvia (2008).
11. Kaufman & Rowe (Creating Your Spotlight workbook, in progress).
12. Bera (2017).
13. Green (2003) and Kaufman, Beghetto, & Watson (2016).
14. Gardner (1993).
15. MacRae & Gillespie Sells (2017, p. 18).
16. Beghetto (2014).
17. Dunning, Johnson, Ehrlinger, & Kruger (2003) and Kruger & Dunning (1999).
18. Kaufman & Beghetto (2013).
19. Laurents, Styne, & Sondheim (1994/1959, p. 47).
20. Laurents, Styne, & Sondheim (1994/1959, p. 65).
21. Laurents, Styne, & Sondheim (1994/1959, p. 102).
22. Godden & Baddeley (1975).

References

Bandura, A. (1997). *Self-efficacy: The exercise of control*. New York, NY: Macmillan.
Beghetto, R. A. (2006). Creative self-efficacy: Correlates in middle and secondary students. *Creativity Research Journal, 18*, 447–457.
Beghetto, R. A. (2014). Creative mortification: An initial exploration. *Psychology of Aesthetics, Creativity, and the Arts, 8*, 266–276.
Bera, M. (2017, March 24). 10 embarrassing anonymous audition stories. *Actor Aesthetic*. Retrieved from https://www.actoraesthetic.com/blog/10-embarrassing-audition-stories
Dunning, D., Johnson, K., Ehrlinger, J., & Kruger, J. (2003). Why people fail to recognize their own incompetence. *Current Directions in Psychological Science, 12*, 83–86.
Flavell, J. H. (1979). Metacognition and cognitive monitoring: A new area of cognitive developmental inquiry. *American Psychologist, 34*, 906–911.
Gardner, H. (1993). *Creating minds*. New York, NY: Basic Books.
Glăveanu, V. P. (2014). Revisiting the "art bias" in lay conceptions of creativity. *Creativity Research Journal, 26*, 11–20.
Godden, D. R., & Baddeley, A. D. (1975). Context-dependent memory in two natural environments: On land and underwater. *British Journal of Psychology, 66*, 325–331.
Green, J. (2003, July 6). A complicated gift. *New York Times*. Retrieved at http://www.nytimes.com/2003/07/06/magazine/a-complicated-gift.html
James, B. (2003). *The new Bill James historical baseball abstract* (rev. ed.). New York, NY: Free Press.
Karwowski, M., Czerwonka, M., & Kaufman, J. C. (2020). Does intelligence strengthen creative metacognition? *Psychology of Aesthetics, Creativity, and the Arts, 14*, 353–360.

Karwowski, M., & Kaufman, J. C. (Eds.) (2017). *The creative self: How our beliefs, self-efficacy, mindset, and identity impact our creativity.* San Diego: Academic Press.

Kaufman, J. C. (2019). Self assessments of creativity: Not ideal, but better than you think. *Psychology of Aesthetics, Creativity, and the Arts, 13,* 187–192.

Kaufman, J. C., & Beghetto, R. A. (2013). In praise of Clark Kent: Creative metacognition and the importance of teaching kids when (not) to be creative. *Roeper Review, 35,* 155–165.

Kaufman, J. C., Beghetto, R. A., & Watson, C. (2016). Creative metacognition and self-ratings of creative performance: A 4-C perspective. *Learning and Individual Differences, 51,* 394–399.

Kaufman, J. C., Glăveanu, V., & Baer, J. (Eds.) (2017). *Cambridge handbook of creativity across domains.* New York, NY: Cambridge University Press.

Kaufman, J. C., & Rowe, D. P. (in progress). *The creating your spotlight workbook.* Retrived from https://creatingyourspotlight.com/

Kruger, J., & Dunning, D. (1999). Unskilled and unaware of it: How difficulties in recognizing one's own incompetence lead to inflated self-assessments. *Journal of Personality and Social Psychology, 77,* 1121–1134.

Laurents, A., Styne, J., & Sondheim, S. (1994). *Gypsy.* New York, NY: Theatre Communications Group. Original version published in 1959.

MacRae, T., & Gillespie Sells, D. (2017). *Everybody's talking about Jamie.* London: Samuel French.

Plucker, J. A., Beghetto, R. A., & Dow, G. (2004). Why isn't creativity more important to educational psychologists? Potential, pitfalls, and future directions in creativity research. *Educational Psychologist, 39,* 83–96.

Sforzini, H. (2011, November 23). Five musicians with missing and damaged fingers, *Paste Magazine.* Retrieved from https://www.pastemagazine.com/blogs/lists/2011/11/five-musicians-with-missing-and-damaged-fingers.html

Silvia, P. J. (2008). Discernment and creativity: How well can people identify their most creative ideas? *Psychology of Aesthetics, Creativity, and the Arts, 2,* 139–146.

Tierney, P., & Farmer, S. M. (2002). Creative self-efficacy: Its potential antecedents and relationship to creative performance. *Academy of Management Journal, 45,* 1137–1148.

Chapter 8

Crying on Cue
Monitoring Your Mood

Eliza Doolittle (*My Fair Lady*), Success
Bruce Bechdel (*Fun Home*), Suppress
Myth: Bad Moods are Always Bad
Activity: A Showtune for Every Mood; What Would Norma Desmond Do?

Eliza Doolittle is a woman of strong emotions. Indeed, the libretto of *My Fair Lady* is eager to infuse her emotions in the stage directions.[1] As we meet her, we see her go from terrified to hysterical to appalled to melancholic to overwhelmed with wonder to desperate – and this kaleidoscope takes place in the first scene. Soon enough (and, again, we are only using the exact words used to describe her moods), she is also triumphant, suspicious, angry, explosive, rageful, hopeful, and so many more. Her final mood, as she returns to Higgins, is gentle and understanding.

Many characters have intense emotions; Sweeney Todd's intensity outstrips Eliza's. What makes Eliza special, and our Success mode for this chapter, is that her moods and emotions propel her to act. She is the one who seeks out Higgins for lessons. Although it is his bet with Colonel Pickering that spurs the action forward, it only occurs because Eliza tracks Higgins down and negotiates for his services. Eliza then spends hundreds of hours learning and practicing how to speak and behave properly before winningly convincing onlookers of her high status at Ascot and then an embassy ball. She uses her fury, her hope, and her exhilaration to keep challenging herself.

If Eliza can use her emotions to accomplish so much, so can you. First, let's distinguish between an emotion and a mood. Although we use them interchangeably in daily life, they have slightly different meanings. Emotion tends to be targeted at a person or event, whereas a mood is more like your default setting.[2] For example, you might feel the emotion of happiness if someone offers you a piece of chocolate cake, a sincere compliment, or a hug. If you are just hanging out and generally cheerful, that's being in a happy mood. Most of what we'll actually be talking about in this chapter is mood; even if it sometimes creeps into what might technically be called emotion, we'll stick to mood for simplicity's sake.

What mood do you associate with being creative? When all of the juices are flowing, are you more likely to be happy? Angry? Do you need to feel sad in order

DOI: 10.4324/9781003389668-11

to write a sad song? Do you need to feel joy to portray joy on stage? One of the most famous acting techniques, the Method, is devoted to the idea that the actor should embody the emotion that the character is feeling.[3] If a character is furious, the actor needs to feel furious. Some have suggested that the principles of Method acting can be used to teach people to feel empathy.[4] There are clearly positives that can emerge from Method acting – but how slavishly must one feel tied to feeling angry or sad in the name of art?

When we think of moods, the most obvious split might be good vs bad – or, as scholars like to label them, positive vs negative moods. What type of mood is most associated with being more creative? Certainly, there is compelling evidence suggesting that positive moods (such as happy, calm, joyful, or relaxed) are more associated with creative performance than negative moods (such as angry, sad, fearful, or anxious).[5] One in-depth study e-mailed workers at a large organization surveys about their daily activities for anywhere from 9 to 38 weeks. These responses were then coded for creative performance and mood; being in a positive mood was connected to being creative (albeit not necessarily to the moments of being the most creative).[6] Negative mood showed no association.

Why might being happy make someone more creative? There are many reasons that have been proposed. Before we dive into them, we want to note that most of this work is on people being creative during a research experiment. This distinction is important because for a study, people solve artificial problems or respond to open-ended questions. Even if someone loves being creative and enjoys these tasks, it is still a world away from pursuing your passion. The way that you might think of many alternate uses for a random object is different from how you might choreograph a dance that has obsessed you for the last two months. Doing a creative exercise alone, with a paper and pencil (or laptop), is a different beast from performing in front of a large audience and feeding off that energy.

With these caveats, let us discuss some possible reasons. Two are straightforward. When we're feeling happy we might be more likely to explore and think in a flexible manner.[7] Another possibility is that when we are happy our brains release more dopamine (a feel-good chemical), which can make it easier for us to switch back and forth between different types of thinking.[8] The third is a bit nuanced; we hope you will find this concept as intriguing as we do.

Might happy people be more creative because they want to maintain their good mood[9]? If you're happy, the argument goes, you want to stay happy. So if you're asked to be creative, you will do whatever it takes to hold onto your good mood – which in this case, would be making the creative activity fun and doing your best. In contrast, sad people usually do not want to stay sad, so anything goes.[10] As the song goes, if they like riding fast cars or singing old hymns or enjoying bare limbs, who would oppose? We know Cole Porter would not.

This idea introduces some interesting hiccups (and it is important to note that although we're talking about creativity, these broad concepts apply to anything where persistence is key). One study asked people to do a slightly odd task, finding similarities and differences between television shows (like *The Simpsons* and *Cheers*). People in a happy mood anticipated this activity to be fun, and they were more creative than people in a sad mood. However, if they were convinced that moods could be frozen (i.e., their moods would not change regardless of what they did), there was no difference between the happies and the sads.[11]

> Creativity Hurdle to Leap: Take advantage of a happy mood and burst out with many ideas right from the beginning!

Myth: Bad Moods Are Always Bad

A trickle-down effect of happy people's desire to maintain their mood is that they will indeed try very hard at first, but may be less likely to persist.[12] One study asked people to do a creative activity and stop whenever they felt was a good time to stop. In contrast to what you might expect, happy folks stopped sooner than the sad folks.[13] Even when there aren't instructions given, the advantage that happy people have over sad people not only goes away but actually becomes reversed over time. Happy people are more creative initially, but if you simply allow more time than usual then the happy people will slow down (or quit). People in a bad mood, however, aren't satisfied. They keep plugging along and trying. If they are given enough time, their output may exceed happy people.[14] If a problem needs a creative solution and it is fairly open with few constraints, maybe happy is better. But if you have many hurdles and obstacles and need a creative solution, then you want an unhappy person who will brood and overanalyze.[15]

Musical theatre is replete with characters who face hardships, rejection, low beginnings, and even outright hatred, yet who are still brimming with determination, persistence, and occasionally fury. They may not necessarily turn to creativity as their outlet, but we see many instances of bad moods (and circumstances) leading to stronger resolve. Sometimes characters have hardscrabble beginnings yet are determined to persevere. We can return to *My Fair Lady*'s Eliza Doolittle, as well as *Funny Girl*'s Fanny Brice, *In the Heights*'s Vanessa, and the titular *Unsinkable Molly Brown*. Others face huge hurdles yet vow to keep fighting; think of *Ragtime*'s Coalhouse Walker, *Ride the Cyclone*'s Ocean Rosenberg, *Into the Woods*' Witch, *Gypsy*'s Mama Rose, or *Evita*'s... well, Evita. Then there are the characters who have experienced devastating personal rejection yet respond with a devastating song to make it clear they are not defeated: *Dreamgirls*' Effie, *Nine*'s Luisa, *A Little Night Music*'s Charlotte, *Waitress*' Jenna, *Follies*' Phyllis, and *La Cage Aux Folles*' Albin.

> Creativity Hurdle to Leap: Let your bad moods help you persist with your creativity!

Beyond Happy and Sad

If we talk about good or bad moods, you know what we mean. But more recently, a different dichotomy has emerged: activated vs deactivated moods. What does that mean? Well, we can certainly define the terms. Activation level is how much you are gathering up your energy and thoughts to focus on a goal.[16] When you are highly activated, your heart might start to pound and your blood pressure may go up.[17] At these times, you may be able to think more flexibly and better access your working memory.[18] More importantly, this state is at the crux of musical theatre! Nearly every song comes from an activated state.

Let's explore this idea a little bit. If we think about emotions that are both positive and activated, we tend to come to happiness, elation, and joy (we're not going to distinguish among these). Perhaps the most commonly understood type of showtune is the "I Want" song, which almost always is a character who wants to do or achieve something that will make them happy (or happier). The happiness aspiration can be more general ("Wouldn't It Be Loverly" from *My Fair Lady* or "On the Other Side of the Tracks" from *Little Me*) or targeted at somewhat specific ("Part of Your World" from *The Little Mermaid* or "Somewhere That's Green" from *Little Shop of Horrors*) or very specific (the titular song from *Paint Your Wagon*, "Maybe" from *Annie*, or "I Hope I Get It" from *A Chorus Line*). They can even be anticipatory, as in "Something's Coming" from *West Side Story*.

Not quite as ubiquitous are songs about feeling pure happiness in the moment. Many are about being in love (or lust) – *She Loves Me*'s title song, *I Do, I Do!*'s "My Cup Runneth Over," *Sweet Charity*'s "I'm a Brass Band," *Fun Home*'s "Changing my Major," *Song and Dance*'s "Unexpected Song," *South Pacific*'s "I'm in Love with a Wonderful Guy" or *Fiddler on the Roof*'s "Miracle of Miracles." A select few capture the joy of accomplishment (*They're Playing Our Song*'s "They're Playing My Song") or simply the pure elation of a beautiful day (*Oliver!*'s "Who Will Buy" or *Oklahoma!*'s "Oh, What a Beautiful Mornin'").

You can also be activated with a negative emotion, such as anger, which might get you riled up for different reasons.[19] Angry songs may not be as plentiful as joyful songs but they are memorable. A number of them express fury at men, whether directed at all men (*Kiss Me, Kate*'s "I Hate Men"), a romantic partner (*Follies*' "Could I Leave You?" or *Nine*'s "Be On Your Own"), a boss/mentor (*My Fair Lady*'s "Just You Wait," *The King and I*'s "Shall I Tell You What I Think of You," or *Mack and Mabel*'s "Wherever He Ain't") – or both (*Dreamgirls*' And I Am Telling You I Am Not Going). Some show anger or even hatred for society at large (*Sweeney Todd*'s "Epiphany," *Godspell*'s "Alas For You," *Into the Woods*' "Last Midnight," or *Wicked*'s "No Good Deed" – and why isn't a mash-up of the last two songs popular as a "bad witch" number?).

Anger consumes a lot of cognitive and emotional resources,[20] which has its own impact on creativity. People who are angry will be much more creative at first (similar to joy), particularly if the anger is related to the creative task at hand.[21] It is important to note that anger is more depleting for naturally agreeable and friendly people, and may not even provide an initial creative bump.[22] After this initial potential spark (which may produce less structured ideas), creative output rapidly plummets.[23] Indeed, if we reflect on our anger songs, many do not lead to sustained productivity. Sweeney Todd ends "Epiphany" ready to slit the throats of the whole world, but within five minutes he's swapping cannibalistic puns with Mrs. Lovett. Where's the follow through? Anger may start you off on your creative journey but it will not sustain you.

> Creativity Hurdle to Leap: Don't seek out reasons to be angry – but if you are, lash out with creative ideas, not your fists!

The Dangers of Passivity

There are different degrees to which you can be activated. If you are so over the moon with happiness or anger to such an extent that you can't even understand what's going on around you, you're not going to be at your creative peak.[24] However, feeling the high arousal that comes when your heart is racing is typically better for creativity.

What about deactivated moods, when your heart isn't racing a mile a minute? If they are positive, then you feel calm, relaxed, and content. We have a few of these songs in musical theatre, from *Girl Crazy*'s "Bidin' My Time" to *The Most Happy Fella*'s "Standing on the Corner" to *The Golden Apple*'s "Lazy Afternoon" to *The Fantasticks*' "Soon It's Gonna Rain." These may be nice feelings, but they are not conducive to being creative.[25] Similarly, feeling a deactivated and negative mood such as sadness (*The Best Little Whorehouse in Texas*'s "Hard Candy Christmas," anyone?) is also not associated with higher creativity.

Indeed, think about our suppress model for this chapter, Bruce Bechdel from *Fun Home*. The story is told from his daughter Alison's point-of-view at three different ages (and, indeed, she can be a bit passive at times). Bruce, stuck in a time period that is not accepting of his sexual orientation, is married with three children. He has a few different possible options. He could suppress his sexuality and focus on his children, his work at the funeral home, and his passion for restoring houses. He could be true to himself and, at potential great personal cost, pursue a chance at real love. Instead, he has stays in a loveless marriage and affairs with much younger men which turn into scandals. When his daughter Alison realizes she is a lesbian and comes out to him, he had an opportunity to reclaim his identity. However, they do not even have a conversation about this issue; one of the most powerful songs in the show, "Telephone Wire," is about them both being passive and noncommunicative, sharing a car ride with only brief and superficial chit chat. Bruce's only action to change his life is, alas, to commit suicide by stepping in front of a truck, leaving Alison to puzzle over their unresolved relationship. His inaction and tragic death inspired Alison's first great work (the graphic novel that is the source material for the musical), but that has been his only legacy.

Another example is Eponine from *Les Misérables*. She endures many obstacles and hardships, yet remains resilient and sweet. There is a reason why she is a popular choice for the show's favorite; many relate or admire to her unrequited yet devoted love. How many of us have never felt like a victim? We are not criticizing her, however; her defining emotions throughout the show are loneliness and grief as she pines for Marius as he can only think of Cosette. Her two solo songs ("On My Own" and "A Little Fall of Rain") are some of the musical's saddest moments.

As a person, she is kind and admirable; however, she accepts her lot in life. Eponine notes she could've been a student but is unable to pursue that. She doesn't fight for Marius's love. She alternates between accepting he may never see her in that way and hoping that her deeds will have him recognize her goodness. For a character who is active in helping others, she is passive about pursuing her own interests. Ultimately, like Bruce Bechdel in *Fun Home*, she is unable to reach her dreams.

> Creativity Hurdle to Leap: Deactivated, passive emotions may not help you reach creative heights!

Activity: A Showtune for Every Mood

We've talked about how different moods are associated with creativity. We've also just listed a whole bunch of showtunes that are associated with different moods. But these are just our picks. Let's turn the focus to you.

Any musical theatre lover has their go-to showtunes for different situations and emotions. There are the songs we sing loudly in the car or shower, the songs we groove to while we cook or clean, and the songs we listen to on repeat during times of heartbreak or struggle. Let's figure out the showtunes (or any song, of course) you associate with different moods.

Pure, unfettered joy. Happiness. Sheer delight. Name your tunes!

_____

_____

_____

_____

_____

Anger. Rage. Burning contempt. Fierce hatred. Name your tunes!

_____

_____

_____

_____

Now think about when you create. Try to imagine the last few times you've been excited about your own ideas. Where were you? What was the situation? Try to place yourself mentally back in that moment.

Perhaps the emotions that come to mind are similar to either happiness or anger, and the songs may overlap. But – either way – what showtunes come to you as you recreate your more recent creative inspirations?

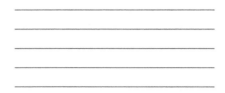

You can go a lot of different directions with these songs. Maybe these are tunes that can inspire you to be creative by listening to them; perhaps you can flesh these out into a full playlist to listen to either before or while you create. Or, perhaps, you can look at these songs and see patterns of nuanced emotions present. What do your choices tell you about your creative process – and yourself?

Think of your playlist as your one-person show. These mood songs can serve many functions. Sing them out loud to feel inspired! Or use them to shift your feelings into a new space from which you feel your creativity bubble over. Maybe your songs can represent the exact emotion you are experiencing and let you feel it completely to either revel in that mood – or else move on. These songs can take center stage or be background music or serve as the overture to the show that is your creative journey.

Creativity Hurdle to Leap: Let showtunes inspire emotion – and creativity!

How Creativity Can Enhance Mood

We've talked about how specific moods can help you be more creative. What about the other way around? Can you use your creativity to feel better? As tempted as we are to say "no" and move to the next section, the answer is that there are ways it does. Indeed, there are many different pathways.

We have just discussed how an activated, negative mood (in other words, being really angry) can increase creativity. But how can creativity bring us down from the ledge? One way is through cognitive reappraisal. This strategy is designed to help us see an emotional situation from other points of view with the purpose of reducing or changing its impact.[26] So, in other words, we might be feeling angry or upset or sad. However, we are able to imagine alternate explanations or reasons that might underlie the situation.

Think of Morales in *A Chorus Line*. When she sings "Nothing," she remembers being a young drama student who is struggling to find success in

Mr. Karp's improvisation class. She can't connect to exercises such as pretending to be on a bobsled or imagining being an inanimate object. When Mr. Karp and the class turn on her, she experiences tremendous self-doubt and wonders if she is in the right profession. It is then that she uses cognitive reappraisal: What if, instead of her being a terrible young actress, it is instead that Mr. Karp is a bad teacher? Perhaps her strengths do not work with his teaching style, and his inability to be flexible and work with her reflects *his* failure, not hers. She changes classes and when we meet her in the show, she has achieved a small modicum of success.

A terrific footnote to this example is that there was a revue directed by Martin Charnin in 1983 called *Upstairs at O'Neals*. There is a marvelous song called "Something," written by Denis Markell and Douglas Bernstein, that offers yet a different appraisal: The story from Mr. Karp's point of view. In their spin on the story, the teacher only wants her to find her voice and use her imagination to create something. He doesn't understand her reticence; what Morales considers bullying is, to him, extra attention. In this version of events, Morales perhaps had an inaccurate cognitive reappraisal.

How is cognitive reappraisal linked to creativity? Remember our discussion of divergent thinking, in which people give many different responses to open-ended questions? It turns out that there are some underlying abilities that cognitive reappraisal and divergent thinking share.[27] For one, both require someone to inhibit or repress the most obvious answers. Let's say you want to think of many original responses to, for example, potential uses for a pen. You would need to mentally avoid, or at least not linger on, a pen's primary function of writing.

In addition, both require you to sift through your mental filing cabinet of memory to find the best possible responses. So if you are trying to think of uses for a pen, you would need to access lots of past memories from your own life or books you read or movies you've seen to pull out additional uses for a pen. Indeed, this cognitive attribute (called long-term storage and retrieval) is linked to creativity both conceptually[28] and in research studies.[29] In part, because both divergent thinking and cognitive reappraisal rely on these abilities, the two constructs have been shown to be linked.[30]

> Creativity Hurdle to Leap: Your creativity can help you find alternate explanations for otherwise upsetting events!

Finding the Good in the Bad

Cognitive reappraisal also underlies a coaching technique that Dana likes to use. All of us suffer losses in our lives, from minor (losing out on an audition or promotion) to devastating (the death of a loved one). When Dana is working with someone who is struggling, he asks them to imagine their life up to that point as a musical. He suggests breaking up their life show into different sections and considering them as scenes or acts, depending on the purpose and the person's age. The goal is to divide a person's life into chunks of about five to eight years.

Dana asks them to consider and analyze each chunk of time. He asks them to remember and recount highlights and positive memories that might bear fruit in their present life, from insights to strengths to teachings. Then Dana asks them to think of a negative life event that they continue to think about or that still has an impact. The temporal distance can help the person work through the first few scenes.

For each dark memory, Dana asks if they might be willing to consider the positive impact. Much as several different characters in *Merrily We Roll Along* keep insisting that various bad happenings are, rather, the best thing that might have occurred, Dana suggests that they think about what has been gained or how they have grown because of the incident. Crucially, he does not push this technique. Some losses or traumas are so completely terrible that there may be nothing redeeming in the slightest; the purpose of this technique is not to minimize someone's suffering. Indeed, Dana's clients are typically not experiencing or recovering from active trauma.

For most people, for most of their scenes, there is a benefit to be found. Minor events are easy to untangle. The job (or role) you lost may have freed you up for an even better opportunity. A small medical emergency may lead to better long-term health habits. For more major events, the connections may take longer but are often there. Again, we are not suggesting that every loss or rejection or setback you've experienced is actually a blessing in disguise. Losing a parent, sibling, or close friend is devastating (let alone a partner or child). Rather, consider such after-effects more of a silver lining. Maybe your takeaway is that you are stronger than you think you are or that you shouldn't be afraid of the unknown. If nothing else, people can recognize their own resilience and that their current battle is one they should be able to handle.

There is a solid body of research on a phenomenon called post-traumatic growth. When someone undergoes trauma (whether from a specific incident, such as surviving Hurricane Katrina,[31] or from a more chronic situation, such as a physical illness or struggle[32]), they may change in a positive way. As they heal, think, talk, and cope, there may be beneficial side effects,[33] such as changes for the better in how they see the world, themselves, and the people around them.[34]

What helps people attain post-traumatic growth? Well, there are many paths – and it might not shock you to find out that creativity is one of them.[35] We've already talked about cognitive reappraisals and how your creativity can help you reevaluate past events; another relevant idea is emotional creativity. Many of you have heard of emotional intelligence (EI), which is being able to understand and read other people's emotions and regulate and accurately express our own.[36] Emotional creativity (EC) is being able to feel, process, and convey emotions in new and original ways. Often people with high EC will be able to experience several different emotions at once, reflecting a nuance and complexity that many others do not possess.[37]

Usually, when we're trying to give an example of a core creativity concept, we have to think of one that relates to musical theatre. But the study we just cited actually uses a musical theatre example already (it may not be a coincidence that the lead author, Zorana Ivcevic, is one of James's dearest friends). Zorana and her colleagues contrast emotional intelligence and emotional creativity by noting that someone with high EI auditioning for a musical might be aware they are feeling nervous and anxious and channel those feelings into their audition song. Someone who is also high on EC could feel a plethora of less-common emotions. For example, maybe they note the silliness of the contrast between their own tension and the boredom or relaxation of the creative team. Or, perhaps, a cross between embarrassment at giving a personally subpar performance and pride at knowing even a mediocre delivery is still outstanding compared to the other auditioners.

Often someone with high EC, incidentally, will do well in auditions because they make interesting choices. Think of a Sweeney Todd who, as he approaches the explosive ending of "Epiphany," goes small instead of big. It can sound like an agonized prayer. One of our favorite examples is when the late and much-missed Angela Lansbury played Mama Rose in the West End and Broadway revivals of *Gypsy*. Arthur Laurents wrote in *Mainly on directing* that he worked closely with Lansbury to refine the powerhouse "Everything's Coming Up Roses." As her Mama Rose belted out the climax, the audience poured out raptured applause. Lansbury seemed to acknowledge the love by stopping the show and taking bows; at first glance, it looked as though she broke character. Except she continued to frantically bow even as the clapping died down; as Laurents describes it, she ended on a final bow to complete silence, with a huge smile still fixed on her face. The audience got chills with the dawning realization that it was always Mama Rose taking a bow in an empty theatre.[38]

Creativity Hurdle to Leap: Flexing your emotional creativity can help you rebound and thrive from trauma!

Emotional creativity is a main determinant of whether people who have experienced trauma can find that silver lining and have post-traumatic growth.[39] One study, for example, looked at how people coped during the COVID-19 pandemic and subsequent lockdown. Emotional creativity was a key way that people helped maintain their mental health.[40]

Perspective-Taking, Creativity, and Feeling Good

Both cognitive appraisals and post-traumatic growth involve switching up your perspective on life events. Indeed, think about the song we mentioned earlier, "Something" from *Upstairs at O'Neals*. It offers a new perspective. The act of perspective-taking is when we try to see, feel, and understand the world from someone else's point of view.[41] Perspective-taking is not only related to creativity but has been suggested as a component of the creative process itself.[42] Indeed, one creativity exercise that can help start the juices flowing is to think about a story from a minor character's perspective. There are many classic plays that use this trope, perhaps most notably Tom Stoppard's *Rosencranz and Guildenstern are Dead*. *Wicked* is one of several musicals that also relies on perspective-taking, such that there are now many folks who can't watch the original *Wizard of Oz* without seeing the Wicked Witch as a tragic character.

Perspective-taking comes from the heart and the head. Someone who is able to truly understand another person's viewpoint will have more compassion (although it is not the same thing as being empathetic, which refers more to feeling what someone else feels[43]). People who are able to see another's perspective are better able to not rely on stereotypes.[44] Indeed, there are interventions designed to reduce prejudiced views that ask people to consider two traits that would stereotypically be in contrast, such as a female mechanic or a hippy lawyer; such exercises also increase people's creativity.[45] There are a number of creativity-related traits that join with perspective-taking in reducing bias, such as not needing too much structure,[46] being open to new experiences,[47] and being able to think flexibly.[48]

With all of these benefits (for your creativity and otherwise), working on increasing your perspective-taking skills is a worthwhile endeavor. Our next activity will offer some tools that, of course, will make you feel like you are on stage. Let's go ahead and improvise a little!

> Creativity Hurdle to Leap: Taking new perspectives can boost your creativity – and more!

Activity: What Would Norma Desmond Do?

One way you can boost your perspective-taking is to think about what other people might think, say, feel, or do in a particular situation. For this activity, we're going to offer a cornucopia of musical theatre icons for you to consider. Let's start by finding an area where you feel stuck or blocked. Maybe it's something huge, like you're working on your great novel and haven't written for a month. Maybe it's something small, like a minor task you keep postponing or a conversation you need to have.

Let's call this area the "Block." First off, the Block shouldn't be inextricably linked to anxiety or any other strong emotion; you should be able to talk about it in a neutral way. If you're putting off going to the doctor for chest pains, put down this book and go to the doctor! Emotions are bound to arise, but our goal is to have you be able to explore a variety of perspectives about your Block without getting stuck or returning to the same mindset.

Now we want you to consider the Block. What is your current perspective? Consider your thoughts, feelings, actions, plans, inner dialogues. It is important to articulate this current point of view as a snapshot to use as a reference point.

1   What are you feeling about the Block? Is there anything in particular that worries you or excites you? What emotions are coming up as you talk about the Block?

2   As you consider tackling the Block, what are you thinking? What is your take or impression? What is your gut/"belly button" feeling about what to do next?

3   What are your goals after you get through your current Block? What do you want to be the ultimate outcome? What would constitute "winning" for you in this situation?

Now we're going to introduce you to the world's most colorful life coaches: Your Broadway legends! For each Broadway legend, we've given you their name, a slogan, what their first thought or advice might be, and a question they might ask. Note that we are not necessarily endorsing these questions or perspectives!

For each one, try to answer their question. If you are feeling up to it, also try write out what they might specifically suggest about how to overcome your Block.[49]

Mary Poppins, *Practically perfect in every way*
Try a spoonful of sugar and everything is possible.
What if you took the simplest path?

Eponine, *On her own*
Try pretending that you don't feel pain.
What if you put your needs second?

Alexander Hamilton, *In the room where it happens*
Try taking your shot and playing the game.
What if you go for it?

Norma Desmond, *Ready for her closeup*
Try never saying goodbye to the little people in the dark.
What if you are already the biggest star to someone?

Belle, *Strange but special*
Try finding the good in what seems to be bad.
What if you are overlooking hidden beauty?

Evan Hansen, *Waving through a window*
Try believing that someone will hear you.
What if you reached out your hand for help?

Tracy Turnblad, *Not stopping the beat*
Try taking to the dance floor.
What if nothing held you back?

Elle Woods, *Omigod!*
Try having your outside reflect what is in you.
What if you found your own true style?

Seymour Krelborn, *Sweet understanding*
Try lifting up your head and not pretending.
What if things were bad but will now be okay?

Feel free to think of what other characters might ask and suggest! Maybe they can help you overcome your Block.

Creativity Hurdle to Leap: Tackle creative blocks by trying the views of musical theatre legends!

In Praise of Distracting via the Arts

We've talked about reappraising and taking new perspectives. Sometimes, however, you can use your creativity to positive ends in an even more straightforward way: By distracting yourself. We are not saying to go to the extremes of Elder McKinley in *The Book of Mormon* and simply try to turn off all of your feelings. However, a momentary distraction can elevate your mood. Much of the research underlying this next part now is specifically focused on the visual arts. However, the core principles have been extended to enough other areas (including writing) that it is likely anyone who engages in the arts, in general, will find comparable benefits. The quick takeaway is that drawing, writing, or generally being creative in artistic areas will make you feel better if you are sad, angry, or anxious.[50]

We know a bit about how to get the most possible benefit from your artistic endeavors. For example, let's say you're feeling sad and want to feel better. Does it matter if you actually draw something or just copy shapes? Yes – unsurprisingly, it's better to actually use your creative muscle.[51] But here's a tidbit that may be less intuitive. If you are drawing to feel better or improve your mood, you might try to distract yourself or to express your emotions. We are used to the core tenets of talk therapy that tell you to let it all out and unload your emotional baggage. Yet it turns out that art for distraction's sake is actually better at increasing your positive emotions and decreasing your negative emotions.[52] Indeed, trying to distract your way to happiness can come in many ways. You can draw (either creating your own design or coloring one in[53]), write (either a narrative or poem[54]), talk, or even just think.[55]

Think about *In the Heights*, when Abuela Claudia has died and Usnavi is talking about moving and it's a hot and gross day in the neighborhood. Daniela rouses everyone into cheering up by singing and dancing "Carnival del Barrio." Unlike many other musical numbers when characters make themselves feel better by singing and dancing, Daniela and the others are firmly aware that they themselves are doing so; it is a diegetic number. In *Sweeney Todd*, Mrs. Lovett distracts Sweeney Todd's raging anger with humor in "A Little Priest;" however, to them, it is just a funny conversation. Sondheim's genius is reserved for us.

> Creativity Hurdle to Leap: To use the arts to help your mood, focus on happy distractions over emotional catharsis!

Moving Forward

What we feel when we create matters. Positive moods can help us start out strong, whereas negative moods can keep us plugging away, and activated moods can sometimes help most of all. We have led you through the chicken-and-the-egg interactivity of creativity and your mood and emotions. But even though we point out the occasional benefits of bad moods, it is much more essential, on a larger level, to protect your mental health. This process includes being resilient, engaging in self-care, and seeking meaning in your life. Contrary to popular myth, most geniuses aren't "mad" – let alone the rest of us! You can live your most fulfilled and happy life and let your creativity flourish.

Notes

1 Lerner & Loewe (1956).
2 Baas (2019).
3 Stanislavski (1988/1936).
4 Verducci (2000).
5 Estrada, Isen, & Young (1994), Isen, Daubman, & Nowicki (1987) and Isen, Labroo, Durlach (2004).
6 Amabile, Barsade, Mueller, & Staw (2005).
7 De Dreu, Baas, & Nijstad (2008).
8 Ashby, Isen, & Turken (1999).
9 Hirt et al. (1997).
10 Wegener & Petty (2001).
11 Hirt, Devers, & McCrea (2008).
12 Kaufmann (2003).
13 Hirt, Melton, McDonald, & Harackiewicz (1996).
14 Gasper (2004) and Kaufmann & Vosburg (2002).
15 Kaufmann & Kaufmann (2014).
16 Baas, DeDreu, & Nijstad (2011b).
17 Lang & Bradley (2010).
18 Baas (2019).
19 Baas, DeDreu, & Nijstad (2008).

20 Nijstad, Stroebe, & Lodewijkx (2003).
21 Strasbaugh, & Connelly (2022).
22 Kao & Chiou (2020).
23 Baas, De Dreu, & Nijstad (2011a).
24 De Dreu, Baas, & Nijstad (2008).
25 Baas (2019).
26 McRae, Ciesielski, & Gross (2012) and Wolgast, Lundh, & Viborg (2011).
27 Fink et al. (2017).
28 Schneider & Flanagan (2015) and Schneider & McGrew (2012).
29 Avitia & Kaufman (2014).
30 Rominger et al. (2018).
31 Metzl (2009).
32 Tolleson & Zeligman (2019).
33 Tedeschi, Shakespeare-Finch, Taku, & Calhoun (2018).
34 Jayawickreme et al. (2021).
35 Forgeard (2013, 2019).
36 Salovey & Mayer (1990).
37 Ivcevic, Bracket, & Mayer (2007).
38 Laurents (2009).
39 Orkibi & Ram-Vlasov (2019).
40 Zhai et al. (2021).
41 Stietz, Jauk, Krach, & Kranseke (2019).
42 Glăveanu (2015).
43 Decety & Jackson (2006).
44 Galinsky & Moscowitz (2000).
45 Gocłowska & Crisp (2013).
46 Gocłowska, Baas, Crisp, & de Dreu (2014).
47 Gocłowska, Baas, Elliot, & De Dreu (2017).
48 Gocłowska, Crisp, & Labuschagne (2013).
49 Kaufman & Rowe (Creating Your Spotlight workbook, in progress).
50 Drake (2019), Genuth & Drake (2021) and Turturro & Drake (2022).
51 De Petrillo & Winner (2005) and Drake & Winner (2013).
52 Drake, Hastedt, & James (2016) and Drake & Winner (2012).
53 Forkosh & Drake (2017).
54 Fink & Drake (2016).
55 James, Drake, & Winner (2018).

References

Amabile, T. M., Barsade, S. G., Mueller, J. S., & Staw, B. M. (2005). Affect and creativity at work. *Administrative Science Quarterly*, *50*, 367–403.

Ashby, F. G., Isen, A. M., & Turken, A. U. (1999). A neuropsychological theory of positive affect and its influence on cognition. *Psychological Review*, *106*, 529–550.

Avitia, M. J., & Kaufman, J. C. (2014). Beyond g and c: The relationship of rated creativity to long-term storage and retrieval (Glr). *Psychology of Aesthetics, Creativity, and the Arts*, *8*, 293–302.

Baas, M. (2019). In the mood for creativity. In J. C. Kaufman & R. J. Sternberg (Eds.), *Cambridge handbook of creativity* (2nd ed., pp. 257–272). New York, NY: Cambridge University Press.

Baas, M., De Dreu, C. K. W., & Nijstad, B. A. (2008). A meta-analysis of 25 years of mood-creativity research: Hedonic tone, activation, or regulatory focus? *Psychological Bulletin*, *134*, 779–806.

Baas, M., De Dreu, C. K., & Nijstad, B. A. (2011a). Creative production by angry people peaks early on, decreases over time, and is relatively unstructured. *Journal of Experimental Social Psychology, 47*, 1107–1115.

Baas, M., De Dreu, C. K. W., & Nijstad, B. A. (2011b). When prevention promotes creativity: The role of mood, regulatory focus and regulatory closure. *Journal of Personality and Social Psychology, 100*, 794–809.

De Dreu, C. K. W., Baas, M., & Nijstad, B. A. (2008). Hedonic tone and activation in the mood-creativity link: Towards a dual pathway to creativity model. *Journal of Personality and Social Psychology, 94*, 739–756.

De Petrillo, L., & Winner, E. (2005). Does art improve mood? A test of a key assumption underlying art therapy. *Art Therapy, 22*, 205–212.

Decety, J., & Jackson, P. L. (2006). A social-neuroscience perspective on empathy. *Current Directions in Psychological Science, 15*, 54–58.

Drake, J. E. (2019). Examining the psychological and psychophysiological benefits of drawing over one month. *Psychology of Aesthetics, Creativity, and the Arts, 13*, 338–347.

Drake, J. E., Hastedt, I., & James, C. (2016). Drawing to distract: Examining the psychological benefits of drawing over time. *Psychology of Aesthetics, Creativity, and the Arts, 10*, 325–331.

Drake, J. E., & Winner, E. (2012). Confronting sadness through art-making: Distraction is more beneficial than venting. *Psychology of Aesthetics, Creativity, and the Arts, 6*, 251–266.

Drake, J. E., & Winner, E. (2013). How children use drawing to regulate their emotions. *Cognition and Emotion, 27*, 512–520.

Estrada, C., Isen, A. M., & Young, M. J. (1994). Positive affect influences creative problem solving reported source of practice satisfaction in physicians. *Motivation and Emotion, 18*, 285–299.

Fink, A., Weiss, E. M., Schwarzl, U., Weber, H., de Assunção, V. L., Rominger, C., Schulter, G., Lackner, H. K., & Papousek, I. (2017). Creative ways to well-being: Reappraisal inventiveness in the context of anger-evoking situations. *Cognitive, Affective, & Behavioral Neuroscience, 17*, 94–105.

Fink, L., & Drake, J. E. (2016). Mood and flow: Comparing the benefits of narrative versus poetry writing. *Empirical Studies of the Arts, 34*(2), 177–192.

Forgeard, M. (2019). Creativity and healing. In J. C. Kaufman & R. J. Sternberg (Eds.), *Cambridge handbook of creativity* (pp. 319–331). New York, NY: Cambridge University Press.

Forgeard, M. J. C. (2013). Perceiving benefits after adversity: The relationship between self-reported posttraumatic growth and creativity. *Psychology of Aesthetics, Creativity, and the Arts, 7*, 245–264.

Forkosh, J., & Drake, J. E. (2017). Coloring versus drawing: Effects of cognitive demand on mood repair, flow, and enjoyment. *Art Therapy, 34*, 75–82.

Galinsky, A. D., & Moskowitz, G. B. (2000). Perspective-taking: Decreasing stereotype expression, stereotype accessibility, and in-group favoritism. *Journal of Personality and Social Psychology, 78*, 708–724.

Gasper, K. (2004). Permission to seek freely? The effect of happy and sad moods on generating old and new ideas. *Creativity Research Journal, 16*, 215–229.

Genuth, A., & Drake, J. E. (2021). The benefits of drawing to regulate sadness and anger: Distraction versus expression. *Psychology of Aesthetics, Creativity, and the Arts, 15*, 91–99.

Glăveanu, V. P. (2015). Creativity as a sociocultural act. *The Journal of Creative Behavior, 49*(3), 165–180.

Gocłowska, M. A., Baas, M., Crisp, R. J., & de Dreu, C. K. W. (2014). Whether social schema violations help or hurt creativity depends on need for structure. *Personality and Social Psychology Bulletin, 40*, 959–971.

Gocłowska, M. A., Baas, M., Elliot, A. J., & De Dreu, C. K. W. (2017). Why schema-violations are sometimes preferable to schema-consistencies: The role of interest and openness to experience. *Journal of Research in Personality, 66,* 54–69.

Gocłowska, M. A., & Crisp, R. J. (2013). On counter-stereotypes and creative cognition: When interventions for reducing prejudice can boost divergent thinking. *Thinking Skills and Creativity, 8,* 72–79.

Gocłowska, M. A., Crisp, R. J., & Labuschagne, K. (2013). Can counter-stereotypes boost flexible thinking? *Group Processes & Intergroup Relations, 16,* 217–231.

Hirt, E. R., Devers, E. E., & McCrea, S. M. (2008). I want to be creative: Exploring the role of hedonic contingency theory in the positive mood-cognitive flexibility link. *Journal of Personality and Social Psychology, 94,* 214–230.

Hirt, E. R., Levine, G. M., McDonald, H. E., Melton, R. J., & Martin, L. L. (1997). The role of mood in qualitative aspects of performance. *Journal of Experimental Social Psychology, 33,* 602–629.

Hirt, E. R., Melton, R. J., McDonald, H. E., & Harackiewicz, J. M. (1996). Processing goals, task interest, and the mood-performance relationship: A mediational analysis. *Journal of Personality and Social Psychology, 71,* 245–261.

Isen, A. M., Daubman, K. A., & Nowicki, G. P. (1987). Positive affect facilitates creative problem solving. *Journal of Personality and Social Psychology, 52,* 1122–1131.

Isen, A. M., Labroo, A. A., Durlach, P. (2004). An influence of product and brand name on positive affect: Implicit and explicit measures. *Motivation and Emotion, 28,* 43–63.

Ivcevic, Z., Brackett, M. A., & Mayer, J. D. (2007). Emotional intelligence and emotional creativity. *Journal of Personality, 75,* 199–235.

James, C., Drake, J. E., & Winner, E. (2018). Expression versus distraction: An investigation of contrasting emotion regulation strategies when drawing, writing, talking, and thinking. *Empirical Studies of the Arts, 36,* 162–179.

Jayawickreme, E., Blackie, L. E., Forgeard, M., Roepke, A. M., & Tsukayama, E. (2021). Examining associations between major negative life events, changes in weekly reports of post-traumatic growth and global reports of eudaimonic well-being. *Social Psychological and Personality Science,* doi: 19485506211043381.

Kao, C. C., & Chiou, W. B. (2020). The moderating role of agreeableness in the relationship between experiencing anger and creative performance. *The Journal of Creative Behavior, 54,* 964–974.

Kaufman, J. C., & Rowe, D. P. (in progress). *The creating your spotlight workbook.* Retrived from https://creatingyourspotlight.com/

Kaufmann, G. (2003). Expanding the mood-creativity equation. *Creativity Research Journal, 15,* 131–135.

Kaufmann, G., & Kaufmann, A. (2014). When good is bad and bad is good: Mood, bipolarity, and creativity. In J. C. Kaufman (Ed.), *Creativity and mental illness* (pp. 205–235). New York, NY: Cambridge University Press.

Kaufmann, G., & Vosburg, S. K. (2002). The effects of mood on early and late idea production. *Creativity Research Journal, 14,* 317–330.

Lang, P. J., & Bradley, M. M. (2010). Emotion and the motivational brain. *Biological Psychology, 84,* 437–450.

Laurents, A. (2009). *Mainly on directing: Gypsy, West Side Story, and other musicals.* New York, NY: Alfred A. Knopf.

Lerner, A. J., & Loewe, F. (1956). *My fair lady.* New York, NY: Coward-McCann.

McRae, K., Ciesielski, B., & Gross, J. J. (2012). Unpacking cognitive reappraisal: Goals, tactics, and outcomes. *Emotion, 12*, 250–255.

Metzl, E. S. (2009). The role of creative thinking in resilience after hurricane Katrina. *Psychology of Aesthetics, Creativity, and the Arts, 3*, 112–123.

Nijstad, B. A., Stroebe, W., & Lodewijkx, H. F. M. (2003). Production blocking and idea generation: Does blocking interfere with cognitive processes? *Journal of Experimental Social Psychology, 39*, 531–548.

Orkibi, H., & Ram-Vlasov, N. (2019). Linking trauma to posttraumatic growth and mental health through emotional and cognitive creativity. *Psychology of Aesthetics, Creativity, and the Arts, 13*, 416–430.

Rominger, C., Papousek, I., Weiss, E. M., Schulter, G., Perchtold, C. M., Lackner, H. K., & Fink, A. (2018). Creative thinking in an emotional context: Specific relevance of executive control of emotion-laden representations in the inventiveness in generating alternative appraisals of negative events. *Creativity Research Journal, 30*, 256–265.

Salovey, P., & Mayer, J. D. (1990). Emotional intelligence. *Imagination, Cognition and Personality, 9*, 185–211.

Schneider, W. J., & Flanagan, D. P. (2015). The relationship between theories of intelligence and intelligence tests. In S. Goldstein, D. Princiotta, & J. A. Naglieri (Eds.), *Handbook of intelligence* (pp. 317–340). New York, NY: Springer.

Schneider, W. J., & McGrew, K. (2012). The Cattell-Horn-Carroll model of intelligence. In D. Flanagan & P. Harrison (Eds.), *Contemporary intellectual assessment* (3rd ed., pp. 99–144). New York, NY: Guilford.

Stanislavski, K. (1988/1936). *An actor prepares*. London: Methuen.

Stietz, J., Jauk, E., Krach, S., & Kanske, P. (2019). Dissociating empathy from perspective-taking: Evidence from intra- and inter-individual differences research. *Frontiers in Psychiatry, 10*.

Strasbaugh, K., & Connelly, S. (2022). The influence of anger and anxiety on idea generation: Taking a closer look at integral and incidental emotion effects. *Psychology of Aesthetics, Creativity, and the Arts, 16*(3), 529–543.

Tedeschi, R. G., Shakespeare-Finch, J., Taku, K., & Calhoun, L. G. (2018). *Post-traumatic growth: Theory, research, and applications*. London: Routledge.

Tolleson, A., & Zeligman, M. (2019). Creativity and posttraumatic growth in those impacted by a chronic illness/disability. *Journal of Creativity in Mental Health, 14*, 499–509.

Turturro, N., & Drake, J. E. (2022). Does coloring reduce anxiety? Comparing the psychological and psychophysiological benefits of coloring versus drawing. *Empirical Studies of the Arts, 40*, 3–20.

Verducci, S. (2000). A moral method? Thoughts on cultivating empathy through Method acting. *Journal of Moral Education, 29*, 75–86.

Wegener, D. T., & Petty, R. E. (2001). Understanding effects of mood through the elaboration likelihood and flexible correction models. In L. L. Martin & G. L. Clore (Eds.), *Theories of mood and cognition* (pp. 177–210). Mahwah, NJ: Erlbaum.

Wolgast, M., Lundh, L. G., & Viborg, G. (2011). Cognitive reappraisal and acceptance: An experimental comparison of two emotion regulation strategies. *Behaviour Research and Therapy, 49*, 858–866.

Zhai, H. K., Li, Q., Hu, Y. X., Cui, Y. X., Wei, X. W., & Zhou, X. (2021). Emotional creativity improves posttraumatic growth and mental health during the COVID-19 pandemic. *Frontiers in Psychology, 12*.

Part III

Your Creative Life

Chapter 9

Leaving the Drama on the Stage

The Myth of the Mad Genius

>
> Celie (*The Color Purple*), Success
> Norma Desmond (*Sunset Boulevard*), Suppress
> Myth: Artists Have to Suffer
> Activities: Let's Put On a Show!; The Auditorium and the Affirmation

What is art without suffering? The idea of the mad genius has been with us since the days of Socrates, Plato, and Aristotle. Their core idea was that the poets and philosophers were inspired by demons who were serving the will of the gods, and these proffered gifts were only available to those who could be empty vessels, such as people who were asleep – or who were mad.[1] Even today, when we know the only empty vessels are the cretins who talk during the ballads, the tortured artist stereotype remains an easy trope.

There are so many real life stories we could discuss, but since we're chatting about musicals, Norma Desmond, this chapter's Suppress model, is a perfect example. As those who have seen *Sunset Boulevard* will remember, Norma was a silent movie icon whose star floundered both with age and the advent of talkies. She is shielded by misguided protection from her butler Max (a former legendary film director and Norma's ex-husband), who keeps her mailbox supplied with fake fan mail. When a perceived potential comeback lands in her driveway in the form of screenwriter Joe Gillis, she uses all of the weapons in her arsenal to woo him and get him to revise her screenplay about Salome. She is a bit off from the beginning – we meet her singing a dirge for her late pet monkey – but she increasingly devolves over the course of the show. By the end, as the police come to arrest her, she sees the flashes of newsreel cameras as her long-anticipated spotlight.

There are many themes to take away from Norma and *Sunset Boulevard*. Does Norma completely lose touch with reality because of a broken heart? The depths of her fall from grace? Max's enabling? Joe's selfish handling of their relationship? Or, instead, is it that anyone who has the creativity and star power to "make it" also has a well of darkness that can emerge at any time? Many shows, indeed, have characters whose creativity and success (or desire for stardom) are tempered by very negative traits – from the near-sociopathic J. Pierrepoint Finch's manipulations (*How to Succeed in Business Without Really Trying*) to Evan Hansen's

DOI: 10.4324/9781003389668-13

depression, anxiety, and low self-esteem (*Dear Evan Hansen*) to Mama Rose's breakdown (*Gypsy*) to Eve's backstabbing and shameless lying (*Applause*).

These legends (on-stage and off-stage) make their way into our current beliefs and behavior. We want to first preface by highlighting what we are *not* going to be talking about. In no way are we intending to disparage or further stigmatize people struggling with genuine mental illness. We are solely discussing how people think about their mental health and how that impacts their life choices. Further, we are *not* talking about eccentricities, particularly ones that are chosen as a way to stand out from the crowd. The theatre people who dye their hair shocking colors or wear outrageous outfits or adapt quirky behaviors are usually doing so by choice – either because they enjoy it or because it makes them memorable. Unless such behavior negatively influences their quality of life or ability to function, there is absolutely no harm whatsoever. Idiosyncrasies are the spice of life.

Here is an example of our distinction. Method acting is a technique that has created many superstars and helped many actors become their best self. If you are playing a vegetarian, for example, and you decide to become a vegetarian in real life for the duration of the role, there is no harm in that whatsoever. It may even improve your health. However, if you are playing a violent drunk in a show, and you decide to drink too much and beat up people… That's hurting yourself and others.

There are many ways in which the myth of the tortured artist (or the mad genius) can hurt theatre folks. Consider Fanny Brice's plaintive lament upon being offered her first big break by Ziegfeld in Isobel Lennart's libretto of *Funny Girl*: "Where's the knock-backs you are supposed to learn from? I haven't suffered enough yet." The line gets a good laugh, but it hides a potentially dangerous truth. As we have mentioned, the Faustian bargain – selling one's soul to the Devil to achieve success – is relied on heavily in the arts and occasionally in science.[3] If someone truly embraces the myth, it can lead to both passive and active self-harm, as well as harming others. We don't intend to make this chapter a scare piece a la *Reefer Madness*, but hashing out legend from fact is important. First, let's do an activity that can also serve as a thought exercise on this topic.

Creativity Hurdle to Leap: Be aware of the dangers of the mad genius stereotype!

Activity: Let's Put On a Show!

Imagine that you are writing a musical with us. It's going to be about a singer who struggles but makes it and what happens afterwards. Let's call our hero by the name "Hero" (no points for originality).

Even before the curtain rises, the story has begun.
What is Hero's backstory?

1 Hero was burdened with a demanding father who was never satisfied with anything they did.

2 Hero grew up in a poor household where the bills were always a challenge but everyone loved each other.
3 Hero lost their parents as a baby and grew up in a series of orphanages and foster homes.
4 Hero had an alcoholic mother who was abusive and prone to outbursts.

Hero keeps plugging along until they discover their calling.
How does this happen?

1 Hero finds out that art is a way to escape all the terrible things surrounding them.
2 With the help of a kindly mentor, Hero discovers they have artistic gifts that can help others.
3 Hero is pushed into the spotlight by a relative who seeks financial gain.
4 Hero decides to pursue their art despite all of their friends and relatives saying that they are crazy and will not make it.

Hero does end up getting a big break and does well. As their career rises, they must make important professional and personal choices.
Which one of the following feels right?

1 Hero finds a forbidden love which could end their career.
2 A bad influence from Hero's past emerges and needs their help.
3 As Hero continues rising, they find that one of their biggest supporters has a dark secret.
4 A health crisis threatens all the success that Hero has accomplished.

As the audience watches with bated breath, everything comes to a climax.
Which one feels the most natural to you?

1 Hero chooses career success at the price of everything else; they become a legend, but are completely alone.
2 Hero picks the honorable solution but in the process loses their gift.
3 Hero finds a clever way to balance their life and the show ends with them in love, surrounded by friends, and at the top of their career.
4 Just when it seems that Hero has overcome their past, they die in a tragic and slightly ironic way.

Step back and look at your four answers. We intentionally did not include any path that would be considered "pure Norman Rockwell." Out of the 256 possible scenarios you could have chosen, there is quite a range. You could have picked a story in which Hero faced important obstacles yet ended up ahead and happy. Alternatively, you could have doomed Hero to a life of struggle and tragedy.

Overall, what type of life did you choose for Hero? We are not trying to create a hidden Rorschach test. We're not going to look at your choices and tell you what you're going to have for breakfast tomorrow. And musicals certainly can be the height of tragedy, even to the point of camp. However, what might this say about how you view somebody who wants to be an artistic success?

Think about what you felt to be the most natural story line. Does an artist need a terrible backstory? Does an artist need to choose between their personal and professional lives? Can you be a success and still have a happy ending?

If you want to go back and update your choices knowing our goals, please do. Some pathways may still feel unnatural. For example, clasp your hands together and see which thumb is on top. Now re-clasp your hands with the other thumb on top. This second way probably feels weird. It's not good. It's not bad. It's just not your preferred way of holding your hands together. Similarly, you may instinctively gravitate to a hero's journey succeeding or ending in tragedy. There are many reasons – and many of these have nothing to do with this chapter – but think for a moment whether you see pursuing an artistic career as a choice that must cost the hero. The idea that success must come at a price makes for fun melodrama but not for great life decisions.

We spoke to West End star Rosemary Ashe (the original Carlotta in *Phantom of the Opera*; original London casts of *Witches of Eastwick* and *Mary Poppins*) and her joy from life was contagious:

> I'm pretty positive and have realized how important it is to try and turn a negative situation around. Of course, I don't always succeed; I am only human. Why waste time on bad situations and flaky people? You can't change the way people behave, but you can change how you react. I try to put that into practice! Hopefully, I can keep this balance of my life going as long as possible. One day the phone will stop ringing, as it does for most people, but I think I'll be ready for it. I already get huge amounts of pleasure from ordinary day to day things – I feel very lucky.

> Creativity Hurdle to Leap: Consider your instincts about whether a successful artist can be happy!

Myth: Artists Have to Suffer

Scientific research is not immune to good stories. The "mad genius" concept has been studied for decades, and it is here that we can see things getting tricky. It is a better story to discover that creative people are mentally ill than if you find no connection. There are many studies (often based on biographies or scant records of dead people) that claim to find a connection between extreme creative genius and mental illness.[4] But the more you dig into the research, the more mistakes and often bizarre decisions you find. For example, someone may be posthumously classified as having depression because he was sad after his child died.[5] Many women of days gone by were considered to be hysterical because they dared to have opinions.

Current studies are scattershot. Some studies find that creative people may be a little neurotic, depressive, or anxious, but the effects are comparatively tiny.[6] Certainly, many people in the arts will be moody or irritable or tend to obsess a little. But that is a world away from clinical-level bipolar disorder or depression (which would require hospitalization). Similarly, the slight association between creative people and minor mental health issues does not even mean that one causes the other. Creativity and mental illness may simply share some attributes. One is what is called latent disinhibition, which is a fancy way of saying that you blurt out whatever it on your mind (like the titular character from *Beetlejuice*). Another is when the pathways in your brain are stretchy, allowing different senses to cross over and influence each other. This phenomenon can result in synesthesia, which is when you can see color auras around numbers or taste certain words or have other cases of sense-swapping. A third shared characteristic is the strong desire to seek out new things. These three attributes are related to both creativity and (low levels of) mental illness; they do not cause either one. Higher intelligence and a better memory can help nudge this trifecta toward creativity.[7]

There are some small indicators that creativity and mental illness have some type of connection. However, even many who argue for this type of relationship acknowledge that although it may be true for geniuses, it is not a worrisome issue for everyday creators.[8] If anything, everyday creative people may be more mentally healthy than others, as we will discuss later in this chapter.[9]

Creativity Hurdle to Leap: You do not need to suffer for your art – creativity is barely related to mental illness and is not a requirement!

One brief break from our light tone of theatre talk and the science discussions: If you are experiencing issues with depression or any other mental health problems, reach out. The number for the National Suicide Prevention Lifeline is 1-800-273-8255, or go to http://suicidepreventionlifeline.org. Outside of the United States, you may need to add the country code (011) after dialing 1.

Alcohol, Drugs, and Creativity

Does alcohol and drug use improve theatrical creativity? Certainly, some people might think so. Teens report one main reason for using illegal drugs is to improve their creativity,[10] and nearly half of people asked believed there exists a direct connection between marijuana consumption and creativity.[11] People believe that they are more creative after they smoke marijuana,[12] drink vodka,[13] or take LSD.[14] However, what we believe is not always the truth (indeed, some people insist that *Starlight Express* is Webber's best musical). In all three cases, actual creative output did not differ between people who were stoned, drunk, or high versus those who were sober. In fact, for the vodka study, people were given either tonic water or tonic and vodka and then *randomly* told they were drinking either vodka or tonic water. What they were actually drinking didn't matter – only what they thought they were drinking.

In general, studies on alcohol and marijuana use give us conflicting results. Some show slight benefits[15] and others show a negative impact,[16] particularly for those who use extensively[17] or take harder drugs.[18] Overall, if you're looking to drugs or alcohol as your ticket to awakening your muse, you're looking in the wrong place. Any slight or occasional boosts are strongly offset by the damage to your cognitive abilities caused from repeated use or abuse.[19] In addition, alcohol and drugs make it harder for you to gauge your own creative performance. If you want to grow, you need to understand your strengths and natural limitations (or, as we discussed in Chapter 7, your creative metacognition). Altered states make this type of understanding fuzzy and make it harder to learn and grow from your mistakes.

We emphasize this point because it is easy to simply look at the great theatre legends and draw the wrong conclusion. For example, Stephen Sondheim was well-known for his large alcohol consumption.[20] Once a steady vodka drinker, he grew more prone to wine in later years.[21] Sondheim would continue to drink steadily throughout the writing process, particularly because he believed it helped him loosen up when crafting lyrics.[22] Many other greats, such as Judy Garland, Lorenz Hart, and Barbara Cook, were open about their struggles with addiction. However, there are a couple of important caveats. One, as we have noted, the research does not support any real gain; Sondheim is (as he often was) an anomaly. Second, Garland and Hart were destroyed by their addiction, and Cook was luckily able to overcome hers to have a second career (as have several other active artists who have been open about their own challenges).

Some prescription drugs ranging from beta blockers (often taken for anxiety relief or high blood pressure)[23] to dopamine (used to treat Parkinson's)[24] to Adderall (taken for ADHD)[25] can increase different aspects of cognition, including creativity. One fascinating interaction found with Adderall was that people who were naturally more creative saw a slight decline when on the drug, whereas people who were naturally less creative saw a slight increase. None of these, of course, will turn you into Sondheim (neither will vodka; Sondheim was just Sondheim).

Looking at the larger literature, drugs and alcohol have a very, very slight chance of having a positive impact on your creativity and a much larger chance of damaging either your creativity, your ability to assess your own creativity, or the quality of your life. Even if science endorsed the magic powers or drugs or alcohol, their abuse has so many potential negative consequences on your creativity and your life that it would be a slippery slope. If you responsibly and legally enjoy the occasional drink or recreational high, there's likely no harm – but don't say you're doing it for your art.

Dana has worked with thousands of theatre people both as a composer and as a personal development coach. Hundreds of them have struggled with substance abuse – to alcohol, to party drugs (such as cocaine, crystal meth, ketamine, or ecstasy), or to prescription drugs (such as OxyContin for pain, or Xanax or Klonopin for anxiety). The journey toward addiction usually starts so innocently. It helps people feel comfortable in their own skin, or else facilitates developing instant relationships with other people. It is easy to feel like you are not part of a larger community; indeed, many of us may engage with creative activities for this exact reason.[26] Alcohol and drugs are known as social lubricants for a reason; they lower inhibitions, make you feel secure and connected to other people, and quiet that inner voice that questions whether you actually belong. Unfortunately, what starts as a solution becomes the problem. The drugs and alcohol work until they do not. The very materials that helped inspire you to pursue creative excellence can build new barriers to success.

In musicals, substance abuse is often treated as fodder for thrillers (such as *Jekyll and Hyde*) or comedy (such as *Reefer Madness*). It is only recently, with shows such as *Jagged Little Pill* and *Be More Chill*, that its dangers are treated in a compassionate and serious way. As before, we are again urging anyone who believes or worries about any type of substance abuse. Reach out to someone. The number for the SAMHSA (Substance Abuse and Mental Health Services Administration) is 1-800-662-HELP (4357), or go http://www.samhsa.gov. Outside of the United States, you may need to add the country code (011) after dialing 1[1].

Creativity Hurdle to Leap: Creativity is not a reason to start alcohol or drug dependence. Any slight potential benefit – if it even exists – is not worth the consequences.

Toward the Bright Side

We've written quite a bit about creativity's relationship with mental illness, alcohol, and drugs. It is equally important, though, to talk about the many ways that creativity improves mental health. For all of the stereotypes about creativity and mental illness, creative people have a wide array of tools and benefits that they can use.

Our model for Success for this chapter, Celie from *The Color Purple*, undergoes a series of traumas in her life. Her father is violent and sexually abusive; he impregnates her twice and forces her to give up the children. He makes her marry a man who is arguably worse, and her beloved sister flees to escape their father. Celie perseveres and reaches post-traumatic growth (as we discussed in Chapter 8) and her creativity is one of the ways she succeeds. She discovers a knack for designing clothing and starts a business selling pants for women (which back then was anomalous). When she is eventually reunited with her children and her sister, it is the music of their clapping song game that instantly reconnects them.

There are many other characters from beloved shows that also come to mind who use their creativity to navigate difficult circumstances. Jamie New, from *Everybody's Talking About Talking*, has a dream to be a drag queen and attend his prom in a dress. He encounters obstacles everywhere he looks. His largely absentee father is embarrassed by Jamie's homosexuality, he is bullied for being gay, his teacher scoffs at his ambitions to be a drag performer, and his school forbids him from going to his prom in drag. His creativity, which flourishes under the mentorship of Loco Chanelle, helps him not only survive these hurdles but enables him to persevere, forgive, and shine.

Consider, too, Charity Hope Valentine. She endures a lot of unpleasant and even heartbreaking moments in *Sweet Charity*. The musical opens with her boyfriend pushing her off a bridge and stealing her purse, and somehow the dance hall hostess's situation keeps getting worse. Charity's innocence and good nature (she gives away most of her money to people on the street) make her incredibly likeable – and an easy target. She is swept off her feet by a movie star, only to have to hide in his closet when his girlfriend returns. As her fellow dancers dream of escape, Charity remains in the moment. She is stuck in an elevator with Oscar, an accountant; they begin to date, but she lies about her job. She momentarily quits, but then decides to be honest with Oscar. Although he initially says he still loves her and wants to get married, he ends up pushing Charity in the same lake as the beginning and leaving her.

Charity stays hopeful despite circumstances that would make the most resilient of us crumble. Another musical example is Molly Brown, who is unsinkable both figuratively (she keeps striving toward her dream and her love) and literally (she survives the Titanic). Or think about Belle from *Beauty and the Beast*, the bookish intellectual who immediately volunteers to swap places with her father as the prisoner of the beast. Once imprisoned, she stays positive, marvels at his vast library, enjoys meals with talking silverware, and generally sees the beauty in everything – including, of course, the beast.

If we examine the benefits of creativity, we can find ways to be as resilient as Jamie, unflappable as Charity, as dogged as Molly Brown, and as upbeat as Belle. Creativity is liberating; it can make us feel free and unburdened[27] and can help us replenish our energy at the end of a difficult day at work.[28] Creativity helps us persevere[29] and grow after traumatic events.[30] If we look at arts participation, as we also noted in Chapter 8, we find even more great benefits (we are aware we risk sounding like an infomercial).

Express Yourself

Writing is a great way to express yourself on a regular basis. Indeed, people who write at least a couple of times a week and have some type of narrative woven through their work (from a fictional story to their life events) show an astounding array of physical and mental benefits.[31] This process, called the Writing Cure, works on a vast diversity of populations, from students to prison inmates to cancer patients to people facing unemployment.[32] The narrative element is particularly important for the benefits to occur,[33] in part because it helps improve your working memory.[34] As a result, what is called "cognitive load" is reduced. Imagine your mind is a disheveled closet, with clothes strewn everywhere. Regular expressive, narrative writing – which would include what is

> Creativity Hurdle to Leap: Regularly writing expressively can hold a host of benefits!

popularly known as "journaling" – serves the function of tossing in a bunch of coat hangers and organizing your mental mess. You have more brainpower that you can devote to anything from self-discipline to getting more accomplished.

In Praise of Positive Distraction

Visual art also helps. Several studies have investigated the power of art to improve your mood (at least in the short term).[35] The way in which you make art is important. You can view art as a way to express your emotions or as a way to distract yourself from the ennui of life. Counterintuitively (at least to us), drawing for distraction is much better at making you happier.[36] Indeed, it is common for people to have a mindset that focuses on productivity, hustle, return on investment, and upward advancement – and there is nothing wrong with having this attitude some of the time. In a world filled with stressors, divisions, and new potential catastrophes seemingly around every corner, however, it is okay to breathe. Take a moment to sing, draw, write, dance, build, cook, or invent, even if you're not good at it! It is also okay to consume or passively enjoy activities. If it makes you happy, play on your phone or play board games or watch your show or do jigsaw puzzles. As long as you're not wasting or killing time or actually impacting the work you need to get done, allow yourself to do something purely for pleasure. It's okay.

But wait, you might think! Dana and James, you told us that expressing yourself was good. We did not lie – it absolutely can be. Expressing yourself in writing with a narrative can help you avoid ruminating or dwelling on negative emotions, especially over the long term.[37] But the benefit of positive distraction can be even better, including for writing.[38] Sometimes, the act of drawing or writing or engaging in any type of creative activity can be most helpful when the act itself makes you happy. Other artmaking benefits include higher general well-being[39] and delaying dementia in older people.[40] Viewing art has its own benefits; in what is dubbed The Museum Effect, walking through an art museum helps people feel more interconnected with others.[41]

Music also contributes in its own way toward positive mental health. It can help us better concentrate and pay attention.[42] Singing, like engaging in art, helps older adults maintain their cognition or stave off dementia if it is already present. One study specifically found that singing Rodgers and Hammerstein and other showtunes is especially helpful.[43] Listening to music helps one become more mindful and live in the present moment[44] and can help us not focus on sad or unpleasant thoughts.[45] However, we should point out that listening to angry or sad music can make you feel worse.[46] So if you are in a dark place, maybe avoid a playlist of *Sweeney Todd*'s "Epiphany," *Les Misérables*'s "Empty Chairs at Empty Tables," *The Color Purple*'s "Hell No!," or *Mack and Mabel*'s "Wherever He Ain't"?

> Creativity Hurdle to Leap: The arts can help distract you in a wonderful, positive way!

Moving toward Meaning

You may be wondering about theatre itself, given we have just covered writing, art, and music. Although there have been fewer studies, what exists is positive. One of the biggest benefits is that theatre training and participation can help people read and understand others, and develop strategies to help control and express their own emotions.[47] In general, theatre education – like arts education – brings with it a host of different intellectual, social, and emotional benefits.[48] Even just attending live theatre helps us see other people's perspectives,[49] feel more empathetic,[50] be more tolerant of others,[51] and generally be more altruistic and helpful[52]

Finally, creativity can be a source of finding meaning in your life. As John Barrowman shared on Dana's podcast *Take It From the Top*:

> I've never really thought about what my life purpose is. But I know why I've been put on the planet: To entertain people, [whether] through a book or a TV show or a musical or a recording or a podcast.

Indeed, recent conceptions of meaning include purpose as a key component, along with coherence and significance.[53] These roughly map onto our past, present, and future. Coherence is whether we can make sense of what has happened to us in our past. Are our responses and actions defensible or understandable, even if they're not ideal? We cannot control many life events – we lose people, we make mistakes, bad things happen. But can we look back and understand or even grow from tragedy? Significance is having a life worth living in the present day. Do we experience joy, connections, love, and enriching experiences? Purpose, as Barrowman expresses, is whether we have goals and ideals for our future. Do we know what we still want to accomplish in our time on Earth? Whether we are young or old, do we aspire to reach new heights and continue toward specific aims? These do not need to be career-based or based on ambition; they could be intensely personal goals.

There are many ways to reach coherence, significance, and purpose – a few examples include religion or spirituality, children, or altruistic work.[54] Creativity is another pathway.[55] Many of these boil down to the idea of symbolic immortality – we are the only species that knows we are mortal and going to die. How do we handle this knowledge and not go insane? It is by finding a substitute way of living forever – leaving a legacy and an impact on others that will outlive us. Most of us do not have the luxury of being creative geniuses and contributing a work of such beauty and profundity that we know people will continue to appreciate it a hundred years hence. How, then, can we reach this symbolic immortality?

One is to hone down how we want to impact others. What would we say? Let's finish off this chapter with an activity!

Activity: The Auditorium and the Affirmation

Imagine that everyone you love is gathered in the first several rows of a gigantic auditorium. Behind them are rows of people who you know, who you respect, or are well-known in their field. Even further behind these people are masses of others – the folks you pass on the street, those from other cities and other countries, and maybe those yet to be born. The entire crowd is hanging on your every word.

We are not trying to trigger a panic attack. Let us assume this audience is friendly and you have as much time as you want to prepare. But once you are ready, you have five minutes to impart your thoughts to the crowd. These five minutes can be anything. Wisdom you have learned, advice to offer, or encouragement to share. After you have spoken, these people will be impacted. They will listen to you. On their way out of the auditorium, they will be handed a framed affirmation of between 15 and 20 words of your choice. They will then hang this affirmation in a prominent place in their home.

We are aware we are placing quite a bit of imaginary responsibility in your lap. But nonetheless, we'd like to try.

First, sketch out what message you'd like to convey in your five minutes. What do you want them to take away from your talk? Think of some ideas!

If you are stuck, perhaps try answering some of these questions:

1 What would you like to provide for these people? Inspiration? Comfort? Tips? Advice? Something else?

2 What emotion or emotions do you want to provoke in your audience?

3 What action would you want these people to go home and do?

4 If the crowd truly listens to you, how might they interact with other people differently? How might they now treat each other?

> Creativity Hurdle to Leap: Find the meaning behind your creative pursuits! Let your creativity enrich and soothe your emotional well-being!

5 Are there any existing stories, proverbs, messages, anecdotes, or quotes that you fervently believe in and would like to reinforce with your speech?

Finally, what would your affirmation say? Try to stay between 15 and 20 words, but if you go longer or shorter, we won't tell!

Moving Forward

The myth of the mad genius is ultimately harmful for any artist. It is easy to hear stories of legends who suffered for their art and went through extensive loss or bouts of poor mental health. The actual evidence for any of these ideas being true is shockingly sparse. Pursuing the arts can help your body, mind, and soul. Nevertheless, many aspiring theatrical artists feel like they must make a Faustian bargain and sell their souls, well-being, and happiness in order to find success. However, the existence of brilliant but troubled creators does not mean that their challenges in any way helped their careers. Successful artists who are happy and content may not yield exciting headlines but are much more common. Do not suffer needlessly! Your art should be a source of joy and satisfaction, not an ambition that requires an entrance fee. Indeed, creativity can help you find your meaning in life.

Part of reaching meaning is looking back on your life and understanding and appreciating your travels. One inevitable part of the journey is navigating the bumps and figuring out when it is time to shake things up. Real life is complicated and messy; creative lives are no exception. When do you persist and when do you alter your goals? Indeed, changing your path can reflect an evolution of yourself and your values. The impetus for you going into theatre in the first place may no longer be true. Career trajectories are rarely smooth, and knowing how to navigate a nonlinear path can help you find your ideal spotlight.

Notes

1. Becker (2014).
2. As quoted in Spencer (2008, n.p.).
3. Gardner (1993).
4. See a summary in Kaufman (2014, 2022).
5. Schlesinger (2020).
6. Taylor (2017).
7. Carson (2011, 2019).
8. Silvia & Kimbrel (2010).
9. Kaufman (2023) and Simonton (2014).
10. Novacek, Raskin, & Hogan (1991).
11. Benedek et al. (2021).
12. Bourassa & Vaugeois (2001).
13. Lapp, Collins, & Izzo (1994).
14. Janiger & de Rios (1989).
15. Humphrey, McKay, Primi, & Kaufman (2015) and Schafer et al. (2012).
16. Kowal et al. (2015) and Plucker & Dana (1998).
17. Bourassa & Vaugeois (2001).
18. Colzato, Huizinga, & Hommel (2009) and Colzato, Ruiz, van den Wildenberg, & Hommel (2011).
19. Gutwinski et al. (2018) and Sagar & Gruber (2018).
20. Rich (2000).
21. Barnett (2012).
22. "6 facts" (2013).
23. Smyth & Beversdorf (2007).
24. Polner, Nagy, Takáts, & Kéri (2015).
25. Farah, Haimm, Sankoorikal, & Chatterjee (2008).

26 Kaufman (2023).
27 Goncalo, Vincent, & Krause (2015).
28 Eschleman, Madsen, Alarcon, & Barelka (2014).
29 Metzl (2009).
30 Forgeard (2013).
31 Pennebaker (1997) and Travagin, Margola, & Revenson (2015).
32 Lepore & Smythe (2002).
33 Kaufman & Sexton (2006) and Pennebaker & Seagal (2002).
34 Klein & Boals (2001).
35 De Petrillo & Winner (2005) and Drake (2021).
36 Drake, Coleman, & Winner (2011), Drake, Hastedt, & James (2016) and Drake & Winner (2012).
37 Nolen-Hoeksema, Larson, & Grayson (1999).
38 Drake & Hodge (2015).
39 Liddle, Parkinson, & Sibbritt (2013).
40 Roberts et al. (2015).
41 Smith (2014).
42 Rodríguez-Carvajal & de la Cruz (2014).
43 Maguire et al. (2015).
44 Diaz (2013).
45 Carlson et al. (2015).
46 Miranda (2021).
47 Goldstein & Winner (2012).
48 Winner, Goldstein, & Vincent-Lancrin (2013).
49 Troxler et al. (2022).
50 Lewandowska & Węziak-Białowolska (2020).
51 Greene, Erickson, Watson, & Beck (2018).
52 Rathje, Hackel, & Zaki (2021).
53 Martela & Steger (2016).
54 Lifton (1979).
55 Kaufman (2018).

References

"6 facts you might not know about Stephen Sondheim." (2013, December 9). *TheatreMania*. Retrieved from https://www.theatermania.com/new-york-city-theater/news/6-facts-you-might-not-know-about-stephen-sondheim_66847.html

Barnett, L. (2012, November 27). Stephen Sondheim, composer – portrait of the artist. *The Guardian*. Retrieved from https://www.theguardian.com/culture/2012/nov/27/stephen-sondheim-portrait-artist

Becker, G. (2014). A socio-historical overview of the creativity-pathology connection: from antiquity to contemporary times. In J. C. Kaufman (Ed.), *Creativity and mental illness* (pp. 3–24). New York: Cambridge University Press.

Benedek, M., Kastendiek, M., Ceh, S., Grabner, R., Krammer, G., Lebuda, I., Silvia, P. J., Cotter, K., Li, Y., Hu, W., Martskvishvili, K., & Kaufman, J. C. (2021). Creativity myths: Prevalence and correlates of misconceptions on creativity. *Personality and Individual Differences, 182*, 111068.

Bourassa, M., & Vaugeois, P. (2001). Effects of marijuana use on divergent thinking. *Creativity Canadian Journal of Psychiatry / La Revue Canadienne De Psychiatrie, 56*, 144–153.

Carlson, E., Saarikallio, S., Toiviainen, P., Bogert, B., Kliuchko, M., & Brattico, E. (2015). Maladaptive and adaptive emotion regulation through music: A behavioral and neuroimaging study of males and females. *Frontiers in Human Neuroscience, 9*, 466.

Carson, S. H. (2011). Creativity and psychopathology: A shared vulnerability model. *The Canadian Journal of Psychiatry / La Revue Canadienne De Psychiatrie, 56,* 144–153.

Carson, S. H. (2019). Creativity and mental illness. In J. C. Kaufman & R. J. Sternberg (Eds.), *The Cambridge handbook of creativity* (pp. 296–318). New York, NY: Cambridge University Press.

Colzato, L. S., Huizinga, M., & Hommel, B. (2009). Recreational cocaine polydrug use impairs cognitive flexibility but not working memory. *Psychopharmacology, 207,* 225–234.

Colzato, L. S., Ruiz, M. J., van den Wildenberg, W. P., & Hommel, B. (2011). Khat use is associated with impaired working memory and cognitive flexibility. *PloS one, 6,* e20602.

De Petrillo, L., & Winner, E. (2005). Does art improve mood? A test of a key assumption underlying art therapy. *Art Therapy, 22,* 205–212.

Diaz, F. M. (2013). Mindfulness, attention, and flow during music listening: An empirical investigation. *Psychology of Music, 41,* 42–58.

Drake, J. E. (2019). Examining the psychological and psychophysiological benefits of drawing over one month. *Psychology of Aesthetics, Creativity, and the Arts, 13,* 338–347.

Drake, J. E. (2021). How drawing to distract improves mood in children. *Frontiers in Psychology, 12,* 78.

Drake, J. E., Coleman, K., & Winner, E. (2011). Short-term mood repair through art: Effects of medium and strategy. *Art Therapy: Journal of the American Art Therapy Association, 28,* 26–30.

Drake, J. E., Hastedt, I., & James, C. (2016). Drawing to distract: Examining the psychological benefits of drawing over time. *Psychology of Aesthetics, Creativity, and the Arts, 10,* 325–331.

Drake, J. E., & Hodge, A. (2015). Drawing versus writing: The role of preference in regulating short-term affect. *Art Therapy, 32*(1), 27–33.

Drake, J. E., & Winner, E. (2012). Confronting sadness through art-making: Distraction is more beneficial than venting. *Psychology of Aesthetics, Creativity, and the Arts, 6,* 251–266.

Eschleman, K. J., Madsen, J., Alarcon, G. M., & Barelka, A. (2014). Benefiting from creative activity: The positive relationships between creative activity, recovery experiences, and performance-related outcomes. *Journal Occupational and Organizational Psychology, 87,* 579–598.

Farah, M.J., Haimm, C., Sankoorikal, G. & Smith, M.E. & Chatterjee, A. (2008). When we enhance cognition with Adderall do we sacrifice creativity? A preliminary study. *Psychopharmacology, 202,* 541–547.

Forgeard, M. J. C. (2013). Perceiving benefits after adversity: The relationship between self-reported posttraumatic growth and creativity. *Psychology of Aesthetics, Creativity, and the Arts, 7,* 245–264.

Gardner, H. (1993). *Creating minds.* New York, NY: Basic Books.

Goldstein, T. R., & Winner, E. (2012). Enhancing empathy and theory of mind. *Journal of cognition and development, 13,* 19–37.

Goncalo, J. A., Vincent, L. C., & Krause, V. (2015). The liberating consequences of creative work: How a creative outlet lifts the physical burden of secrecy. *Journal of Experimental Social Psychology, 59,* 32–39.

Greene, J. P., Erickson, H. H., Watson, A. R., & Beck, M. I. (2018). The play's the thing: Experimentally examining the social and cognitive effects of school field trips to live theater performances. *Educational Researcher, 47*(4), 246–254.

Gutwinski, S., Schreiter, S., Priller, J., Henssler, J., Wiers, C. E., & Heinz, A. (2018). Drink and think: Impact of alcohol on cognitive functions and dementia–evidence of dose-related effects. *Pharmacopsychiatry, 51*(04), 136–143.

Humphrey, D. E., McKay, A. S., Primi, R., & Kaufman, J. C. (2015). Self-reported drug use and creativity: (Re)establishing layperson myths. *Imagination, Cognition, and Personality, 34*, 181–203.
Janiger, O., & de Rios, M. D. (1989). LSD and creativity. *Journal of Psychoactive Drugs, 21*, 129–134.
Kaufman, J. C. (Ed.) (2014). *Creativity and mental illness*. New York, NY: Cambridge University Press.
Kaufman, J. C. (2018). Finding meaning with creativity in the past, present, and future. *Perspectives on Psychological Science, 13*, 734–749.
Kaufman, J. C. (2022). Creativity and mental illness: So many studies, so many scattered conclusions. In J. A. Plucker (Ed.), *Creativity and innovation: Theory, research, and practice* (2nd ed., pp. 83–88). Waco, TX: Prufrock Press.
Kaufman, J. C. (2023). *The creativity advantage*. New York, NY: Cambridge University Press.
Kaufman, J. C., & Sexton, J. D. (2006). Why doesn't the writing cure help poets? *Review of General Psychology, 10*, 268–282.
Klein, K., & Boals, A. (2001). Expressive writing can increase working memory capacity. *Journal of Experimental Psychology: General, 130*, 520–533.
Kowal, M., Hazekamp, A., Colzato, L., van Steenbergen, H., van der Wee, N. J., Durieux, J., Manai, M., & Hommel, B. (2015). Cannabis and creativity: Highly potent cannabis impairs divergent thinking in regular cannabis users. *Psychopharmacology, 232*, 1123–1134.
Lapp, W. M., Collins, R. L., & Izzo, C. V. (1994). On the enhancement of creativity by alcohol: Pharmacology or expectation? *American Journal of Psychology, 107*, 173–206.
Lepore, S. J., & Smyth, J. M. (2002). *The writing cure: How expressive writing promotes health and emotional well-being*. Washington, DC: APA Books.
Lewandowska, K., & Węziak-Białowolska, D. (2020). The impact of theatre on empathy and self-esteem: A meta-analysis. *Creativity Research Journal, 32*(3), 237–245.
Liddle, J. L., Parkinson, L., & Sibbritt, D. W. (2013). Purpose and pleasure in late life: Conceptualising older women's participation in art and craft activities. *Journal of Aging Studies, 27*, 330–338.
Lifton, R. J. (1979). *The broken connection*. New York, NY: Simon & Schuster.
Maguire, L. E., Wanschura, P. B., Battaglia, M. M., Howell, S. N., & Flinn, J. M. (2015). Participation in active singing leads to cognitive improvements in individuals with dementia. *Journal of the American Geriatrics Society, 63*, 815–816.
Martela, F., & Steger, M. F. (2016). The three meanings of meaning in life: Distinguishing coherence, purpose, and significance. *The Journal of Positive Psychology, 5*, 1–15.
Metzl, E. S. (2009). The role of creative thinking in resilience after hurricane Katrina. *Psychology of Aesthetics, Creativity, and the Arts, 3*, 112–123.
Miranda, D. (2021). Neuroticism, musical emotion regulation, and mental health. *Psychomusicology: Music, Mind, and Brain, 31*(2), 59–73.
Nolen-Hoeksema, S., Larson, J., & Grayson, C. (1999). Explaining the gender difference in depressive symptoms. *Journal of Personality and Social Psychology, 77*, 1061–1072.
Novacek, J., Raskin, R., & Hogan, R. (1991). Why do adolescents use drugs? Age, sex, and user differences. *Journal of Youth and Adolescence, 20*, 475–492.
Pennebaker, J. W. (1997). Writing about emotional experiences as a therapeutic process. *Psychological Science, 8*, 162–166.
Pennebaker, J. W., & Seagal, J. D. (1999). Forming a story: The health benefits of narrative. *Journal of Clinical Psychology, 55*, 1243–1254.

Plucker, J. A., & Dana, R. Q. (1998). Alcohol, tobacco, and marijuana use: Relationships to undergraduate students' creative achievement. *Journal of College Student Development, 39,* 472–481.

Polner, B., Nagy, H., Takáts, A., & Kéri, S. (2015). Kiss of the muse for the chosen ones: De novo schizotypal traits and lifetime creative achievement are related to changes in divergent thinking during dopaminergic therapy in Parkinson's disease. *Psychology of Aesthetics, Creativity, and the Arts, 9,* 328–339.

Rathje, S., Hackel, L., & Zaki, J. (2021). Attending live theatre improves empathy, changes attitudes, and leads to pro-social behavior. *Journal of Experimental Social Psychology, 95,* 104138.

Rich, F. (2000, March 12). Conversations with Sondheim. *New York Times Magazine.* Retrieved from https://www.nytimes.com/2000/03/12/magazine/conversations-with-sondheim.html

Roberts, R. O., Cha, R. H., Mielke, M. M., Geda, Y. E., Boeve, B. F., Machulda, M. M., Knopman, D. S., & Petersen, R. C. (2015). Risk and protective factors for cognitive impairment in persons aged 85 years and older. *Neurology, 84,* 1854–1861.

Rodríguez-Carvajal, R., & de la Cruz, O. L. (2014). Mindfulness and music: A promising subject of an unmapped field. *International Journal of Behavioral Research and Psychology, 2,* 1–9.

Sagar, K. A., & Gruber, S. A. (2018). Marijuana matters: Reviewing the impact of marijuana on cognition, brain structure and function, & exploring policy implications and barriers to research. *International Review of Psychiatry, 30*(3), 251–267.

Schafer, G., Feilding, A., Morgan, C. J., Agathangelou, M., Freeman, T. P., & Curran, H. V. (2012). Investigating the interaction between schizotypy, divergent thinking and cannabis use. *Consciousness and Cognition, 21*(1), 292–298.

Schlesinger, J. (2020). *The insanity hoax: Exposing the myth of the mad genius* (rev. ed.). New York, NY: Shrinktunes Media.

Silvia, P. J., & Kimbrel, N. A. (2010). A dimensional analysis of creativity and mental illness: Do anxiety and depression symptoms predict creative cognition, creative accomplishments, and creative self-concepts? *Psychology of Aesthetics, Creativity, and the Arts, 4,* 2–10.

Simonton, D. K. (2014). The mad-genius paradox: Can creative people be more mentally healthy but highly creative people more mentally ill? *Perspectives on Psychological Science, 9,* 470–480.

Smith, J. K. (2014). *The museum effect: How museums, libraries, and cultural institutions educate and civilize society.* Lanham, MD: Rowan & Littlefield.

Smyth, S. F., & Beversdorf, D. Q. (2007). Lack of dopaminergic modulation of cognitive flexibility. *Cognitive and Behavioral Neurology, 20,* 225–229.

Spencer, C. (2008, May 10). Funny Girl: Poignant, funny, wonderful. *The Telegraph.* Retrieved from https://www.telegraph.co.uk/culture/theatre/drama/3673274/Funny-Girl-Poignant-funny-wonderful.

Taylor, C. L. (2017). Creativity and mood disorder: A systematic review and meta-analysis. *Perspectives on Psychological Science, 12,* 1040–1076.

Travagin, G., Margola, D., & Revenson, T. A. (2015). How effective are expressive writing interventions for adolescents? A meta-analytic review. *Clinical Psychology Review, 36,* 42–55.

Troxler, R., Goldstein, T., Holochwost, S., Beekman, C., McKeel, S., & Shami, M. (2022). Deeper engagement with live theater increases middle school students' empathy and social perspective taking. *Applied Developmental Science.* doi: 10.1080/10888691.2022.2096610

Winner, E., Goldstein, T. R., & Vincent-Lancrin, S. (2013). *Art for art's sake? The impact of arts education.* Paris: OECD Publishing.

Chapter 10

Taking Your Show on the Road
Know When to Make a Change

Cassie (*A Chorus Line*), Success
Father (*Ragtime*), Suppress
Myth: Persistence is Always Good
Activity: The Change Flowchart

It may have lost its longest-running Broadway show crown many moons ago, but *A Chorus Line* remains one of the ultimate "Broadway" Broadway musicals. Even with its 1970s setting firmly in place and dating it a bit, the messages are eternal. A more nuanced counterpoint to the world of *42nd Street*, *A Chorus Line* takes place at an audition for a new Broadway show. It focuses on the lives of the ensemble members, from younger, aspiring novices to professional veterans. When we first meet her, Cassie initially seems out of place. She has already had several featured parts on Broadway and pursued television and movie work.

Nevertheless, Cassie is treading the boards and hoping to get a job in the chorus for a show directed by her ex, Zach. Why? "I can't get a job," Cassie says. "It would be nice to be a star… But I'm not, I'm a dancer."[1] We discussed the sliding spectrum of the SpotLight model in Chapter 4, and Cassie was our actual example of going from Lead to Supporter. Although it has some negative connotations, much like a former major league baseball player staying in the minor leagues, it represents a much-needed survival skill.

It is not easy to admit failure. We have emphasized the importance of acceptance, flexibility, and adaptation, but there are times when it is impossible to not feel like you are letting people down. Cassie has been set up to be the next Broadway star – certainly by Zach, as well as her friends, fans, and likely the critics. It's all about perspective. A Local player debuting in a Broadway ensemble may be the happiest person in the world. A Lead acting in the same role may feel like it is a step backward. Cassie has to acknowledge (as she does, to Zach) that she is not a great actress, did not succeed in Hollywood, and is not a Star. She needs money, but even more than that she needs to be dancing and working in a show again.

Cassie demonstrates very sharp metacognition (as we discussed in Chapter 7); she is aware of her strengths and weaknesses. Further, she is rewarded for her self-insight. At the end of the show, when Zach announces the chosen actors, Cassie is on the list. She is back on Broadway, even if it is in a different type of role.

One of the many actors who made his Broadway debut in the original run of *A Chorus Line* was Scott Wise. Wise then joined the Broadway ensemble of *Cats* (which would eventually break the record for longest-running Broadway show before being beaten by *Phantom of the Opera*), *Song and Dance*, and the infamous flop *Carrie*. When he was cast in *Jerome Robbins' Broadway*, he won rave reviews and won the Tony Award for Best Featured Actor. After going on the national tour for the show, his next Broadway role was in the hit *Guys and Dolls* revival with Nathan Lane and Faith Prince – in the ensemble. Wise would continue to do seven more Broadway shows (as of this writing), being nominated for two more Tony awards – but also continuing to rejoin the ensemble. He's also succeeded in other arenas, from choreography to teaching. Many actors might have been tempted after winning a Tony Award to hold out for star billing in their next show – and many actors therefore would never have returned to Broadway. Scott Wise, in contrast, has gone on to have a long and prosperous career.

Changing Roles Over Time

It is not only the move from Star to Lead or Lead to Supporter that can be a difficult change. Sometimes it is the type of role. There is a point where an actor stops getting the role of Tommy Albright in *Brigadoon* and instead is offered the part of Mr. Lundie. Such an evolution is part of life and can result in some delightful casting choices. In Dana's musical *The Witches of Eastwick*, Peter Jöback created the role of the naïve young Michael on the West End in 2000. In 2019, he played the older, demonic Darryl Van Horne (originally played by Ian McShane). James saw a terrific production of *Flower Drum Song* in the early 1980s at the (much missed) Starlight Bowl in San Diego that starred Pat Suzuki as Madame Liang. In 1958, Suzuki created the role of Linda Low, singing "I enjoy being a girl."

Such progressions are common. Daisy Eagan went from creating the role of Mary Lennox in *The Secret Garden* on Broadway to playing Martha in regional productions. Andrea McArdle, the original titular star of *Annie* on Broadway, would play the Star-to-Be in the 1999 television adaptation and has played Miss Hannigan in many regional productions. She was initially cast as Eleanor Roosevelt for the 2021 television adaptation but had to drop out, thereby missing out on completing the matched set. To name but two instances of an actor going on to play his character's father: The original *Pippin*, John Rubinstein, was a replacement Charlemagne in the 2013 revival, and Chip Zien, the original Baker in *Into the Woods*, played the Mysterious Man (also known as – spoiler alert – the Baker's father) in a 2012 Central Park production.

These are fun and memorable, but it can also be difficult to realize you no longer are getting the same roles you once did. Whether it is because of age, physical changes, or vocal shifts, there are many reasons why you may not be getting seen for the same roles you once did. There are dangers in trying to be what you can no longer be. It is easy to imagine a 45-year-old dancer being unable to perform the same fancy tap moves such as scissor steps, cramp rolls, or buck triple times that he did when he was 16 years old. The body ages and muscles ache and they generally don't listen to the brain's commandments quite as well as they once did.

The same is true for singing. If you keep singing with identical techniques to the ones you first learned, you will hurt yourself. Your vocal folds have to make a myriad of micro-adjustments to make specific sounds. As a singer, you must control your air flow with your diaphragm and create vowels with the shape of your tongue, lips, and vocal cavity. As we age, our vocal cords thicken and become less flexible and our diaphragms can weaken. The inside of our mouth and our lips and our tongues change as we get older.[2] If you keep pushing yourself to sing in the same way, you can damage your voice. Your voice may develop wobbles and obvious register breaks. It is important to recognize these shifts that occur with age lest it become a psychological hindrance. Consider that opera star Sherrill Milnes was relieved to find out his vocal difficulties were due to leaks in his capillaries – simply because he was terrified it was in his head.[3]

Our body changes with age and throughout history people have always tried to resist. Consider how a boy soprano will suddenly be unable to make the same sounds when his voice breaks. It is why castrati used to be so popular. Unless you are willing to go to similar ends, you have the accept your body for what it is. Even though many people feel a stigma about getting older, there should be no shame in aging.[4] Consider Patti LuPone. She joined John Houseman's Acting Company at age 23 and got her first Tony nomination three years later for *The Robber Bridegroom*. When she was 30, she created the iconic Broadway role of Evita (winning her first Tony). She kept up a string of successes, including creating Fantine in London's *Les Misérables*. However, her best-known achievement in her 40s was creating Norma Desmond in London's *Sunset Boulevard* – and, famously, not being invited to recreate the role in the United States (just as she was not asked to recreate *Evita* on the silver screen). LuPone kept going past these setbacks, embracing roles written for women of a certain age. Her magnificent takes on *Gypsy*'s Mama Rose and Joanne in *Company* led to her second and third Tony awards (the latter at age 73).

It is essential at this point to note that successful aging does not only happen to those who are already established stars like LuPone. It is never too late to pursue a career or avocation in the performing arts. Although there are certainly many stories of actors who began as children, there are also many examples of those who have hit success despite pursuing other careers first. Jessica Vosk, for example, worked on Wall Street until she was 27. She was economically successful but more and more miserable. She decided to pursue her lifelong dream of the stage, even though she had no manager or agent and was not part of any union. Despite being often ineligible for many of the auditions she wanted to pursue, she was cast in the musical *Five Course Love* – and used her background in finance to negotiate getting her Equity card with the role.[5] Vosk has gone on to be a longtime Elphaba in *Wicked* and appears in multiple Broadway shows; she made her Carnegie Hall debut in 2021.

There are many such stories. John Mahoney was a teacher and editor who started acting at age 37. Although he is best known for his Emmy-nominated role in *Frasier*, Mahoney started on the stage. He was a member of the famed Chicago Steppenwolf Theatre and won a Tony Award for his star turn in John Guare's *House of Blue Leaves*. Another example is Bruce Sabath (2008 *Company* revival, 2019 Yiddish *Fiddler on the Roof*), who worked for American Express for years before his wife convinced him to stop complaining and follow his passion.[6]

Scholarly research supports the importance of later-in-life contributions, particularly in the arts. Although some scientific fields (such as physics) are known to peak quite early, there is much more leeway in the arts. Well-known creators in the arts are usually most prolific in their 40s, and (on average) produce more in their 60s than in their 20s.[7] Cinematic composers tend to be nearly 40 years old before having their first hit.[8] There is also the idea of the swan song (i.e., one last production or performance or creation). A large study of classical composers found that their last work was more likely to be higher than their other pieces on aesthetic significance and subsequent popularity.[9]

> Creativity Hurdle to Leap: Change is natural, whether it is the prominence of the part, the type of role, or simply the aging process. Change can also bring you into the spotlight!

Changing Focus within Theatre

There are many other types of change besides the types of roles you play. Consider the fundamental way in which you are part of the theatre. There are so many different lives one can pursue in the theatre. We have largely focused on actors in this book, with some forays into the adventures of directors, producers, writers, and composers. But there are so many more. As we discussed in Chapter 1, there is a whole world behind the scenes and in front of the house. From sound mixers to publicity managers to costume designers, there are hundreds of people who are essential to a show succeeding. They may not get the direct applause that an actor does, but anyone working in the theatre will attest to how a terrific lightning designer can be the difference between a show being fine or amazing.

Particularly in the Local world, where theatre may be smaller (but also outstanding), a show may not be able to run unless company members can assume multiple roles. Often, simply to have a functional community theatre, you need to have a group of people who not only have the passion to act, sing, and dance but also the ability and desire to make the technical, financial, and practical sides of the show work.

Often, people behind the scenes can make or break a show. For example, when Dana's show *Blackbeard* premiered at the Signature Theatre in Virginia in 2019, a host of talented creators all contributed. So many were amazing, but one who stands out to Dana – despite receiving fewer public accolades – was lighting designer Chris Lee. The costume and set designs (correctly) received a nice amount of publicity, but without Lee's talents, the set would have looked like dark debris. His lighting brought out the vivid colors and textures of the fabric. The underlighting on the set's edges created an undulating effect that gave the illusion of a ship genuinely floating in waves at sea. The lighting helped set the scene, whether dramatic, exciting, or foreboding. Theatre is at its essence a collaborative process, and the importance of each role cannot be emphasized enough.

Many people discover their passion is actually for a less glamorous side of the theatre. A terrific example is James Gardiner. In 2008, in his early 20s, he co-authored the Broadway musical *Glory Days*. Although the show was a regional hit at the Signature Theatre, it did not receive good reviews on Broadway and lasted only one performance. How does someone recover from this type of a setback? Some people might give up and leave theatre altogether. Others might toil away and keep writing in hopes of a comeback. Gardiner had the insight that he truly loved the process and production of making theatre. He did not want to simply keep writing to avoid being labeled a failure. Today he works for the same Signature Theatre as their deputy director of creative content and publicity.[10]

There are many other jobs within the realm of theatre. Actors can become writers, directors, or choreographers. Show creators can take their turn on stage. Most choreographers have started as dancers (and many continue to do both). Anyone can decide to become a mentor, either short-term or long-term, and switch their focus toward being a teacher or coach for acting, voice, composition, dance, or writing. So many people discover joys, discoveries, and career highlights by trying their hand at a new facet of theatre.

Jim Walton created the lead role of Frank Shephard in the original *Merrily We Roll Along* and has continued a long and storied career on Broadway and around the world (including the 2021 filmed production of *Come From Away*). However, he has continued to find new challenges to pursue.

> He told us, "I've been more focused on writing, composing, writing music and lyrics for many years," It slowly kind of crystallized more towards that... This is my true calling. When I'm writing, I'm in a creative act. It feels like I'm just happy all the time. I have more of what feels like a healthy ambition, and I have more control over what I say.

Some of Walton's shift has come with age and as his roles as an actor have changed:

> As an actor (and more so over the last 10 to 15 years), it feels to me that less is asked of me and my skills. This means it's gotten a little too easy. I need a challenge in order to feel that my contribution is worthy... Writing offers me that. Here's a fun idea; how am I going to do that?... I feel reborn each time I'm writing a new song. It's like magic.

Other theatre people have gone into academia and work at a university of college while still remaining in the game. Kaitlin Hopkins, who originated roles in *Bat Boy – The Musical, The Great American Trailer Park Musical*, and *Bare: a pop opera*, created the BFA Musical Theatre program at Texas State University and has won awards for her teaching. She has also branched out to other areas, which we will discuss in the next section. She kindly spoke to us and shared,

> I think it is the same part of my brain that I use to perform and teach... I'm always having crazy ideas of things I want to do and see if I like them or want to pursue them further. I just love brainstorming.

Hopkins is not the only dual performer-professor. Danny Gurwin, who starred on and off Broadway in shows ranging from *A New Brain* to *Forbidden Broadway* to *A Little Night Music*, is an Associate Professor in the School of Theatre, Film, and Television at the University of Arizona. Jay Berkow, author of *What a Wonderful Feeling* and other shows, is a Professor at Western Michigan University. Lara Teeter, Tony-nominated for *On Your Toes*, heads the Musical Theatre program at Webster University. Robert Westenberg, who created key roles in Broadway's *Into the Woods, Sunday in the Park with George*, and *The Secret Garden*, teaches musical theatre at Missouri State University.

Other performers become coaches. Perhaps one of the most successful is Matt Farnsworth. He has been a successful Broadway actor (his credits include *Cats, Tommy*, and the original cast of *Curtains*), but his greater fame is as a vocal coach. He worked with the original cast of *Rent*, and a small sampling of his clients include Sara Bareilles, Dove Cameron, and Tony Award winner Ali Stroker. Anne Runolfsson was Julie Andrews' standby in *Victor, Victoria*, among many other credits. She now runs her own vocal studio and her clients include Tony nominee Susan Egan. Other notable performers-turned-coaches include David Sabella (*Chicago*), the late Elly Stone (*Jacques Brel is Alive and Well and Living in Paris*), and Joshua Finkel (*Kiss of the Spiderwoman*).

Another pathway is to become an artistic director of a theatre. David Drake, author of *The Night Larry Kramer Kissed Me* and an actor/director, is the artistic director of the Provincetown Theatre. Terrence Mann, the three-time Tony nominee who created roles in Broadway's *Les Misérables, Beauty and the Beast, Cats,* and so many others, served as the Artistic Director of the Connecticut Repertory Theatre's Summer Series.

Some performers become casting agents. Dave Clemmons was in the original Broadway casts of *The Scarlett Pimpernel* and *The Civil War*; now he runs his own casting agency (he did *Brooklyn* and *Ring of Fire*) and is a Broadway producer (with such credits as *Beautiful* and *Once*). Kelly Crandall D'Ambroise (Broadway's *The Boy From Oz*) was at one point Signature Theatre's resident casting director. Anthony Christian Daniel went from acting in regional theatres to casting for the Ogunquit Playhouse.

Performers also often turn to writing – sometimes primarily to give themselves a vehicle, but other times creating shows that become very well known. In straight plays, this phenomenon is almost common; Pulitzer Prize-winners Bruce Norris (*Clybourne Park*), Tracy Letts (*August: Osage County*), Stephen Adly Guirgi's (*Between Riverside and Crazy*) are but a few of many actors who have found notably more success as a playwright. It is not quite as common in musical theatre but there are still many inspiring stories.

The most obvious answer is Lin-Manuel Miranda, who defies any attempt to be categorized. He (of course) has written and starred in two (as of this writing) classic musicals – *In the Heights* and *Hamilton*. As in every other way, however, Miranda is an outlier. Do not assume you will be the next Lin-Manuel Miranda. Hunter Foster has starred on Broadway (in *Urinetown* and the revival of *Little Shop of Horrors*, among others) and written shows such as *Summer of '42*. Ed Dixon has appeared in many, many Broadway shows (such as a long-running replacement Thénardier in *Les Misérables*) and also written several musicals, including *Fanny Hill*. He also wrote and starred in a one-man show called *Georgie*, about his relationship with the legendary yet troubled actor George Rose.

> Creativity Hurdle to Leap: There are so many ways to stay involved in the theatre, whether as ways to supplement performing or discover new challenges!

Activity: The Change Flowchart

As we think about different types of career changes and evolutions, it is important to think about when is the right time to shake things up. Just as there is a difference between sensible risk-taking and silly risk-taking (as we mentioned in Chapter 5), so too is there a difference between changing for the right reasons and changing because it is something to do. Keep your results from the Pick Your Quartile (Chapter 1 activity) handy, and work on the flow chart to see our recommendations!

Your Creative Life

We hope this activity gets the change juices flowing.
What did you think? Did you end up in a place you would have predicted?

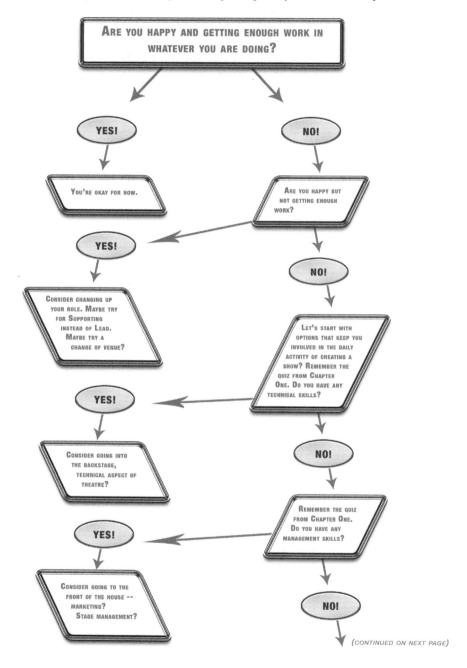

(CONTINUED ON NEXT PAGE)

Taking Your Show on the Road: Know When to Make a Change 175

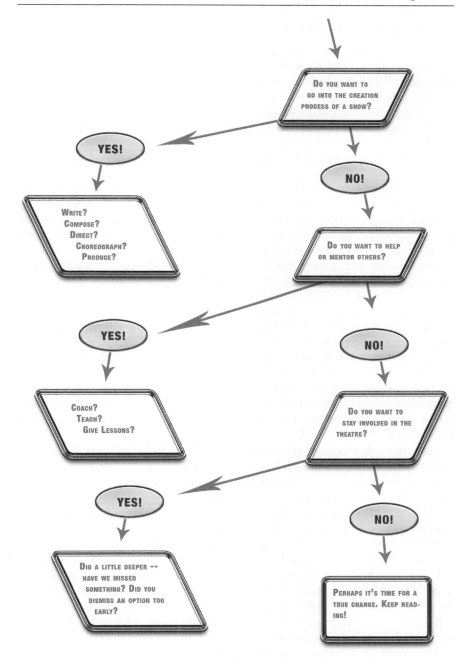

Figure 10.1 The Change Flowchart. © Kaufman and Rowe (Creating Your Spotlight workbook, in progress)

Knowing When to Change Big

Let's think about Father from *Ragtime*, our Suppress example for this chapter. At the beginning of the show, Father seems to have it all. He is well-off, has an adoring wife and son, and gets to go on exciting adventures with Admiral Peary to the North Pole. As he sails away, his world has already begun to shift when the immigrant Tateh and his daughter arrive in New York. Little by little, in his absence, life goes on. Mother finds an infant buried alive and ends up welcoming his mother (Sarah) and the child into her home. Sarah's love, Coalhouse Walker, shows up at Mother's house to woo Sarah back. He becomes part of the family's lives.

The situation continues to change, often for the worst. Coalhouse is driving Sarah around in his new Model T Ford when he is stopped by a group of racist firemen. They insult him and, when he goes in search of a policeman, destroy his car. Coalhouse pursues justice; when Sarah runs up to a prominent politician to ask for his help, she is beaten and killed. Younger Brother has discovered politics via Emma Goldman and become an activist. Coalhouse switches to seeking vengeance and targets any and all firemen. Younger Brother has gotten involved in political activism. Meanwhile, Tateh has found success by cutting silhouettes and in the process inventing a type of animated movie.

Father had now returned to find his life turned upside down. His wife has agency and makes her own decisions. There is an African American baby living in his house. When he takes his son to a baseball game, he is dismayed to discover the genteel game he remembered is now played and cheered on by immigrants. His nephew, Younger Brother, volunteers to help Coalhouse and uses his explosives knowledge (gained from working in Father's factory) to help build bombs to step up the attacks on the firemen. When Father takes his family to Atlantic City, Mother meets the now-wealthy Tateh.

Although Father has been resisting change, he still has a good heart. When Coalhouse (and Younger Brother) are surrounded by police in J. P. Morgan's library, Father volunteers to act as a go-between. After negotiating a peaceful surrender, he is horrified to see the police essentially kill Coalhouse in cold blood. Father has finally begun to change, but it is too late. He again travels abroad, but this time on the *Lusitania*. When it sinks, he dies. Mother marries Tateh and they form a new, blended family. They watch their children – an upper class boy, an immigrant girl, and an African American toddler – play together.

Father is in no way a bad person. Yet as the world moves on and immigrants and African Americans begin (slowly) gaining status and respect, he is absent. His orderly world has been shaken up. Although, at last, he does act in a noble way, his way of life is part of the past. His story ends in the show, whereas Mother, Tateh, and their children continue journeying on.

Sometimes, performers with thriving careers try their hand at something very different while still active. Kaitlin Hopkins, who as we mentioned earlier is a successful academic, also invented Fontus Green Apple throat lozenges. They are the official lozenges of *Hamilton* and many other Broadway shows.

The performer-entrepreneur link may seem unusual, but as Hopkins told us, the connection was straightforward:

> The reason I branched out was because I had a need and there wasn't anything available on the market to fill it that worked for me.... I wanted an all-natural [throat lozenge] that addressed dry mouth while also providing hydration/lubrication. Most lozenges have menthol, which dries out the vocal cords more, and sugar, which coats the cords and makes me have to clear my throat, which can create swelling. So I made what I needed, and I got lucky that there was a market for them. They are great for allergy sufferers and kids, because there is no sugar and they taste amazing.

Hopkins also co-founded Living Mental Wellness, a company that offers an evidence-based mental wellness curriculum for performing artists. Again, this company sprang from a need that she noticed. At Texas State University, she wanted to

> address stress-related issues that actors struggle with, and just sending them to the counseling center didn't work for me. [The center] wasn't prevention-based; it was more of an intervention once things were already in crisis mode. I wanted to offer tools that were long-term solutions to help manage their lives and careers from the beginning of their training. I ended up collaborating with experts in that field to create a program that I now teach to all our incoming freshman.

When she saw the program was working, she worked to expand it for other groups (including athletes, pre-med students, and others facing high levels of stress). It now offers a teacher certification program to allow people at other institutions to implement it elsewhere.

The astute reader may note that back in Chapter 1, we mentioned that domains tend to be distinct; being creative in acting may not mean you are creative in math. Hopkins is a rare exception who reached a high level of success across multiple domains. She often forged her own path based on what she saw was lacking. This scope and breadth of accomplishment do not need to be your starting goal – but there is a great deal to be learned from her story.

Other performers have also turned to different fields. Kelly Lester has won an L. A. Stage Alliance Ovation Award – and was Princess Puffer in a magnificent production of *The Mystery of Edwin Drood* that James saw at the Connecticut Rep –developed EasyLunchboxes, a best-selling line of products. Justin "Squigs" Robertson continues to act in musical theatre but has seen his hobby of drawing cast pictures for each of his shows take off and become the talk of the town as his renderings of Broadway casts have become the new Hirschfelds. Betsy Struxness (original Broadway cast of *Hamilton*) is also a successful photographer. Actress Maura Knowles is also a writer, composer, and the CEO of Mac-n-Mo's, a health and wellness coaching company.

Change is hard. Extreme, career-shifting change is even more difficult. To paraphrase *Promises, Promises,* one of the hardest things is to know the right time to leave. There will be times in most people's lives when a major change is needed. James, for example, has one friend who was a ballet dancer and broke her foot, and another one who was a top-ranked minor league baseball player. Both went on to get their Ph.Ds. in Psychology. Theatrical lives are the same.

As with James's friends, sometimes injuries can lead performers to seek new careers. Wanda Richert (Broadway's *42nd Street* and a longtime Cassie in *A Chorus Line*) was injured on stage and ended up turning to spirituality and becoming an interfaith reverend. Theatrical careers – particularly those heavily reliant on physicality and dance – can sometimes end prematurely. It is never good to overly dwell on negative possibilities, but it is also important to be prepared. Organizations such as Dancers Over 40 offer a variety of resources to help mature artists continue their work, pursue related work in creative fields, and potentially transition to other areas.

It is essential to note that such transitions can be phenomenal successes. Many performers have amazing second acts in totally different fields. To give but a few examples: Michael Maguire, who earned a Tony Award for creating Enjolras in *Les Misérables* on Broadway, is now a leading family lawyer. Another performer who also found success in family law (perhaps a curious pattern?) is the late Jane Ohringer, who created the Broadway role of the Mistress in *Evita*, singing "Another Suitcase in Another Hall." Jere Shea, the original Giorgio from Broadway's *Passion*, works in the non-profit sector helping to raise money for museums and other worthy causes. Ben Wright, the original Jack in Broadway's *Into the Woods*, became a financial advisor who now owns his own company, Dye Creek Capital.[11]

> Creativity Hurdle to Leap: Know when branching out to new areas can enrich your career – or offer a hint for a new one.

Myth: Persistence Is Always Good

Most of the career changes and adjustments we've discussed in this chapter are done when still being active in the theatre. You can find a second (or third) creative outlet or financial resource and continue your theatrical life. Sometimes, however, the natural arc of your career has reached its end. There are many ramifications of this progression. Some are personal and related to how you define your life and identity, and we will address these issues in depth in the next chapter. But much comes down to what you see as success compared to failure. It is tempting to look at any outcome with the lens that being able to continue acting (or staying in the theatre) is the definition of being successful. Indeed, we hailed the importance of persistence back in Chapter 5, and it is absolutely an essential skill in living a life in the theatre. But it is not always the right direction. Consider the question of how you frame your career.

We are a funny species. We can look at the exact same facts and see victory or defeat based on how they are framed. For example, we will paraphrase a classic social science experiment in which people taking part in a study were asked to imagine a scenario about a terrible outbreak of a disease which can potentially kill 600,000 people.[12] We should note that this study was conducted many decades ago, before the 2020 coronavirus pandemic caused so much suffering around the world.

Participants were then presented with two possible scenarios. In the first one, more time is spent researching a vaccine, but as a result, 200,000 people will definitely be saved. In the second, a vaccine is developed much quicker, allowing a 1/3 probability that all 600,000 people will be saved and a 2/3 chance that no one will be saved. When people heard this scenario, approximately 3/4 chose the first option – to take the safe path and make sure you save people.

The other half of the study participants were told of the same disease outbreak but offered a slight variation in the outcomes. The vaccine that would take longer to develop, they were told, would definitely kill 400,000 people. The vaccine that would be offered sooner would give a 1/3 chance that no one will die and a 2/3 probability that all 600,000 people would die. The respondents gave diametrically opposite answers as their earlier counterparts. Approximately 3/4 selected the *second* option, to take the risk.

You may notice that these are the exact same odds for each scenario – all that changed was whether the information was presented in a positive framework (people being saved) or a negative framework (people dying). There are other messages that can be taken away (if a problem is presented as a potential gain, people are conservative and averse to risk; however, if presented as potential loss, people are more likely to gamble and take a chance). The even broader take-home point is that everything depends on how a problem is framed.

Think about Yul Brynner, Rex Harrison, and Carol Channing playing the same roles (in *The King and I, My Fair Lady*, and *Hello, Dolly*, respectively) for decades and decades, well past the age range for the character. You can look at them as the ultimate success: They found a part that became such a quintessential signature piece that they always had steady work and adoring fans. Generations and generations got to share the same magnificent experience of seeing their idols live on stage. But you can consider such a choice as representing stagnation. Many actors keep playing the same role over and over again without pursuing new and daring opportunities. Contrast that scenario with John Cullum. He may not have ever had his own Henry Higgins (although we are partial to Charlie Anderson in *Shenandoah*), yet by continuing to take chances and innovate, he found his own path to greatness. At an age when most actors would be happy finding any work, Cullum was lending respectability and gravitas to bold and controversial shows such as *Urinetown* and *The Scottsboro Boys*.

Creativity Hurdle to Leap: Know when it is essential to be persistent and keep trying, and know when you are being stagnant and inert!

Is it better to stick to the tried and true or to experiment? Is it better to go out on top or to enjoy the spotlight and share your triumphs as many times as possible? In the end, of course, the only one who can answer that is you. But it is not a simple question.

Moving Forward

In the real world, creative lives are bumpy. There is no ideal or traditional career trajectory. Actors become playwrights. Dancers become choreographers. Many theatrical people become mentors, teachers, or coaches. Some second careers are complete switches, such as going into business. Staying the course when the surrounding field is changing may not produce the best results.

The exploration of the myth of this chapter brings us to a larger issue which we will continue to explore. It is easy to root your identity in the vision of yourself as a certain type (as we discussed in Chapter 7). Identity development is linked with creativity; some have argued that forming our identity is itself a creative act.[13] It is possible to see the process of change (whether toward a different role in the theatre, a different theatre-related career, or an entirely new pathway) as losing a central part of your identity. If you are left with these feelings, it may also feel like you are losing part of your creativity.

However, staying fixed and fighting change is not something a creative person tends to do.[14] We are not saying change is always the answer. But it is important to recognize that making a change does not mean that you have failed. Sometimes, staying in the same place is the wrong choice. There are times when change represents the right pathway and should be embraced. Just as we discussed the difference between risk-taking and sensible risk-taking in Chapter 5, so too is there change and sensible change. Ultimately, it is all up to you – as we will explore in the next (and final) chapter.

Notes

1. Kirkwood, Dante, Hamlisch, & Kleban (1975, p. 93).
2. Butler, Lind, & VanWeelden (2002).
3. Tommasini (1994).
4. Chasteen & Cary (2015).
5. Calfas (2019).
6. Kaufman (2008).
7. Simonton (1997).
8. Simonton (2007).
9. Simonton (1989).
10. Butler (2019).
11. Fountain (2014).
12. Tversky & Kahneman (1981).
13. Barbot & Heuser (2017).
14. Öllinger, Jones, & Knoblich (2008).

References

Barbot, B., & Heuser, B. (2017). Creativity and identity formation in adolescence: A developmental perspective. In M. Karwowski & J. C. Kaufman (Eds.), *The creative self* (pp. 87–98). San Diego, CA: Academic Press.

Butler, A., Lind, V. A., & VanWeelden, K. (2002). Research on the aging voice: Strategies and techniques for healthy choral singing, *Proceeding of the Phenomenon of Singing International Symposium III*, 42–50.

Butler, I. (2019, July). One night wonder. *Topic magazine*. Retrieved from https://www.topic.com/one-night-wonder

Calfas, J. (2019, January 19). She was stuck in a job that gave her panic attacks. Now she's the star of 'Wicked' on Broadway. *Money*. Retrieved from http://money.com/money/5506347/jessica-vosk-wicked-broadway/

Chasteen, A. L., & Cary, L. A. (2015). Age stereotypes and age stigma: Connections to research on subjective aging. In M. Diehl & H.-W. Wahl (Eds), Research on subjective aging: New developments and future directions. *Annual Review of Gerontology and Geriatrics* (vol. 35, pp. 99–119). New York, NY: Springer

Fountain, B. (2014, December). Give my regards to Broadway. *Wrightsville Beach Magazine*, *15*, 68–69.

Kaufman, S. B. (2008, November). Better late than never. *Psychology Today.* Retrieved from https://www.psychologytoday.com/us/articles/200811/better-late-never

Kirkwood, J., Dante, N., Hamlisch, M., & Kleban, E. (1975). *A chorus line*. New York, NY: Applause.

Öllinger, M., Jones, G., & Knoblich, G. (2008). Investigating the effect of mental set on insight problem solving. *Experimental Psychology*, *55*, 269–282.

Simonton, D. K. (1989). The swan-song phenomenon: Last-works effects for 172 classical composers. *Psychology and Aging*, *4*, 42–47.

Simonton, D. K. (1997). Creative productivity: A predictive and explanatory model of career trajectories and landmarks. *Psychological review*, *104*, 66–89.

Simonton, D. K. (2007). Cinema composers: Career trajectories for creative productivity in film music. *Psychology of Aesthetics, Creativity, and the Arts*, *1*, 160–169.

Tommasini, A. (1994, October 9). As the limelight fades, a star lowers his sights. *New York Times*. Retrieved from https://www.nytimes.com/1994/10/09/arts/as-the-limelight-fades-a-star-lowers-his-sights.html

Tversky, A., & Kahneman, D. (1981). The framing of decisions and the psychology of choice. *Science*, *211*, 453–458.

Chapter 11

Dreaming Your Dream
Your Journey of Success

Professor Harold Hill (*The Music Man*), Success
Benjamin Barker (*Sweeney Todd*), Suppress
Myth: Greatness is Always Great
Activity: Rodgers and Hammerstein Value Wheel

When we first meet Harold Hill in *The Music Man*, he is much like a theatrical performer. He travels from town to town and plays a role there. He wins over people with his natural charisma before moving on to the next project and starting all over again. By many metrics, he is successful. Hill has discovered a plan that works and he repeats it (or a variation) with a new audience over and over again. Judging from his preference for the sadder but wiser girls, he may well be having brief romances (or one night stands) in each new town. Although he does not seem to be incredibly wealthy, he is definitely making money and, perhaps, spending it on enjoyable pursuits. There are many people who would kill for this life.

When Hill runs into his former colleague Marcellus Washburn in River City, Iowa, he finds that Marcellus has settled down (with his boss's niece, Ethel Toffelmier). Hill's immediate reaction is "Gone legitimate, huh? I knew you'd come to no good.[1]" Hill is not bothered by being a con man and promising things he cannot deliver. After he has sold his uniforms and instruments, he is long gone from a town before they find out he has no intention of actually teaching the children how to play.

There is no reason to think that River City will be any different from past towns. However, what makes Hill our Success model for this chapter is that he is able to recognize when his needs and values have changed – and then modify his behavior accordingly. He initially sees Marian Paroo, the local librarian, as yet another foil to be deceived. But little by little, he finds himself falling in love with Marian. When another salesman exposes him as a con, the rational response would be to sneak out of town – his friend Marcellus has helped arrange it, and even Marian, knowing the truth, wants him to save his own skin. But he can't.

When Marian's younger brother, Winthrop, confronts the scam artist and calls him a liar and crook, Hill does not deny it. Yet when Winthrop questions the existence of the marching band, Hill tells him, "I always think there's a band, kid.[2]"

DOI: 10.4324/9781003389668-15

In this moment, we start seeing beneath the veneer and realize that perhaps Hill has not been fulfilled as he's escaped from place to place. Part of him may secretly want to stay and lead a children's marching band (or, perhaps, he is simply an excellent liar, even to a child). As Marian defends Hill to the angry, rapidly growing mob, he decides to join Marcellus in going legit and openly declares his love for Marian.

Thankfully, unlike *Annie* or *Bye Bye Birdie*, there has been no push for a sequel to *The Music Man* (just endless revivals). If there was one, would Hill still be contentedly married to Marian and in charge of a mediocre band? Would he be plotting one last scheme? Would his ultimate destination be to settle in River City and be a family man, or will he always be a vagabond at heart? With luck, we will never know and always picture him at the end of *The Music Man*, delightedly leading an off-tune group of young musicians. Let us assume that Hill is where he wants to be. In order to get there, he had to reevaluate what success meant to him. It was no longer something to be measured in money or the adrenaline thrill of stealing. Instead, success for Hill became the quiet life of living in a small town, knowing love and his place in the world.

There are two Harold Hills in *The Music Man*. At the beginning, he is nomadic, fine with any limitations or missing pieces in his life, and disdains roots and commitment. At the end, he is happy to give up the excitement of his old life for the sweet comfort and companionship he has found in Iowa. It is important to note that although Harold Hill's inner success comes with winding down, this type of self-discovery can come in many different forms. You can also think of Leo Bloom from *The Producers*. At the beginning, he is a shy accountant with seemingly unattainable dreams of producing on Broadway. By the end, after his adventure with Max Bialystock, *Springtime for Hitler*, and prison, Bloom is a big-time producer who is happily married to leading actress Ulla. The key is each character has found their true bliss – whether it is a quieter life or the brassiest life imaginable.

Short-Term vs Long-Term

How do you know which Harold Hill you are right now? One way to consider the issue is in the ideas of Hedonia and Eudaimonia.[3] Harold Hill starts in Hedonia and ends in Eudaimonia. Hedonia is based in pleasure and short-term gratification, whereas Eudaimonia is more about life satisfaction and long-term happiness. Hedonia is eating a hot fudge sundae, embracing a new lover, or going on a shopping spree. Eudaimonia is reaching a sense of belonging in family or friends, feeling like you are making the world a better place and finding a sense of life being worthwhile.

We are not saying that Hedonia is wrong or sinful. A life spent avoiding any indulgences is not the goal. Any extreme is likely to not being desirable. If Hill immediately gave up his scams, settled down, adopted three children, tithed 20% of his band earnings to charity, and spent his weekends at a soup kitchen, he may quickly decide that this life is not for him and go back to the hustle. We need pleasure, just as we need fulfillment. The key is to find the right balance between Hedonia and Eudaimonia that works best for you.

You can find your life's purpose in many places. Think about your goals for when you are 75 years old. Maybe you want to be sitting on your porch next to your life partner, watching your grandkids play in your front yard while cookies are baking in your oven. Maybe you want to be touring and doing a one-person show of your best stories and songs to sold-out, adoring crowds every night. Both are great goals. Both are a blend of pleasure and fulfillment.

It is not unreasonable to start thinking about where you want to end up, even at an early age. What are you willing to do? What are you willing to give up to get to that goal? So many life dreams can have hidden costs or require more advance planning than you might think. Fixating on a single dream without considering that your own values may change over time can lead to poor outcomes. For example, do you want to have kids? Some people decide to postpone having children or outright choose to not have them. It is very important to note that this is a wonderful and correct decision for many, many people. We are in no way judging people based on whether or not they have kids. But either choice is hard to undo.

It is obviously impossible to undo having kids once you have them; you can't exactly drop your five-year-old off at a boarding school with $20 and a note saying "Good luck!" The other side also can be also difficult to reverse. Many people wait to have kids until they are older, only to discover that fertility is not always a given. Others intend to have children in the distant future but do not act until it is too late. Understanding your needs for family, children, and friends is essential to having a healthy and enjoyable career (and life).

West End star Rosemary Ashe spoke to us about her illustrious career and life. Her candid insight illustrates the importance of knowing yourself:

> She told us, "It is very difficult for a partner to understand 'the pull of the theatre,'". My first marriage failed because my husband didn't understand I had to do what I had to do, and I ended up having a 'showmance,' which wrecked everything. My second husband felt lonely and *he* looked elsewhere, whilst I was busy doing eight shows a week! I am now fortunate to have a partner who understands my needs. He has no problem with my performing and being away sometimes. The problem he *does* have with me is that I have so many friends. Not having had children (I never wanted any), my friends are my family and they vary in age from their 20s to 80s. Mostly they are in the same profession, but not all. I usually 'collect' a new person from every show I do. Sometimes, I admit, it is exhausting keeping up with them all and my partner then feels neglected, so I have to really watch that. Having said that I feel the balance of my life just now, seems ideal.

Creativity Hurdle to Leap: All choices require giving something up. Reflect on what you most want for your later life!

Legacies

In Chapter 9, we discussed issues of meaning. We need to feel like we can understand our lives, that they are worth living, and that we have goals for the future. Such needs can include wanting to leave some type of legacy that we leave behind. Children represent one possible legacy; at its most biological, it is spreading your genetic material and ensuring that a part of you will live on. Yet Darwin be damned, any way in which we influence the lives of others is a legacy. Whether it is adopting or fostering children, donating your time to help others, or mentoring younger colleagues or students, these actions will make you live on in the hearts and minds of other people after you are gone. There is also the power of your creative work – your legacy could be how your performances are remembered by audiences in years to come or how your behind-the-scenes efforts are revived and produced down the line. Remember the two dream scenarios for 75 years old (watching grandkids with your life partner or sold-out tours)? They both offer legacies, just different types.

Nothing is guaranteed. You might have a football team's worth of children, be the greatest parent in the world, and yet end up saddled with ungrateful brats who want nothing to do with you. Your creative work is even more of a crapshoot. The Pulitzer Prize for Drama, one of the highest annual honors for plays, was first given more than 100 years ago (in 1918). Some of the pre-1940 winners are still legendary, such as Eugene O'Neill's *Anna Christie*, Thornton Wilder's *Our Town*, and Hart and Kaufman's *You Can't Take It with You*. Yet so many early winners are virtually forgotten today. *Craig's Wife*, by George Kelly (Grace's uncle – really), was adapted into three movies. *Hell-Bent Fer Heaven*, by Hatcher Hughes, featured George Abbott and Clara (Auntie Em) Blandick. Other Pulitzer Prize winning playwrights include Paul Green, Owen Davis, Jesse Lynch Williams, and Zoe Akins. Maybe you've heard of all of them (and we love you for it), but these ones have stumped us.

The Systems theory of creativity offers an explanation for the fickle ways that some theatre is remembered and others forgotten.[4] It discusses creative work as being the interaction between the creator, the gatekeepers (i.e., critics, funders, and other decision-makers), and the field (i.e., consumers). The creator – and the product – stay the same over time. But the gatekeepers and the field do not. Theatre critics from 1927 may have seen Paul Green's *In Abraham's Bosom* and been moved by its portrayal of an African American trying to succeed despite Jim Crow laws. More modern critics would likely find the lead character to be portrayed in an inaccurate and condescending way. Audiences once loved the Ziegfeld Follies – and there will always be a segment who enjoy those types of shows – but modern audiences accustomed to the fleshed-out characters and gripping stories from shows such as *Oklahoma!, Gypsy, West Side Story, Sweeney Todd*, or *Hamilton* may have little use for simple song and dance.

Consider *Two Gentlemen of Verona*, with music by *Hair's* Galt MacDermott and lyrics by *Six Degrees of Separation*'s John Guare. It originally opened in Central

Park, produced by Joe Papp in association with the New York Shakespeare Festival, before moving to Broadway. Many other shows, such as *Hair, A Chorus Line*, the revised *Pirates of Penzance, Drood*, and *Runaways*, followed a similar path. *Two Gentlemen of Verona* was a hit with audiences and critics and won the 1972 Tony Award for Best Musical. It defeated other shows you may know – *Follies* and *Grease*. Over the last several decades, musical theatre gatekeepers have changed and undoubtedly would recognize *Follies* as the superior work. Similarly, the field of theatergoers has evolved and would likely gravitate toward *Grease*. Meanwhile, *Two Gentlemen of Verona* was revived in 2005 off-Broadway but is otherwise largely forgotten.[5]

Some creative works are eternal and will continue to resonate for future generations. Others are a product of their times and may be a historical curiosity but little else. It is important to note that the original reception of a work is still related to its eventual success. One study of operas found that the length of the original run helped predict how often they were performed in modern repertoires.[6] Indeed, in going through the list of Tony winners, most are still reasonably well-known.

Taking a step back, however, the bottom line is that your career must have meaning to you. If you are looking to your work to be your lifeline and your ticket to immortality, it's a lottery even for the best and brightest. Make a list of any theatre person currently alive who you think will be remembered in 100 years. We guarantee you there's at least one entry on the list who will be long-forgotten.

Are we saying you should give up? Are we saying that if the odds are incredibly against your creative contributions standing the test of time then any hope for a meaningful legacy is gone? Of course not. James has two paintings by his Grandma that are hanging in his living room as he and Dana write these words. Objectively, the paintings are mediocre. If they were by someone else, he would have no interest in displaying them. But they are a reminder of his Grandma Blanche and her kindness and passion, and they are colorful and bright and they make him smile when he looks at them. Dana has his mother's paintings in most rooms of his apartment. Some are beautiful and some are not. All of them are copies of other, better known paintings – a creativity researcher might mark her down for that (although, as we note in Chapter 7, replications are still creative!). Somewhere in the middle of a legacy of creative contributions and a legacy from personal connections are these paintings. They are still appreciated as art by both James and Dana – but also as memories of a loved one.

> Creativity Hurdle to Leap: No legacy is guaranteed, so make sure that the journey is also a meaningful experience.

Myth: Greatness Is Always Great

There are many harmful myths about genius or great creators. The most prevalent – which we have already discussed a bit – is that you do not need to be a genius (or Legend) to be creative (Chapters 4 and 7). Further, the idea of the mad genius is hugely overstated (Chapter 8). We are going to tackle a couple of different other myths about being a great creator here.

It is easy to have an idealized version of what a great (or good) creator is like. It is easy to think of every Sondheim lyric being brilliant or every Richard Rodgers tune being a delight. Part of that image may include each show taking a great deal of time and care. Someone who creates many different works is sometimes seen as overexposed or even a formulaic hack. It is easy to wonder if someone who is very prolific is giving it his or her "all."

The science suggests otherwise. The most creative people are also the most productive.[7] The best creators crank out a lot of work. There are many different nuances to explore in this bit of information. It is absolutely okay if you take a long time to create something. You should not feel at all embarrassed if you are a composer who needs months to finish a song or a performer who needs many extra rehearsals. However, if you work fast it does not mean your output is sloppy or of lower quality. It is hard for us to find examples in musical theatre, to be honest, but most people do not want to admit that a piece was written quickly. It can come off as arrogant and, even worse, can make people dismiss its quality.

Sylvester Stallone, who many readers may not remember was nominated for an Oscar for writing the original *Rocky*, once said: "I'm astounded by people who take 18 years to write something. That's how long it took that guy to write *Madame Bovary*, and was that ever on the best-seller list?[8]" He comes off sounding stupid and cocky – and yet remember that he wrote one of the most iconic scripts in movie history in just three days. Imagine if Lin-Manuel Miranda began bragging he wrote *Hamilton* in one afternoon (he has *not* made such a claim) – how would that impact your opinion on the show? Would it change how you viewed Miranda himself? Maybe it would cement his genius to you, or perhaps it would make you doubt your appreciation of the show.

We have a number of other stereotypes about "great" creators or "great" works should be like. It is easy, for example, to dismiss simplicity. Sondheim's brilliance is his intricate complexity. Yet consider one of the classic songs by a theatrical composer, Harold Arlen's "Over the rainbow." The melody itself is very basic, yet uses notes that span an octave over the first word "Some…. where." This distance allows us to better remember the tune. The simplicity of the melody places the E. Y. Harburg's lyrics front and center. It gives an extra emphasis to Dorothy's yearning. The first notes represent a large musical gesture which is then followed by smaller ones that explain the sources of Dorothy's longing.

When Dana composed "Dance with the devil" from *Witches of Eastwick*, he tossed around several ideas with his lyricist, John Dempsey. John had the title and Dana set a simple melody to that phrase and repeated it multiple times. Dana was ready to move on, thinking it was too basic, yet John wanted to explore this version more. The multiple small repetitions created the rhythmic impact of a single, large musical gesture that worked for an infectious production number.

Great creators can work fast, they can work in a simple way, and they can also work in a wide variety of styles for many different outcomes. Sometimes that can mean indulging in a little fun. Stephen Sondheim had already written the lyrics for

Gypsy and *West Side Story* when he teamed up with composer Mary Rodgers to contribute "The boy from..." for *The Mad Show*. Using the pseudonym Esteban Rio Nido (a direct translation of his name), the song was a parody of "The girl from Ipanema." The joke (a little less funny now) is that the girl was pining for a man with obviously homosexual tendencies. *A Funny Thing Happened on the Way to the Forum* came out the same year.

Many theatrical greats have also written side projects, changes of pace, and whimsy. It is not unusual to see some of our great writers working on Disney films (the roster includes Alan Menken Howard Ashman, Tim Rice, Stephen Schwartz, Lin-Manuel Miranda, and so many more). David Yazbeck, the Tony Award-winning creator of *The Full Monty* and *A Band's Visit*, has also worked in rock and roll (including collaborating with New Wave band XTC) and co-wrote the theme song to *Where in the World is Carmen Sandiego*. Maury Yeston (*Nine, Titanic*) took an unusual route to being a Broadway composer; he spent years as a Yale professor – and composed most of the "Star Wars Christmas Album." Richard Adler (*Damn Yankees*) produced and staged Marilyn Monroe singing "Happy Birthday" to John F. Kennedy.

A final implication of great creators being more likely to be prolific is that they are more likely to fail. If you do more, you will make more mistakes. So a lot of the best theatre people have done a lot of crap. Obviously, deciding what constitutes a poor showing versus an underappreciated great work is quite subjective. There are always those who will insist that *Starlight Express* is Andrew Lloyd Webber's best work. Rather than us dish on our least-favorite work (that will be saved for the audiobook version), we will instead note that creators at all levels should embrace and learn from mistakes.[9]

> Creativity Hurdle to Leap: Brilliant creators are also prolific creators. Don't be afraid to crank out new work!

What Is Success?

We've circled around this question throughout the book: What does success mean to you? The answer can change across our lives. Perhaps growing up, your goal was to be a Superstar who becomes a Legend. Some people will continue to have that goal their entire lives, making every decision with an eye toward center stage. Others will gradually shift. There are many different reasons for such changes.

Some people may become disenchanted with the system; the sacrifices and compromises needed to live that reality may become more than they are willing to endure. Just as greatness is not always great, greatness is also not easy. It can require an obsession that may be akin to walking in a straight line with blinders on to prevent any distraction – and yet that may make some miss out on life.

Others may still love theatre but not feel the need to sacrifice everything to reach the pinnacle. As with James Gardiner, the co-author of *Glory Days* who we discussed about in Chapter 9, the only reason to stay on the fast track may be to prove yourself. Yet many reach a point where there is nothing to prove. They are happy and content and may get their validation and fulfillment from other sources, whether a different facet of the job or from other parts of their life (such as family, friends, hobbies, or service).

Still others may find they enjoy aspects of being a Lead, Supporter, or Local even more. For example, is it better to play Sky Masterson or Sarah Brown in *Guys and Dolls* in a production in Columbus, Ohio, or to play Angie the Ox or Ferguson the Hot Box Dancer in a production off-Broadway? Is it better to do a one-person show where you sing your favorite songs that best show off your voice to a local audience of seniors or students, or to keep singing 16 bars in audition after audition in hopes of joining a Broadway ensemble? The answer, of course, is it entirely depends on you. Many would rather have a crack at the greatest roles or have control over their set list in exchange for playing on a smaller stage.

What is satisfying at age 22 may not be satisfying at age 46 or age 71. One of Dana's good friends is Marta Sanders, who is a renowned cabaret artist, top NYC tour guide, and was in the original Broadway cast of *Best Little Whorehouse in Texas*. She told him once that at a certain point, your life shifts from "what may be" to "what is." This sentiment may strike younger readers as a little bit of a downer, yet we find it actually may enable happiness more. It is not that there is a certain point at which you should give up – we are not endorsing that idea at all! – but, rather, there is a time to take stock and make sure that what you are doing brings you joy and meaning. If you have been treading the boards for 30 years and you still love it, *keep doing exactly that*! But if you reach a point where you are only doing it in hopes that you will catch a big break that will bring you pleasure, you are taking a risk. "We think that our creative persona is all that is important and all that we are – our identity," Marta told Dana. "We learn that we're much more than that. Nurturing our other roles, sister, daughter, neighbor, and friend is what gives substance to our lives and work." As we age, she adds, we are less encumbered by other people's opinions. We end up competing with ourselves – which makes it easier emotionally.

André Ward, whom we quoted earlier on handling rejection, also spoke eloquently on keeping personal and professional identity separate after a period of being away from Broadway:

> For so many creative people, the line between who you are and what you do is so enmeshed that when what you do seemingly isn't there, then who are you? So for me it was about unpacking who I am without this thing called Broadway. I found out that I am still a loving friend, a brother, a partner, and a great spiritual force in the world that has love to give. Your strength comes in knowing that no matter what happens, no matter how many no's you get, you are enough who you are. Just as you are born, you are enough. You are loved and you are enough. That has been the biggest revelation to me as I have grown up in this business. The more I learned that I'm enough, the better my life is – no matter what job I have.

Marta also told Dana, "People do what they want; the rest is just excuses." Indeed, we believe that talent is rarely discovered by chance. The number of actors, directors, writers, and dancers who have stumbled into success is quite small (although they do exist). James always notes that his academic colleagues who always complain about being busy and overworked are rarely the ones who are the most productive. *Everyone* is busy. The difference is that some people are busy and get things done, and others are just busy for the sake of being busy. Indeed, some have suggested that being busy has become a status symbol, with people wanting to appear busy so that others believe they are in demand.[10]

This focus on appearance permeates many dimensions of our lives. For example, it is well-established that people are quite good at impression management and, bluntly, faking their lives on social media.[11] As a result, though, it is harder to find authenticity. Although it is complex and nuanced,[12] increased social media is associated with depression.[13] Most people present their best selves, which means if your friends are in the business, you are faced with a barrage of people posting about getting cast, successes, and raves. It is rare for people to be honest and be equally open about the failed auditions, terrible reviews, and unresponsive audiences. If you are struggling in your career (or life), it is easy to feel like everyone else is successful and happy. This phenomenon makes it harder to accurately gauge other people's success – and, by extension, your own. If you feel as though all of your friends are on their way toward being Legends, a decision to stay Local may make you feel like you have given up. If you keep reading about your Local friends being satisfied and posting pictures of smiling kids, you may wonder if your pursuit of being a Star is an exercise in self-delusion. Seeing only the highlights of your friends' lives induces doubt in any of your decisions.

There are so many questions you can have about your career and your life. Should you aim to be a Star, Lead, Supporter, or Local? What is the ideal work-family life balance? When should you shake up your career by finding a new facet of theatre to explore, moving to the big city or a smaller suburb, or finding a new outlet altogether for your passion and creativity? There are no "correct" answers. The key is finding your own path that lets you get the most out of your abilities, enjoy your passions, and live a life that gives you pride, joy, and meaning.

> Creativity Hurdle to Leap: Success is not one-size-fits-all. It changes by person and over time.

Activity: Rodgers and Hammerstein Values Wheel

As you find the path that is best for you, one of the big decisions is to understand what are the main components that you value and which ones are of less importance. In life, there are many different core values that inspire us. Some of them are closely related (such as striving for both power and personal achievement), whereas others can seem at odds (imagine wanting to conform and wanting to be an individual).[14]

For this activity, we are focusing on eight core career values.[15] Given this book is grounded in musical theatre (which, hopefully, you have noticed by now), we will be presenting a Rodgers and Hammerstein values wheel! We will describe our eight core values below – each encapsulated by a classic Rodgers and Hammerstein song.

Many a New Day (Oklahoma!): Like Laurey, you want to be able to move onward and upward. In your career, you would like to be able to advance up the ladder and have access to new opportunities. You want to work with people who will recognize your talents and help you achieve.

In My Own Little Corner (Cinderella): Like Cinderella, you want a place and home of your own. You want to make enough money that you don't have to worry about how you will pay the next rent check. You want enough of a safety net that if the show closes, you will still be able to put food on the table.

You'll Never Walk Alone (Carousel): Nettie's song reassures Julie that even in the wake of tragedy, an inter-connectedness with the world and others can help us carry on. You want to be in that type of supportive and nurturing environment. You want to feel close to other people. You want to feel relaxed and safe around your colleagues.[16] You want to be able to share the story you are telling with an audience.

A Hundred Million Miracles (Flower Drum Song): Mei Li sings about all of the miracles happening every day; you want to help others find their own miracles. You want to give back and help other people, creatures, or the planet. You want to make the world a better place.

I Whistle a Happy Tune (The King and I): Anna is determined that she and her son walk with determination and confidence even when they are afraid. She has purpose – and so do you. You want to have specific and concrete goals that propel you forward. You also want to be driven by larger dreams and desires.

Sixteen Going On Seventeen (Sound of Music): Rolf sings to Liesl about how he is older and more mature (and therefore wiser, although not wise enough to avoid being a Nazi). Just as Liesl is in the process of growing up and developing, so are you. You want to experience personal and professional growth. You want to learn new talents and strengthen your existing abilities.

It Might As Well Be Spring (State Fair): Margy sings this song as she gets ready to go to the titular fair. She feels such a keen need to explore that it borders on restlessness. Like Margy, you want to break free. You want to be autonomous and in charge of your life. You want to feel like your choices matter and you are the captain of your own ship.

Happy Talk (South Pacific): Bloody Mary encourages Liat and Lt. Cable to dream, make small talk, and fall in love. She wants them to enjoy each other. You also seek out and enjoy pleasure. It could be sensual, as in romance or delicious food and drink. It could be cozy, as in snuggling up to a good book or fine cup of coffee. It could be cultural, as in traveling the world or seeing a great show. You like to enjoy your life.

Now we will ask you to rate yourself on our Rodgers and Hammerstein values wheel two times: Where you see yourself right now ("Current") and where you wish you could be in the near future ("Ideal"). First, we would like you to go through the left side of each category and use the 1–10 scale provided (with 1 being "very low" and 10 being "very high"). Mark where you think you are right now and fill in the blank space up to that point. After you are done, go through the right side of each category and use the scale in the same way to indicate what your ideal rating would be.

We did an example wheel to illustrate what it should look like when you are done. We chose to fill out the wheel as though we were the King of Siam as portrayed in *The King and I*. When the musical opens, the King is a man of tradition, power, and control. He cares about his people but is not especially invested in their personal well-being. He is aware of how he is perceived by the West and wants to be respected. We have filled out the wheel to best reflect this set of values. By the end of the musical, he has softened and been able to appreciate others more. He is focused on legacy and ensuring he has a proper successor. Again, we have tried to complete the "ideal" section of the wheel to reflect this development. Take a look at our "King" example and then do your own in the following empty wheel provided. We are not imposing any exact directions of how you should space out or consider your ratings; theoretically, you could put "10" for every one of the eight values. However, such a decision would kind of feel like cheating and would definitely be boring.

Compare where you are to where you want to be. Where are the biggest gaps? What values do you want to be less focused on? Which values do you want to play a larger role in your life? What are some ways you might get to your "ideal" slate?

One topic to think about is how you would be able to ride your wheel if it was the front wheel of your bicycle. Are you close enough to your ideal that you could get to where you want to go? How balanced is your wheel? Would you have a smooth or a bumpy ride?

Creating and Living in Your Spotlight

In the second half of this book, we spoke more to maintaining and thriving. We highlighted what traits are characteristics of creative people and how your art should not come at the expense of your mental (or physical or spiritual) health. Just as there are many career pathways, so are there many different preferences and styles for how to be creative and live a creative life. In the last two chapters, we have emphasized understanding where are you in your career and where you want to be.

The theme of the first half was exploration. Creativity is like a stretchy and personalized outfit: You can design your own size, style, and look. The second half of the book is about focus. Once you've picked out your creativity wardrobe, make sure it's what you want to wear and make sure it shows you off to the world for

Dreaming Your Dream: Your Journey of Success   193

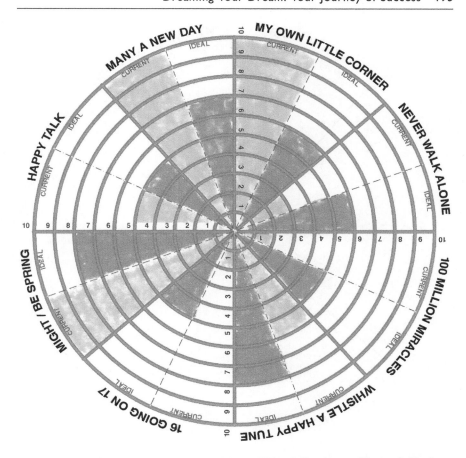

Figure 11.1 Rodgers and Hammerstein Values Wheel, For King of Siam. © Kaufman and Rowe (Creating Your Spotlight workbook, in progress)

the fierce and fancy beast you are. It is never too late to change fashions. Think about your favorite outfit. It is probably the one that you wear for a special night out when you want to look good. Maybe you've had it for years (or you keep buying the latest version). Some looks never go out of style. It might be a classic and one that you will always enjoy and maybe it's the outfit you will be laid to rest in. That is fantastic. But other times, styles get dated. Maybe the robin's egg blue headband and leg warmer combo you rocked a few years ago is no longer getting appreciative stares. It might be time for a switch, whether it is a slight adjustment (maybe try mauve) or a completely new wardrobe. Or, perhaps, the only person's approval you seek is your own, and your outfit is comfortable and you like how it looks. That is okay, too!

194 Your Creative Life

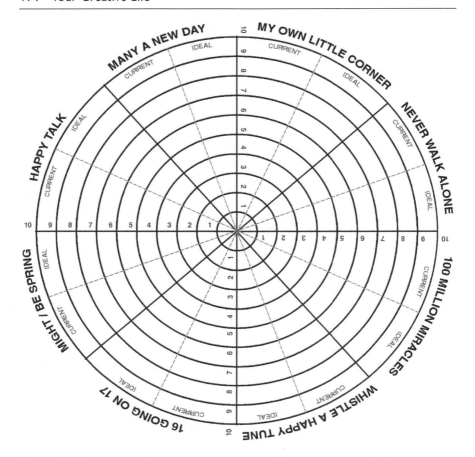

Figure 11.2 Rodgers and Hammerstein Values Wheel, For You. © Kaufman and Rowe (Creating Your Spotlight workbook, in progress)

At the end of the day, we see creativity as a lifestyle. It is a liquid choice. Creativity can be a glass of warm milk, something to comfort you in times of stress. Creativity can be a lazy river, letting you drift and soak in the joys of life. Creativity can be a salve that helps lubricate difficult situations. Creativity can be a palette cleanser, giving you permission to try something completely new. Creativity can be olive oil, a neutral base that can serve as a starting point that allows many different disparate ingredients to marinate together to form a new entity. Creativity can be rocket fuel, helping you launch yourself to the top of your field and be a Star.

If you've stuck with us this far, then you've learned a bit from shared wisdom, lived experience, and scientific foundations. You've engaged in activities and challenges that we designed to help you articulate and discover nuances of not only your own creativity but also your beliefs and values. Our hope is that you are moved to both reflection and action. Whether your next audition, submission, job, performance, or journey is successful is less important than whether it is a step in the right direction. Our belief is that the question is not how you can fix yourself, but how you can take who you are and get the most from it. The goal is not how you can get to some ideal place, but how you can adjust where you are to make it where you want to be. It is our deepest wish that your creativity enriches your life in multiple ways: By bringing personal fulfillment, moments of pure joy, meaningful connections, and a deep sense of purpose.

In short, we want you to create your own spotlight. The brightness, shape, color, placement, and size and entirely up to you.

Notes

1 Willson (1958, p. 30).
2 Willson (1958, p. 150).
3 Disabato et al. (2016) and Tov & Lee (2016).
4 Csikszentmihalyi (1999).
5 Miller (2018).
6 Simonton (1998).
7 Simonton (1977, 1985).
8 Petras & Petras (1993, p. 35).
9 Beghetto (2005) and Hannigan (2018).
10 Bellezza, Paharia, & Keinan (2017).
11 Keep & Attrill-Smith (2017). and Schroeder & Cavanaugh (2018).
12 Aalbers et al. (2019).
13 Brunborg & Burdzovic Andreas (2019).
14 Schwartz (1996) and Schwartz & Boehnke (2004).
15 Amabile & Pratt (2016) and Schwartz & Boehnke (2004).
16 Ford & Sullivan (2004).

References

Aalbers, G., McNally, R. J., Heeren, A., de Wit, S., & Fried, E. I. (2019). Social media and depression symptoms: A network perspective. *Journal of Experimental Psychology: General, 148*, 1454–1462.

Amabile, T. M., & Pratt, M. G. (2016). The dynamic componential model of creativity and associated with modest increase in depression, conduct problems, and episodic heavy drinking. *Journal of Adolescence, 74*, 201–209

Beghetto, R. A. (2005). Preservice teachers' self-judgments of test taking. *The Journal of Educational Research, 98*, 376–380.

Bellezza, S., Paharia, N., & Keinan, A. (2017). Conspicuous consumption of time: When busyness and lack of leisure time become a status symbol. *Journal of Consumer Research, 44*, 118–138.

Brunborg, G. S., & Burdzovic Andreas, J. (2019). Increase in time spent on social media is busyness and lack of leisure time become a status symbol. *Journal of Consumer Research, 44*, 118–138.

Csikszentmihalyi, M. (1999). Implications of a systems perspective for the study of creativity. In R. J. Sternberg (Ed.), *Handbook of creativity* (pp. 313–335). New York, NY: Cambridge University Press.

Disabato, D. J., Goodman, F. R., Kashdan, T. B., Short, J. L., & Jarden, A. (2016). Different types of well-being? A cross-cultural examination of hedonic and eudaimonic well-being. *Psychological Assessment, 28*, 471–482.

Ford, C., & Sullivan, D. M. (2004). A time for everything: How timing of novel contributions influences project team outcomes. *Journal of Organizational Behavior, 21*, 163–183.

Hannigan, S. (2018). A theoretical and practice-informed reflection on the value of failure in art. *Thinking Skills and Creativity, 30*, 171–179.

Keep, M., & Attrill-Smith, A. (2017). Controlling you watching me: Measuring perception control on social media. *Cyberpsychology, Behavior, and Social Networking, 20*, 561–566.

Miller, S. (2018). *Literally anything goes: 14 great oddball musicals and what makes them tick.* Self-published, CreateSpace Independent Publishing Platform.

Petras, R., & Petras, K. (1993). *776 stupidest things ever said.* Davidson, NC: Main Street Books.

Schroeder, A. N., & Cavanaugh, J. M. (2018). Fake it 'til you make it: Examining faking ability on social media pages. *Computers in Human Behavior, 84*, 29–35.

Schwartz, S. H. (1996). Value priorities and behavior: Applying a theory of integrated value systems. In C. Seligman, J. M. Olson, & M. P. Zanna (Eds.) *The Ontario symposium. The psychology of values* (vol. 8, pp. 1–24). Hillsdale, NJ: Lawrence Erlbaum.

Schwartz, S. H., & Boehnke, K. (2004). Evaluating the structure of human values with confirmatory factor analysis. *Journal of Research in Personality, 38*, 230–255.

Simonton, D. K. (1977). Creative productivity, age, and stress: A biographical time-series analysis of 10 classical composers. *Journal of Personality and Social Psychology, 35*, 791–804.

Simonton, D. K. (1985). Quality, quantity, and age: The careers of 10 distinguished psychologists. *International Journal of Aging and Human Development, 21*, 241–254.

Simonton, D. K. (1998). Fickle fashion versus immortal fame: Transhistorical assessments of creative products in the opera house. *Journal of Personality and Social Psychology, 75*, 198–210.

Tov, W., & Lee, H. W. (2016). A closer look at the hedonics of everyday meaning and satisfaction. *Journal of Personality and Social Psychology, 111*, 585–609.

Willson, M. (1958). *The music man.* New York, NY: G. P. Putnam's Sons.

Exit Music
The Show Must Go On

With five minutes to curtain, we feel like we have been on quite a journey with you. What have we covered? We've started with the ways that you can find your own voice and discover the melodies that only you can sing. We've discussed how can you find an ideal balance between your own song and making sure you can still harmonize with others. Then we've talked about how to find what sparks your creativity, how to be in tune with your strengths and weaknesses, and how to engage in the many stages of the creative process.

Creativity can at times feel like a laundry list of instructions. You need to be original and daring, yet also someone who can accommodate and work well with others when needed. You need to be open to new experiences and ideas but also able to be organized and work hard and persevere. You need to pursue your passion yet not be so tied to it that you can't also do the necessarily yet boring parts of the job. You need to leverage feeling happy and sad. You need to know when to distract yourself, when to see things from a new perspective, and when to let yourself heal. You need to have confidence in yourself while also being aware of how you need to grow.

We know that these can feel like one contradiction after another – as though we're asking you to belt like Merman while floating a dulcet high note like Audra. But we're not expecting you to be iconic quite yet. The world may be a stage, but creativity does not have to be. You can be creative in small, personal ways that no one else needs to ever see. That's okay. Just as you might meditate or journal privately, you can have incremental goals to be more creative piece by piece. Try to generate more original ideas on one day. Focus on incisively choosing the best one on day two. Maybe take a week and simply enjoy new experiences every day – eat a meal you've never tried on Monday, listen to a fresh genre of music on Tuesday, explore a different part of your neighborhood on Wednesday, go from a quick hello to a deeper chat with a long-term acquaintance on Thursday, and plan for an adventure-filled weekend on Friday. Pay attention to how you're feeling and what you're thinking. Listen to what your brain and heart are wanting to try or do. How can your actions and beliefs become more aligned with your values and aspirations?

If you're the protagonist of your own musical, what is your "I want" song? How is your character going to grow over the course the show? What will your 11 o'clock number be? Our goal for this book is not to tell what you to do. We have shared what we see as the best of the worlds of art and science with the goal of setting you up for a positive creative journey. It does not matter whether that is a private moment of delight or ambitious project aimed for the whole world – it is your creative spotlight to do with as you wish. If you want to continue the conversation, please check out our website, *Creating Your Spotlight!*, at https://creatingyourspotlight.com/, where we will continue to have activities, blogs, interviews, and other explorations of theatre and creativity.

Places, ladies and gentlemen. Let's go and have a great show!

Index

Note: *Italic* page numbers refer to figures.

25th Annual Putnam County Spelling Bee, The (musical) 96
42nd Street (musical) 96, 167, 178
1600 Pennsylvania Avenue (musical) 54
1776 (musical) 32, 51, 54, 62, 107
1950s musicals 118–112

abacus of balance 38–40, *39*
Abbott, George 185
Acting Company 169
activated *vs.* deactivated moods 133, 134, 136, 143
Adams, Cameron 35
Adler, Richard 188
Ado Annie (fictional character) 45, 47, 54
Agreeableness 75
Ain't Misbehavin' (musical) 61
Akins, Zoe 185
"Alas For You" (song) 133
Alberto, Madalena 97–98
Alexander Hamilton (fictional character) 76–80
Allegiance (musical) 32
Almost, Maine (Cariani) 77
Ambiguity, tolerance of 84
American Express 170
American Horror Story (TV show) 123
And Don't You Ever Forget It (musical) 118
"And I Am Telling You I Am Not Going" (song) 133
Andrews, Julie 2, 172
anger songs 133–134
Anna Christie (musical) 185
Annie (musical) 133, 168, 183
Annie Get Your Gun (musical) 54

"Another Suitcase in Another Hall" (song) 178
anti-creativity bias 33
Apolinar, Danny 50
Applause (musical) 152
Aristotle 151
Arlen, Harold 187
art bias 116
artistic career 154
Ashe, Rosemary 154, 184
Ashman, Howard 188
aspirations 66
Assassins (musical) 76, 107, 123
associative thinking 52–55, 77
Attack of the Clones (movie) 46
attitude 83, 98, 159
August: Osage County (Letts) 77, 173
Avian, Bob 2

Bad Cinderella (musical) 77
bad habits 34
bad moods 132, 143
bad perfectionism 81–83
Band's Visit, A (musical) 188
Bare: a pop opera (musical) 172
Bareilles, Sara 172
Barnum (musical) 54
Barrowman, John 2, 160
Bat Boy – The Musical (musical) 172
Batman (fictional character) 124
Bay Jones, Rachel 110–111
Beautiful (musical) 172
Beauty and the Beast (musical) 66–67, 172
Beetlejuice (musical) 154
Beghetto, Ron 59

200 Index

being creative 33, 35
Belle (fictional character) 158
Be More Chill (musical) 157
Ben Franklin in Paris (musical) 54
"Be On Your Own" (song) 133
Berkow, Jay 172
Bernstein, Douglas 137
Bernstein, Leonard 50, 68
Best Little Whorehouse in Texas (musical) 61, 189
Between Riverside and Crazy (Guirgis) 173
BFA Musical Theatre program 172
"Bidin' My Time" (song) 134
Big-C 59, 60
bipolar disorder 155
Birds of Paradise (musical) 60
Blackbeard (musical) 2, 171
Blandick, Clara 185
Blumenkrantz, Jeff 90
Boggess, Sierra 2, 63
Book of Mormon, The (musical) 142
Borghesi, Leanne 36, 37
Boy From Oz, The (musical) 172
Boyle, T. Coraghessan 22, 123
brainstorming 46, 47, 94
Brice, Fanny 152
Bridesmaids (movie) 46
Brigadoon (musical) 79–80, 82, 168
Broadway 29, 30, 32, 35, 55, 58, 59, 61–63, 69, 80, 81, 107, 110, 167, 168, 170, 171, 178, 189
Brohn, Bill 95
Brooklyn (musical) 172
Brown, Mordecai 117
Bruce Bechdel (fictional character) 134, 135
Brynner, Yul 179
Bye Bye Birdie (musical) 183

Cabaret (musical) 115
"Cabaret" (song) 115
Cal, A Tale of Relative Insanity (musical) 22
Cameron, Dove 172
camping, concept of 78
Candide (musical) 17, 90
career: changes 173, 178; pathways 192; values 190–192
Cariani, John 77
Cariou, Len 68
"Carnival del Barrio" (song) 143
Carousel (musical) 191
Carrie (musical) 168
Casablanca (movie) 46

Cassie (fictional character) 167–168
casting choices 168–170
Cats (musical) 168, 172
Celie (fictional character) 157
censorship 36
"Changing my Major" (song) 133
Channing, Carol 179
Charity Hope Valentine (fictional character) 158
Charnin, Martin 137
Chenoweth, Kristin 17, 18, 61, 62
Chicago (musical) 61, 62
choices *vs.* constraints 37, 107–108
Chorus Line, A (musical) 8, 62, 67, 118, 133, 136–137, 167, 168, 178, 186
Christine Daaé (fictional character) 18
Cinderella (musical) 191
Citizen Kane (movie) 46
City of Angels (musical) 95
Civil War, The (musical) 172
Clemmons, Dave 173
Clybourne Park (Norris) 77, 173
coaching technique 137
cognition 156, 159
cognitive load 158
cognitive reappraisal 136–139
coherence 160
colorblind casting 51
Color Purple, The (musical) 157, 159
Come From Away (musical) 171
commitment 94
community theatre production 17, 30
Company (musical) 67, 69, 169, 170
composer 23, 90, 118–121, 122, 156, 170, 177, 187, 188
Connecticut Repertory Theatre 173, 177
Conscientiousness 75, 79, 81–83
convergent thinking 47
Cook, Barbara 156
"Corner of the Sky" (song) 43
"Could I Leave You?" (song) 133
county fair creativity 59
COVID-19 pandemic 37, 139, 179
Craig's Wife (Kelly) 185
creation types 68–69
creative ability 68
creative activity 131, 132, 157, 159
creative balance 40
creative class 65
creative expression 127
creative investment 32–33
creative pathways 69–70

creative people 33, 34
creative process 40, 47, 55, 90
creative self 116–118
creative styles 68–69
creativity 29, 50, 78, 94, 95, 116, 160, 192; alcohol and drugs 155–157; collaborative 79; and constraints 36–37; definition 8, 36; Eastern conceptions of 36; effortless 125–126; enhancing mood 136–137; everyday 59; expert-level 59; as lifestyle 194; and mental illness 155, 157; personal 59; and perspective-taking 139–140; research 8, 29, 34, 44, 46, 49, 53, 59; Systems theory of 185; theory 32; types of 36, 40, 58
creativity map 9–12
Crown, The (TV show) 77
Crucible, The (Miller) 95
Cullum, John 179
cultures 78–79
Curtains (musical) 172

D'Ambroise, Kelly Crandall 172
Damn Yankees (musical) 107, 188
Dancers Over 40 178
"Dance with the Devil" (song) 108, 187
Daniel, Anthony Christian 173
Davis, Owen 185
Dear Evan Hansen (musical) 111, 152
Deis, Jean 123
dementia 159
Dempsey, John 23, 25, 108, 187
Dench, Judi 115
depression 155, 190
DeShields, Andre 61
designers 7, 51, 76, 170, 171
director 15–16, 22, 35, 45, 47, 54, 55, 58, 69, 80, 81, 84, 93, 95, 98, 109, 117, 121, 124, 126, 170–173, 190
Disney 29, 30, 33, 188
distraction 142–143
diva 34–35
divergent thinking 46, 137
diversity 78–79
Dixon, Ed 173
domains 9, 10, 12, 15, 30, 58, 59, 63, 69, 76, 122, 177
"Don't Rain on my Parade" (song) 17
"Don't Tell Mama" (song) 115
Drake, David 172
Dreamgirls (musical) 132, 133

Driver, Donald 50
driving range activity 99, *100–106*, 107
Drowsy Chaperone, The (musical) 32
Dye Creek Capital 178

Eagan, Daisy 168
Eastern cultures 36, 108
EasyLunchboxes 177
"Easy to Say" (song) 17
Egan, Susan 172
Eliza Doolittle (fictional character) 130
emotional creativity (EC) 138, 139
emotional intelligence (EI) 138, 139
Emotional Stability 75, 83–84
emotions 7, 50, 67, 70, 127, 130–131, 133, 136, 138, 140, 143, 159, 160
Empire Strikes Back, The (movie) 46
"Empty Chairs at Empty Tables" (song) 159
"Epiphany" (song) 133, 134, 139, 159
Eponine (fictional character) 135
Equity-waiver theatres 62
Eudaimonia 183, 184
Eva Peron (fictional character) 96–97
Everybody's Talking About Jamie (musical) 123, 157
"Everything's Coming Up Roses" (song) 17, 139
Evita (musical) 54, 96–98, 178
explicit beliefs 116
expressing yourself 158–159
extraversion 75, 83
extrinsic motivation 90, 94–99, 107, 108, 111

Fanny Hill (musical) 173
Fantaisie-Impromptu Opus 66 in C-sharp minor (piano composition) 92
Fantasticks, The (musical) 36, 134
Farnsworth, Matt 172
Faustian bargain 122, 152, 162
Fennell, Emerald 77
Fiddler on the Roof (musical) 31, 58, 60, 70, 133, 170
Fields, Dorothy 68
finding balance 31–32
Finkel, Joshua 172
Finneran, Katie 61
Fiorello! (musical) 54, 107
First, The (musical) 54
Five Course Love (musical) 169
Fix, The (musical) 22, 23, 25, 94
fixed mindset 110
flexibility 46

202　Index

Flow 91–92, 111, 125
Flower Drum Song (musical) 168, 191
Floyd Collins (musical) 54
fluency 46
Foley, Ellen 62
Follies (musical) 132, 133, 186
Forbidden Broadway (musical) 172
Force Awakens, The (movie) 46
Fosse, Bob 60
Foster, Hunter 172
Four C Model of Creativity 59, 60
Four Guys Named José and una Mujer Named Maria (musical) 32
Frasier (TV show) 169
Freaky Friday (musical) 122
Freaky Friday (Rodgers, novel) 122
Friday the Thirteenth (movie) 46
Friedman, Maria 23
Full Monty, The (musical) 188
functional fixedness 51–52
Fun Home (musical) 133–135
Funny Girl (musical) 132, 152
Funny Thing Happened on the Way to the Forum, A (musical) 31, 188

Gardiner, James 171, 188
Garland, Judy 60–61, 156
Gaston (fictional character) 66–67
Georges Seurat (fictional character) 28
Georgie (Dixon) 173
Gershwin, George 60
Ghostbusters (movie) 46
Girl Crazy (musical) 134
"Glitter and Be Gay" (song) 17
Glory Days (musical) 171, 188
goals 21, 29, 43, 58, 59, 63, 66–68, 80, 83, 91, 93, 98, 108–111, 117, 133, 138, 140, 141, 154, 160, 162, 183–185, 188, 191, 197
Godspell (musical) 133
"Goin' out of My Head" (song) 17
Golden Apple, The (musical) 134
Goodman, Gordon 3
"Good Morning, Baltimore" (song) 75
good perfectionism 81–83
Gordon, Ricky Ian 122
Graff, Randy 80, 95
Grease (musical) 108, 186
Great American Trailer Park Musical, The (musical) 172
Green, Paul 185
Grey Gardens (musical) 32, 54

growth mindset 110
Guare, John 170, 185
Guettel, Adam 122
Guido (fictional character) 18–19
Guirgis, Stephen Adly 173
Gurwin, Danny 172
Guthrie, Woody 52
Guys and Dolls (musical) 168, 189
Gypsy (musical) 2, 124–125, 132, 139, 152, 169, 185, 188

Hair (musical) 51, 111, 185, 186
Hairspray (musical) 75
hallucinogenic drugs 85
Hamilton (musical) 4, 43, 51, 54, 76, 78, 107, 172, 176, 177, 185, 187
Haney, Carol 80
"Happy Birthday" (song) 188
"Happy Talk" (song) 191
Harold Hill (fictional character) 182–183
Harrison, Rex 179
Hart, Lorenz 156, 185
Haworth, Jill 115
Hearn, George 68
Heathers (musical) 96
Hedonia 183, 184
Hell-Bent Fer Heaven (Hughes) 185
"Hell No!" (song) 159
Hello, Dolly (musical) 179
Herman, Jerry 1
Hester, Hal 50
Hip Hop 32
Hitchcock, Alfred 80
Hope Cladwell (fictional character) 37
Hopkins, Kaitlin 172, 176–177
Horn, John 22
Houseman, John 169
House of Blue Leaves (musical) 170
How to Succeed in Business Without Really Trying (musical) 60, 68, 90, 96, 151
Hudson, Jennifer 17
Hughes, Hatcher 185
"A Hundred Million Miracles" (song) 191

idea evaluation 47
idea generation 45–46, 52
I Do, I Do! (musical) 133
"I Hate Men" (song) 133
"I Hope I Get It" (song) 133
"I'm a Brass Band" (song) 133
imaginative thinking 53
Imperfect Action, concept of 125

implementation 47
implicit beliefs 116, 117
In Abraham's Bosom (Green) 185
inappropriateness, risks of 29–31
incubation 47–48, 55
Indiana University 123
"In My Own Little Corner" (song) 191
Inside Out (movie) 50
insight, theory of 48–51
intentional exclusion 65
In the Heights (musical) 32, 78, 132, 143, 172
Into the Woods (musical) 3, 43–44, 62, 132, 133, 168, 172, 178
intrinsic motivation 90–94, 99, 107, 108, 111
"It Might As Well Be Spring" (song) 191
"It's Raining Men" (song) 118
Ivcevic, Zorana 139
"I Want" song 43, 133, 197
"I Whistle a Happy Tune" (song) 191

Jabara, Paul 118
Jackman, Hugh 61
Jacques Brel is Alive and Well and Living in Paris (musical) 172
Jagged Little Pill (musical) 157
Jamie New (fictional character) 157–158
Japanese arts 36
Jean Valjean (fictional character) 69–70
Jekyll and Hyde (musical) 157
Jerome Robbins' Broadway (musical) 168
Jesus Christ Superstar (musical) 3, 16
Jöback, Peter 168
journaling 159
"Just You Wait" (song) 133

Kabuki 36
Kander and Ebb 17
Kaufman, James C. 1, 3, 9, 17–22, 34, 35, 49, 59–63, 66, 77, 123, 125, 159, 168, 177, 178, 185
Kelly, George 185
Kennedy, John F. 188
key change 49
King and I, The (musical) 133, 179, 191, 192
Kiss Me, Kate (musical) 133
Kiss of the Spiderwoman (musical) 172
Knot's Landing (TV show) 52
Knowles, Maura 177
Kudisch, Marc 76

La Cage Aux Folles (musical) 58, 132
LaChiusa, Michael John 122

"Lament" (song) 96, 97
Lane, Nathan 35, 168
Lansbury, Angela 17, 139
L. A. Stage Alliance Ovation Award 177
"Last Dance" (song) 118
Last Jedi, The (movie) 46
"Last Midnight" (song) 133
latent disinhibition 155
Laurents, Arthur 50, 139
Lawrence, Gertrude 60–61
"Lazy Afternoon" (song) 134
lead roles 61–62
League of Regional Theatres (LORT) 62
learning goals 109
Lee, Chris 171
Lee, Gypsy Rose 124–125
legacies 185–186
Legally Blonde (musical) 96
Lennart, Isobel 152
Les Misérables (musical) 29–30, 69–70, 95, 135, 159, 169, 172, 173, 178
Lester, Kelly 177
Lettice and Lovage (Shaffer) 61
Letts, Tracey 77, 172, 173
Light in the Piazza, The (musical) 77
Lion King, The (musical) 62, 69
"A Little Fall of Rain" (song) 135
Little Me (musical) 133
Little Mermaid, The (musical) 63, 133
Little Night Music, A (musical) 132, 172
"A Little Priest" (song) 143
Little Shop of Horrors (musical) 22, 133, 173
Living Mental Wellness 177
Locals 62–63, 67, 68
locus of control 24
Longtime Companion (movie) 77
"Look at Me" (song) 49
Louise, Meryl 3
Love Never Dies (musical) 63
Lucas, Craig 77
LuPone, Patti 35, 61, 111, 169
lyricist 119, 121, 187

MacDermott, Galt 185
Mack and Mabel (musical) 54, 133, 159
Mackintosh, Sir Cameron 2, 22, 23, 53, 95, 108
MacLaine, Shirley 80
Mac-n-Mo 177
"mad genius" concept 151, 154, 162, 186
Mad Show, The (musical) 188
Maguire, Michael 178

Mahoney, John 170
Mainly on directing (Laurents) 139
Mame Dennis (fictional character) 91, 93
Mame (musical) 16, 91, 93
Mamet, David 22
Mamma Mia! (musical) 3, 16
Manhattan Association of Cabarets (MAC) Award 36
Mann, Terrence 172
"Many a New Day" (song) 191
Maria Rainer (fictional character) 92
Markell, Denis 137
Marry Me a Little (musical) 77
Martin, Michael X. 35
Mary Poppins (musical) 2, 154
"Maybe" (song) 133
McArdle, Andrea 168
McCormick, Michael 35
McDonald, Audra 61
McShane, Ian 168
meaning in life 160, 185
Meet Me in St. Louis (musical) 110
"Mein Herr" (song) 115
Memphis (musical) 32
Menken, Alan 188
Mendes, Sam 22, 25
mental health 59, 139, 143, 152, 157, 159, 162, 192
mental illness 34, 152, 154, 155
mental wellness curriculum 177
mentors 21–24
Menzel, Idina 35
Mercer, Marian 61
Merman, Ethel 35, 60
Merrily We Roll Along (musical) 66, 138, 171
metacognition 39, 118, 122–127, 167
Method acting 131, 152
Midnight Madness (movie) 46
Milnes, Sherrill 169
mindset, concept of 110
Minnelli, Liza 62, 115
mini-c 59, 60
"Miracle of Miracles" (song) 133
Miranda, Lin-Manuel 32, 67, 78, 173, 187, 188
Missouri State University 172
Mitchell, Jerry 2, 81
Molly Brown (fictional character) 158
Monroe, Marilyn 188
moods 130, 131, 135–136, 143
Morales (fictional character) 136–137
Mordden, Ethan 31

Mostel, Zero 31
Most Happy Fella, The (musical) 134
motivation 7, 16, 85, 127
Moulin Rouge! (musical) 82
Mount Essex, Shari 3
multicultural understanding 78, 79
Multiple Intelligences 5
The Museum Effect 159
Musical Theatre program 172
Music Man, The (musical) 96, 182–183
"My Cup Runneth Over" (song) 133
Myers–Briggs test 75
My Fair Lady (musical) 130, 132, 133, 179
"My Shot" (song) 43
Mystery of Edwin Drood, The (musical) 50, 69, 177, 186

narrative writing 158, 159
national touring company 30, 61
negative emotion 133, 142
nepotism 65
New Brain, A (musical) 172
New-Different continuum 68
New York Shakespeare Festival 186
Next to Normal (musical) 32
Night Larry Kramer Kissed Me, The (Drake) 172
Nine (musical) 18–19, 132, 133, 188
"No Good Deed" (song) 133
Norma Desmond (fictional character) 151, 169
Norris, Bruce 77, 173
"Nothing" (song) 136

Off-Broadway 17, 18, 22, 50, 62, 186
Ogunquit Playhouse 173
"Oh, What a Beautiful Mornin" (song) 133
O'Hare, Denis 123
Ohringer, Jane 178
Oklahoma! (musical) 45, 54–55, 69, 133, 185, 191
Oliver! (musical) 2, 133
Once (musical) 172
Once on this Island (musical) 43
Once Upon a Mattress (musical) 122
O'Neill, Eugene 185
"On My Own" (song) 135
On Sondheim (Mordden) 31
"On the Other Side of the Tracks" (song) 133
Onward Victoria (musical) 54
On Your Toes (musical) 172
Openness 75–79, 84–86

Openness to Experience 76
Openness to Intellect 76
originality/novelty 8, 15, 17–18, 29, 30, 36, 46
Our Town (musical) 185
"Over the Rainbow" (song) 187

Pacific Overtures (musical) 78
Paint Your Wagon (musical) 133
Pajama Game, The (musical) 80
Papp, Joe 186
Parade (musical) 54, 107
"Part of Your World" (song) 133
passion 90, 92, 96, 97, 108, 111, 171
Passion (musical) 178
passivity 134–135
Past, Expression, Attainability, Constraints, and Ego (PEACE) 38, *39*
Patinkin, Mandy 35
perfectionism 81, 94
performance goals 109
performer 17, 18, 31, 35, 45, 61, 62, 67, 69, 76, 83, 84, 90, 109, 119, 123, 158, 172, 173, 176–178, 182, 187
performing arts 169
persistence 81–83, 178–179
personality 75, 83–85, 127
perspective-taking 139–140
Peter and the Starcatcher (Elice) 51
Peters, Bernadette 35, 61, 62
Phantom Menace, The (movie) 46
Phantom of the Opera (musical) 18, 23, 30, 62, 154, 168
Pippin (fictional character) 43, 44
Pippin (musical) 69, 111, 168
Pirates of Penzance (musical) 186
Pixar 50
Plato 151
pleasure 91
Poland, Albert 22
"Pore Jud is Daid" (song) 55
Porter, Cole 60
Pose (TV show) 82
positive distraction 159
positive emotions 142
positive *vs.* negative moods 131, 134, 136, 143
post-traumatic growth 138, 139
Prelude to a Kiss (Lucas) 77
Prime of Miss Jean Brodie, The (movie) 61
Prince, Faith 168

problem-finding 44, 47
problem-solving 44–48, 52
Pro-c 59
producer 30, 33, 60, 65, 66, 80, 84, 93, 121, 126, 170, 173
Producers, The (musical) 183
Promises, Promises (musical) 61, 177
Promising Young Woman (movie) 77
promotion focus 85
Propulsion Theory 68
prosocial motivation 92
Provincetown Theatre 172
Pulitzer Prize for Drama 185
"Putting it Together" (song) 28

Rachael Lily Rosenbloom (And Don't You Ever Forget It) (musical) 118
Ragtime (musical) 54, 107, 132, 176
Random Random Random exercise 77
redefinition 68
Reefer Madness (musical) 152, 157
regional theatre 99, 109
Reid, T. Oliver 35
reinitiation 69
remote theatrical associations 53–54
Rent (musical) 172
replications 68
Return of the Jedi (movie) 46
Revenge of the Sith (movie) 46
rewards 95, 96, 98–99
Rex (musical) 77
Rice, Tim 97, 188
Richardson, Natasha 115
Richert, Wanda 178
Ride the Cyclone (musical) 132
Ring of Fire (musical) 172
Road to Wellville, The (Boyle) 22
Robber Bridegroom, The (musical) 169
Robertson, Justin "Squigs" 177
Robinson, Jackie 54
Rocky (movie) 187
Rodgers and Hammerstein 190–192
Rodgers, Mary 122, 188
Rodgers, Richard 187
roles: changing 168–170; type of 170–173
Romeo and Juliet (Shakespeare) 68
Rose, George 173
Rosencranz and Guildenstern are Dead (Stoppard) 140
Rowe, Dana P. 1–3, 15–16, 20–23, 25, 33, 48, 49, 51, 53, 54, 61, 63, 77–78, 80, 90, 92–95, 108, 109, 123–125,

206 Index

137–138, 156, 159, 160, 168, 171, 186, 187, 189, 190
Rubinstein, John 168
Runaways (musical) 186
Runolfsson, Anne 172

Sabath, Bruce 170
Sabella, David 172
Sally Bowles (fictional character) 115
Sanders, Ann 35
Sanders, Marta 189, 190
Scarlett Pimpernel, The (musical) 172
Schwartz, Stephen 188
Scottsboro Boys, The (musical) 32, 107, 179
Secret Garden, The (musical) 168, 172
selective combination 48–50
selective comparison 48, 50
selective encoding 48–49
self-beliefs 116, 118, 121, 127
self-confidence 117, 121
self-efficacy 117–118, 121
self-esteem 24, 121
self-perceptions 39
sense-swapping 154
sensible risk-taking *vs.* silly risk-taking 173, 180
Shakespeare, William 50, 69
"Shall I Tell You What I Think of You" (song) 133
Shea, Jere 178
She Loves Me (musical) 133
Shenandoah (musical) 77
short-term *vs.* long-term 183–184
Showboat (musical) 61, 69
Signature Theatre (Virginia) 171, 173
significance 160
Six Degrees of Separation (Guare) 185
"Sixteen Going On Seventeen" (song) 191
Skinner, Emily 15–16
Smith, Maggie 61
Snow-Wilson, Jessica 18
social media 190
Socrates 151
"So Long, Farewell" (song) 92
"Something" (song) 137, 139
"Something's Coming" (song) 133
"Somewhere Over the Rainbow" (song) 43
"Somewhere That's Green" (song) 133
Sommers, Avery 61
Sondheim, Stephen 7, 50, 67, 69, 77, 78, 93, 95, 156, 187
Song and Dance (musical) 133, 168

"Soon It's Gonna Rain" (song) 134
"Sorry-Grateful" (song) 67
Sound of Music, The (musical) 2, 92, 191
South Pacific (musical) 23–24, 133, 191
SpotLight model 55, 59–64, 67, 70
Springtime for Hitler (fictional musical) 183
stage manager 99
Stallone, Sylvester 187
"Standing on the Corner" (song) 134
Star 61, 67, 68
Starlight Express (musical) 107, 188
Star Wars (movie) 46
"Star Wars Christmas Album" 188
State Fair (musical) 191
Steel Pier (musical) 17, 18
Steppenwolf Theatre (Chicago) 169
stereotypes 117, 140, 151, 157
Sternberg, Robert 22
Stone, Elly 172
Stoppard, Tom 140
strengths and weaknesses 118, 122, 125, 127, 167
Stroker, Ali 172
Struxness, Betsy 177
substance abuse 156, 157
success 67–68, 76, 188–190; model 18, 28, 69, 76, 92, 124, 130, 157, 182; pathways to 18–19
Summer of '42 (musical) 173
Sunday in the Park with George (musical) 28, 172
sunk cost fallacy 51–52
Sunset Boulevard (musical) 151, 169
Superman (fictional character) 124
supporters 62, 68
suppress model 23, 28, 34, 43, 66, 79, 96, 134, 151, 176
Suzuki, Pat 168
Sweeney Todd (fictional character) 82, 130, 134, 139
Sweeney Todd (musical) 3, 17, 30, 62, 68, 77, 82, 90, 133, 143, 159, 185
Sweet Charity (musical) 123, 133, 158
Sylvia Plath Effect 34
symbolic immortality 160
synesthesia 154
synthesis 69

Take it From the Top (podcast) 2, 90, 123, 160
Take Me Out (Greenberg) 123
task appropriateness 29, 31, 36, 40, 55, 58
Taymor, Julie 69

Teeter, Lara 172
"Telephone Wire" (song) 134
Texas State University 172, 177
theatre: critics 122, 185; education 160; participation 160; training 160
Theatre World Award 17
theatrical and creative aspirations 58–59; SpotLight model of 55, 59–64, 67, 70
theatrical archetypes 117
theatrical career(s) 178, 180; pursuing 12–15; survey *13–14*, 15
theatrical metaphor 60
"They're Playing My Song" (song) 133
They're Playing Our Song (musical) 133
This is Us (TV show) 123
"This Land is Your Land" (song) 52
Thoroughly Modern Millie (musical) 76
Titanic (musical) 188
Tommy (musical) 172
Tommy Albright (fictional character) 79–80, 82
Tony and Tina's Wedding (musical) 69
Tony Awards 61, 62, 69, 123, 168, 169, 170, 186
Tracy Turnblad (fictional character) 75
"Tradition" (song) 31
traits *vs.* states 85
trauma 138, 139
Trouble with Harry, The (movie) 80
True Blood (TV show) 123
Tune, Tommy 69
Two Gentlemen of Verona (musical) 185, 186

uncertainty 84
"Unexpected Song" (song) 133
University of Arizona 172
unoriginal 4
Unsinkable Molly Brown (musical) 132
Upstairs at O'Neals (musical) 137, 139
Urban Cowboy (musical) 90
Urinetown (musical) 37, 173, 179

values 7, 19, 28, 36, 85, 86, 94, 96, 162, 182, 184, 190–192, 194, 197
Verdon, Gwen 61
versatility 62
Victor, Victoria (musical) 62, 172
visual arts 142, 159
Vosk, Jessica 169–170

"Waiting for Life to Begin" (song) 43
Waitress (musical) 43, 132
Walton, Jim 171–172
Ward, André 82, 189
Webber, Andrew Lloyd 77, 97, 188
Webster University 172
"We Go Together" (song) 108
well-being 159, 162, 192
Westenberg, Robert 172
Western culture 36, 108
Western Michigan University 172
West Side Story (musical) 2, 3, 16, 50, 79, 133, 185, 188
What a Wonderful Feeling (Berkow) 172
"What Baking Can Do" (song) 43
"What I Did for Love" (song) 67
Where in the World is Carmen Sandiego (musical) 188
"Wherever He Ain't" (song) 133, 159
"Who Will Buy" (song) 133
Wicked (musical) 30, 62, 133, 140, 170
Wilder, Thornton 185
Williams, Jesse Lynch 185
Wilson, August 60, 68
Wise, Scott 168
Witch (fictional character) 43–45
Witches of Eastwick, The (musical) 2, 22–23, 49, 95, 108, 154, 168, 187
Wizard of Oz, The (musical) 43, 140
Women on the Verge on a Nervous Breakdown (musical) 111
"I'm in Love with a Wonderful Guy" (song) 133
work-life balance 70, 190
"Wouldn't It Be Loverly" (song) 133
Wright, Ben 178
Writing Cure 158

Yazbeck, David 188
Yeston, Maury 188
You Can't Take It with You (Kaufman/Hart) 185
"You'll Never Walk Alone" (song) 191
You're a Good Man, Charlie Brown (musical) 51
Your Own Thing (musical) 50

Zien, Chip 168
Zippel, David 77
Zombie Prom (musical) 2, 16–18, 22